Played Out on the Strip

Played Out on the Strip

The Rise and Fall of Las Vegas Casino Bands

JANIS L. MCKAY

UNIVERSITY OF NEVADA PRESS

Reno & Las Vegas

University of Nevada Press, Reno, Nevada 89557 USA
www.unpress.nevada.edu
Manufactured in the United States of America
Cover design by Omega Clay
Cover photographs: Signage detail from the Flamingo hotel & casino © Kobby Dagan (*top*);
Horn player © Furtseff (*middle*); New York–New York located on the Las Vegas Strip © GTS
Productions / Shutterstock (*bottom*).

LIBRARY OF CONGRESS CATALOGING-IN-PUBLICATION DATA
Names: McKay, Janis, 1964-
Title: Played out on the strip : the rise and fall of Las Vegas casino bands / Janis L. McKay.
Description: Reno : University of Nevada Press, 2016. | Includes bibliographical references
    and index.
Identifiers: LCCN 2015037826 | ISBN 978-0-87417-999-6 (paper : alk. paper) |
    ISBN 978-1-943859-03-0 (ebook)
Subjects: LCSH: Music—Social aspects—Nevada—Las Vegas—History—20th century. |
    Band musicians—Nevada—Las Vegas. | Casinos—Nevada—Las Vegas.
Classification: LCC ML3917.U6 M23 2016 | DDC 331.7/6178409793135—dc23
LC record available at http://lccn.loc.gov/2015037826

The paper used in this book meets the requirements of American National Standard for
Information Sciences—Permanence of Paper for Printed Library Materials, ANSI/NISO
Z39.48–1992 (R2002). Binding materials were selected for strength and durability.

This book has been reproduced as a digital reprint.

For my parents

Contents

Illustrations follow page 122

Preface

I WILL ALWAYS REMEMBER the first time I played with an orchestra on Las Vegas Boulevard, known as "the Strip," where most of the famous hotels and casinos are located. Newly arrived in Las Vegas with many years of performing experience already under my belt, I had played just about every type of job there was for a bassoonist as an orchestral and freelance musician. Or so I thought.

When I got a call from contractor Johnny Haig to play for Tony Bennett at Caesars Palace, I was thrilled. Tony Bennett had been a soloist for several of the orchestras I had performed with in other cities, and it was always a joy to work with him. He treated his musicians well, and was warm and friendly to everyone. And, of course, he sang beautifully and interpreted lyrics with great style. He is always a class act. So I thought I knew what to expect and looked forward to seeing the backstage of the Caesars Palace showroom.

Rehearsal was quick and easy, as I had anticipated. The musicians in Las Vegas were all seasoned professionals who needed little guidance. Most of them had played for Bennett many times before. The real surprise came later, when I arrived for the first show. Like most professional musicians, I had amassed a quantity of black clothing for performances, items that are meant to help you blend in with all the other musicians on stage or in the pit. Most of my clothes were pretty shabby from years of wear, and all were plain and unornamented in any way.

Looking around at the other musicians backstage, I could see right away that I was out of my league. The women wore sequins, sleeveless and strapless dresses, with big statement jewelry and hair. The men were all equally dressed up, with fancy cufflinks, interesting ties, and expensive shirts: there were no worn-out tuxedos here. As I stood taking it all in, one of the woodwind doublers walked up and said with a laugh, "I see no one has told you about 'Vegas black.'[1]" His name was Jay Volney, and that night was the first of many when Jay told me about performing in Las Vegas. He explained that being in a Las Vegas orchestra was a lot more like being in show business than the kind of classical performing that I was used to doing. The musicians were expected not only to play extremely well, but also to dress the part and to take an active role with the entertainers on the stage if needed.

Over the next few years, I enjoyed hearing Jay's backstage stories, especially those from the golden age of the Las Vegas bands before 1989, the year the corporate hotels began using taped music and synthesizers. As more and more musicians talked to me about those days, it seemed that these stories should somehow be preserved.

I contacted my father, a retired journalist, and suggested that the two of us write this book. I got a one-semester sabbatical from my teaching job at The University of Nevada, Las Vegas, and my parents moved to Nevada for the spring. We began by searching materials housed in the local Las Vegas Musicians Union (American Federation of Musicians [AFM] Local 369 [hereafter the Musicians Union]), but unfortunately most of the records from before 1990 had been destroyed in a fire. Much of the book is based on oral history and so entirely dependent on the memories of the musicians and others with whom we spoke, although we did get independent confirmation when possible.

From the beginning, my mother was also part of this project. My parents had already written one book together, and they were used to working as a team. I welcomed her help as it soon became clear to me that this project was much larger and more daunting than I could have imagined. As we talked to the musicians, we realized that the book would have to be more than a collection of entertaining stories—we would also have to address "the strike of '89."

"The strike of '89" was mentioned over and over by the musicians, with sadness and resignation. It was obvious that this was a major turning point for the Las Vegas musicians and the end of an era. Almost everyone we interviewed became wistful, or angry as they recalled the long strike that ended with many musicians permanently out of work in Las Vegas, replaced by taped and synthesized mechanical sound.

The three of us interviewed our subjects, with my father asking most of the questions while I taped and videotaped the subjects and my mother took notes. I am sure that some people we talked to were a bit overwhelmed to be the focus of so much concentrated attention. Nevertheless, things had been progressing well when my father suddenly passed away.

My mother and I made the decision to finish the book because we knew my father would have wanted it. We also felt a real commitment to the musicians who had shared their lives with us. I missed my father even more than I thought possible as I transcribed the interviews alone. During the interviews, I did not always understand why he had asked certain questions or ignored things that I thought were important. As I began to write, I realized how lucky I was that he had done most of the interviews, with the savvy and skill of a longtime professional. Everything that I needed to know was on tape, just waiting for me. I was also very lucky to have my mother's notes, which saved me weeks of time. As my first reader, she was invaluable.

The process of finishing the manuscript took far longer than originally planned, and some of the people we interviewed have since passed away. The Johnny Haig "Relief" Orchestra was a fixture on the Las Vegas Strip during the 1970s and 1980s, playing a different showroom each night to give the regular house orchestra a night off. Haig Eshow, known as Johnny Haig, is a central figure in this book because of his great contributions to the Las Vegas music world, and I am truly sorry that he did not live to see the finished work. Another musician who died before the work was completed was composer, arranger, and musician Don Hannah. Sadly, Jay Volney did not live to see this book reach publication, either. I wish he could have known that he was the initial inspiration for this book, though I suspect it just would have made him laugh. These tragic losses made me more determined than ever to finish.

I hope this book will be a lasting legacy for all of the musicians who lived and worked in Las Vegas during the golden age. Though I dedicate this book to my father, I write it also for Johnny Haig, Don Hannah, Jay Volney, and all the other great musicians who shared their stories. With thanks.

NOTES

1. A doubler is a musician who plays more than one instrument.

Played Out on the Strip

Introduction

*If the casino hotels get their way and continue to eliminate
musicians in their main showrooms and replace live music with
records and tapes, it will have a devastating effect on both the
music industry and indeed, our entire American culture.*[1]

MARTIN EMERSON, President of the American Federation of
Musicians of the United States and Canada (1987–1991)

*I've got $385 million in construction projects.
At this point I could care less about the musicians.*[2]

JOHN GIOVENCO, Director, Hilton Hotels Corporation, 1980–1992

IN THE LATE 1960s the Nevada state legislature passed two Corporate Gaming Acts, allowing corporations to acquire casinos and access legitimate funding for these ventures for the first time. The mob money had begun to run out and the syndicate casino owners were getting older. For Las Vegas, which was dependent on tourism, this legislation was a life-saving move that led to explosive growth and dramatic changes as corporations invested greater and greater sums, competing with each other to have the biggest and best properties on the Strip.

While no one would argue that the crime syndicates should have remained in control of Las Vegas, many would point out that corporate casino ownership has not necessarily improved the lives of the casino workers. For the musicians who worked in the hotel bands in the golden age of live music in Las Vegas, roughly the late 1940s through 1989, the change in ownership was definitely a change for the worse.

As many as 1,400 to 1,700 local musicians were employed in Las Vegas during the 1960s–1980s. In 1989, in a bid to save money, several corporate

hotel owners sought to replace hotel orchestra musicians with synthesizers and taped music. The hotel musicians reacted with a seven-and-a-half-
month strike that ultimately failed. A large number of musicians lost their
jobs, and many of them left Las Vegas. The results were both long lasting
and far reaching for the entertainment business in Las Vegas, though the
changes here were part of larger changes that have affected the entire live
music industry.

In contrast, most local hotel musicians found that the experiences
of working for "the boys" (the mob owners) were among the best of their
careers. It was in some ways a simpler time, with deals decided by handshake
and no complicated contracts. Musician and contractor Johnny Haig said,
"They had two rules: You don't mess with their women or their money . . . ,
which was understood. [You were fine] as long as you were what they would
call a 'stand up' guy. . . . I never signed a contract."[3]

When my parents and I first began interviewing Las Vegas musicians
in 2005, we knew that there were many musicians with stories to tell who
wanted to talk. After interviewing roughly forty musicians and conducting
other research, we started to notice certain common themes. The most
apparent, and the one that is the overarching theme of this book, is that the
biggest change in the Las Vegas music community happened when corporate owners took over the casinos from the mob owners and the workplace dynamic shifted from a more personal business model to a corporate
one. This shift mirrored the larger shift of the entire Las Vegas business culture. Even as the Las Vegas casino/hotel industry became more respectable,
many of the workers who helped to make Las Vegas succeed found that their
services were no longer valued or needed. There is no doubt that different
ownership led to permanent changes on the Las Vegas Strip.

The syndicate owners respected talent and work ethic and showed their
appreciation in a variety of ways. In contrast, the corporate owners sought to
cut musicians' pay, benefits, job security, and visibility; at their worst, they
made the musicians believe that their life work was unnecessary. The musicians who helped turn Las Vegas into the "Entertainment Capital of the
World" remember when skilled musicians had guaranteed, steady work,
and were appreciated for their contributions. They were able to have stable lives and satisfying careers in an often-mercurial field. They took pride

in knowing that star performers counted on them to provide some of the highest-quality support available anywhere. "There's no way I could have made it in this business without the guys and girls in the back," said Sammy Davis Jr. of the Las Vegas hotel musicians. "I've been a saloon singer for sixty years. Without the ladies and gentlemen of the orchestra I wouldn't have been there sixty days."[4] Local musician Ralph Pressler added, "That whole era back then was really neat . . . because there were so many musicians working full-time, being able to keep their significant others or their spouses at home, raise kids and send them to college."

Job opportunities for working musicians have since been severely limited, compared to what they once were. After the Las Vegas strike in 1989, other cities around the world also began to use taped music and synthesizers. Advances in technology have seemingly replaced the need for musical skill. Specific inventions such as the now-ubiquitous Auto-Tune allow even poor musicians to sound like professionals.[5] According to Frank Leone, president of Musician's Local 369 in Las Vegas from 2000 to 2015, "Prior to recorded sound, musicians were not merely musicians, they were magicians. That was a magical thing that happened when someone came in and played the flute or clarinet. You were a magical person because you had this magical ability to transform the mood. . . . Musicians [now] get treated with indifference because they've made your magical art commonplace, and readily available because of technology. And the end result is that you are treated with indifference." The failure to stop the use of taped music and synthesizers in Las Vegas in 1989 was just one of many developments that contributed to sweeping industry changes, but it was nevertheless significant in a city that has defined itself in part by high-quality entertainment.

Las Vegas is a city that is also defined by rapid change. Numerous writers and historians, including Michael Green, Eugene Moehring, and Hal Rothman have observed the consequences of such astonishing growth. Thomas Ainlay and Judy Gabaldon made this the thesis of their work, *Las Vegas: The Fabulous First Century*: "Las Vegas is unique among cities in America and, at the same time, uniquely American. No other community in the United States—or the world, for that matter—has seen so many dramatic changes in such a short time."[6] It is a chameleon city, ready to provide whatever is desired to the millions of tourists who visit each year. Out with the old and in with the new. Implode, rebuild, and implode again. Historian Hal Rothman noted, "Rapid growth obliterated the old company town and replaced it with the postmodern metropolis, the leading tourist destination in the world and the only city in the world devoted to the consumption of entertainment."[7]

The Las Vegas entertainment industry may sometimes be seen as a microcosm of the industry as a whole. With a few exceptions, most notably in the 1970s and 1980s, Las Vegas entertainment has served as a showcase for current trends. In the 1940s, 1950s, and 1960s there were star performers such as Frank Sinatra. Today, there are celebrity DJs and EDM, Cirque du Soleil and Britney Spears.[8] And, like everything from movies to television shows to books, if a concept is successful, it will be copied and done to death until a new idea comes along. This is one of the only predictable things about Las Vegas: you can count on casinos piling on a lucrative theme.

Nevertheless, there is a palpable nostalgia for Old Las Vegas. People want to believe that the era of the Rat Pack (Frank Sinatra, Dean Martin, Sammy Davis Jr., Peter Lawford, and Joey Bishop) and Elvis can be recaptured, but it is simply not to be. All that remains of that time are the memories, and even those are fading. Some of the musicians who worked in Las Vegas during its golden age of live music are still living and working here, and they have fascinating stories to tell. Many of their stories are collected here in this book. While not as famous as the headliners, hotel musicians were a significant part of the Las Vegas entertainment industry during its heyday. These professionals were around some of the best and most popular performers in the business, often while those performers were at the peak of their fame. They were onstage and backstage for live animal shows, magic shows, comedy shows, dinner shows, lounge shows, impersonator shows, circus shows, topless shows, production shows, and headliner shows.

Are their stories the last remembrances of a dying breed, of a past that will never return? Or, in an ever-changing industry, will we again hear more live music as an antidote to corporate sameness? While the answers to these and other questions about the future of Las Vegas entertainment remain unclear, stories from the past remind us of how Las Vegas originally came to be known as "The Entertainment Capital of the World."

NOTES

1. Timothy Chansud, "Bally's Showroom to be Dark in Wake of Musicians' Strike," *Las Vegas Sun*, August 2, 1989.

2. Michael L. Campbell, "'Last Offer' a Sour Note for Musicians," *Las Vegas Sun*, September 25, 1989.

3. (a) A contractor locates and hires musicians for various jobs. (b) Unless otherwise indicated, quoted material comes from interviews of the named musician. The list of interviewed musicians may be found in the bibliography section of this book. (c) Some musicians have asked to be quoted off the record; in those cases, I simply say the speaker was a musician, contractor, or other without providing any identifying information.

4. David Finnigan, "Strip Headliners Rap Taped Music," *Las Vegas Review Journal*, July 7, 1989.

5. Auto-Tune, a device that automatically corrects pitch inaccuracies, is an audio processor created by Antares Audio Technologies. With Auto-Tune, even an out-of-tune vocal performance can sound correct.

6. Thomas Ainlay and Judy Dixon Gabaldon, *Las Vegas: The Fabulous First Century* (Charleston, SC: Arcadia, 2003), 8.

7. Hal Rothman, *Neon Metropolis* (New York and London: Routledge, 2002), xix.

8. Electronic dance music (EDM), is also known as club music. It is based on a set of percussive electronic music genres created by disc jockeys (DJs).

CHAPTER ONE

....

1900–1950:
From Sawdust Floors
to Carpet Joints

Every night is New Year's Eve in Las Vegas![1]

1930s Saying

[You were fine] as long as you were what they would
call a 'stand up' guy. . . . I never signed a contract.

JOHNNY HAIG, Musician and Contractor

USIC HAS BEEN A PART of Las Vegas life for over a century. Founded in 1905 and incorporated in 1911, Las Vegas is often billed as the "Entertainment Capital of the World." The town of Las Vegas began as a rest stop on the Old Spanish Trail. By the early 1900s it was "little more than a sleepy whistle-stop servicing a railroad."[2] Nevertheless, there was music to be found there. *The Las Vegas Age*, a weekly newspaper published from 1905 until 1924, mentioned the existence of a Las Vegas Symphony Orchestra (most likely a dance band) as early as 1907.[3] One of the earliest editions of the paper, in 1905, included a program for an evening of music celebrating Christmas. Other editions advertised dances with music performed by various bands and orchestras, music teachers for hire, and concerts by local or touring musicians.

The first casino opened in 1906. Shortly thereafter, a fancier casino called the Arizona Club was one of the first to offer music, and employed three pianists.[4] The Arizona Club was located on notorious Block 16, an area originally designated for drinking, prostitution, and gambling. Early casinos appear to have hired musicians mostly to provide background music to the main entertainments of drinking and gambling. A 1912 photograph of the Arizona Club pictures a typical scene, featuring a banjo player and a violinist seated in the middle of the barroom floor while the patrons go about their business. Ed Von Tobel, an early and longtime resident, noted, "We lived on North 3rd Street and quite often in the night time we could hear rink-a-dink piano playing."[5]

Typical hotel saloon entertainment from that time included piano players, "cowboy" singers, dance bands, and small instrumental groups. The Overland Hotel advertised "good music which will add to the enjoyment of the patrons every afternoon and evening" in 1909.[6] The Vegas Park Plunge and Pavilion, a "delightful resort," advertised music for dancing on Wednesday and Saturday evenings.[7] In 1909 the Opera House opened on the second floor of the Thomas Department Store; it served as a performance venue for traveling opera and vaudeville companies and as a center for social and cultural activities.[8] In 1912 or 1913 the Opera House was renamed the Majestic Theater and continued to feature vaudeville acts as well as movies. These types of entertainments were offered through the 1920s and 1930s as Las Vegas grew. In 1924, violin and cornet player J. R. Garehime was persuaded to stay in Las Vegas, and he opened a music and jewelry store on Fremont Street, selling upright pianos, sheet music, and wind-up gramophones.[9] Anyone who could afford to do so could now have music at home.

Nevada legalized gambling in 1931 specifically to attract both long-term investors and tourists to the state. Though Las Vegas had catered to travelers since its beginning, the resort business did not become the dominant industry until the 1940s.[10] Prior to that decade, a number of different industries had helped to build the city, starting with the railroads. The railroad shops were lost after Las Vegas workers joined a large national strike. Union Pacific moved the repair shops to Caliente in an action that many believed to be in retaliation against the strongly pro-union town.[11] Residents tried to attract other businesses in the early 1920s, and tourism was just one of the industries they considered.

Even before the railroad yards were gone, there were early attempts to market Las Vegas as a resort city because of the red-light district clubs on Blocks 16 and 17.[12] The resort idea gained more initiative when the Hoover

Dam project was approved in 1928 and then when gambling was legalized in 1931. The construction of the Hoover Dam helped turn Fremont Street and other parts of Las Vegas into tourist centers.[13] According to historian Eugene P. Moehring, "75 percent of those visiting the Hoover Dam also stopped in Las Vegas and these totals grew every year."[14]

Soon, casinos like the Meadows Club were offering gambling and entertainment, catering to both dam workers and tourists. Built in 1931 on Boulder Highway by the Cornero Brothers, the Meadows provided a more refined option for nightclub entertainment than the Wild West bars and brothels on Block 16. The brothers invested $31,000 building thirty hotel rooms that had running water, plus a nightclub with its own house band. Judy Garland appeared there as a nine-year-old singer in a trio called the Gumm Sisters.[15] Jack Laughlin was hired to produce the "Meadows Revue" in the showroom with music provided by a Los Angeles band.[16]

Once tourism had been established as a viable option for Las Vegas business, the race was on to build the nicest hotel, casino, or nightclub, and owners competed to provide the best entertainment—a competition that has never stopped. All the new entertainment options available in the 1930s inspired the saying, "Every night is New Year's Eve in Las Vegas."[17]

In addition to the regularly hired touring performers and groups, each location that provided musical entertainment usually hired a regular house band that provided both music for featured entertainers and music for dinner and dancing. The growth of tourism thus coincided with the beginnings of the golden age of the casino hotel bands and lounge acts. The Musicians Union was chartered in 1931, the same year that Nevada legalized gambling. The first president was a pianist named Jack Tenny, who composed the popular song "Mexicali Rose" in 1923.[18]

Until around 1934 most of the union members were working regularly and making good wages in the smaller clubs, but this changed when the Hoover Dam construction boom ended. By 1936 many people who had come to Las Vegas and Boulder City to work on the dam were unemployed, and the smaller clubs were no longer able to afford to hire as many musicians. After this, the union reorganized and began to get more serious about seeking to provide a living wage for its members.[19]

In the 1930s and early 1940s some musicians called Las Vegas "the elephant's graveyard." Many of the first players were road musicians with "alcohol problems, personality problems, every other kind of problem you could think of," said Las Vegas musician and contractor Johnny Haig. Most of these early musicians played for dances and provided background music. Once the tourism industry began to take hold in Las Vegas, the hotel owners sought to out-do each other and the need for quality musicians grew. The union musicians were in a perfect position to capitalize on the growth of the resort entertainment industry.

In 1941 Tom Hull built the El Rancho Vegas, considered by most historians to be the first true resort-casino on the Las Vegas Strip, or Highway 91.[20] His sister Sally Stewart was the first entertainment director, and she sought to hire the best performers that were available to serve as a draw for the new casino.[21] The El Rancho had two main entertainment venues: the dinner theater that accommodated three hundred (called the Round-Up Room until 1951, then the Opera House), and Nugget Nell's Cocktail Lounge.[22] Touring headliners Peggy Lee and Sammy Davis Jr. both made their Las Vegas debuts here in 1946.[23] The El Rancho dinner theater also had a regular house entertainment group—Frank Fay and the El Rancho Starlets, backed by the Garwood Van Orchestra.[24] Through the years, various orchestras served as the house band for the El Rancho, including the Carlton Hayes Orchestra, the Al Jahns Orchestra, the Chick Floyd Orchestra, the Sterling Young Orchestra, the Ted Fio Rito Orchestra, the Bob Ellis Orchestra, and the Dick Rice Orchestra, among others.[25]

Also on the Highway 91 Strip, the old Pair-O-Dice Nightclub was replaced in 1942 with a new resort property called the Last Frontier. While the Pair-O-Dice had offered live music like many of the small nightclubs, the owner of the Last Frontier, R. E. Griffith, wanted his entertainment to be as good as or better than what the El Rancho was offering. On a visit to Los Angeles, he heard a talented singer named Maxine Lewis. At his request, Lewis moved to Las Vegas in 1942 to become the entertainment director of the Last Frontier. Lewis later said Griffith hired her because "I knew most everybody in show business." At that time, said Lewis, there were no sidewalks on the Strip—everything was dirt. The customers for the showrooms were still mostly locals, dressed in Western attire. Still, the Last Frontier was a much nicer club than the Pair-O-Dice or the Meadows and it competed directly with the El Rancho for business. Lewis recalled, "We thought it was so gorgeous! And the public thought that."[26] The Last Frontier also hired a regular house band, Gus Martell and his 5th Avenue Orchestra. Its showroom, the Ramona Room, could seat six hundred guests. Lewis was given a large budget and a free hand.[27]

To fill the showroom, Lewis ran advertisements all over the country and traveled to cities like New York and Chicago to see talent agents for new acts. She was the first booker in Las Vegas to hire Liberace. His original contract was for $750 per week, but Lewis thought so much of his act that she doubled his salary to $1,500 per week after his first show.[28] "He was such a great artist. . . . Lovely boy, nice boy."[29]

In addition to its star room, sometime in the early 1950s The Last Frontier opened what was possibly the first true lounge with musical entertainment. Some historians place the birth of the lounge act in Las Vegas in 1953, but longtime Las Vegas resident and entertainment writer Bill Willard said that he knew there was lounge entertainment as early as 1951 because he saw it himself.[30] Nevertheless, the Mary Kaye Trio was the first act to play in the lounge of the Last Frontier. The jazz trio had just ended a successful run in the main showroom, and the owner did not want them to leave. There was already another act booked in the main room for the following two weeks, though. Mary Kaye suggested that a stage be built in the bar area, essentially inventing the entire concept of lounge music. Norman Kaye said, "We were the first lounge group advertised as such. . . . It was a marvelous career for all of us."[31] After that, most hotels included lounges with free entertainment; many hotels still offer free lounge music.

Many of the earliest owners and investors in Las Vegas came from California during and after the late 1930s, when the California state government cracked down on illegal gambling. They saw opportunities to run legitimate businesses in Nevada, where gambling was legal. The 91 Club, the Pioneer Club, the Frontier Club, the El Cortez, and the El Rancho were all owned by men with previous connections to gambling in California. By 1946 the crime syndicate members from the East Coast began to infiltrate the casino business, beginning with Benjamin "Bugsy" Siegel. Soon, the eastern mob controlled virtually all of the sports betting in town.[32] Susan Berman, daughter of mobster and Flamingo executive Dave Berman, remembered that most of the gangsters were happy to have a place where they could live a more normal and settled life. "Life was to be enjoyed with major events, orchestrated perfectly, planned to the smallest detail, no expense spared. And because the gangster/mobsters and their wives were so happy at last to have a place to throw respectable parties, they went all out; no one was ever as proud or as fine hosts as they were."[33]

According to Frank Leone, the Las Vegas Musicians Union president from 2000 to 2015, the real change in Las Vegas entertainment came when Siegel and Billy Wilkerson opened the Flamingo Hotel in 1946, a property that was designed specifically to attract the rich and famous to Las Vegas. The Flamingo was modeled after Miami Beach motels; the owners spent lavishly on food, decoration, and entertainment.[34]

Originally, Wilkerson was the sole owner of the property. He owned several upscale nightclubs in Los Angeles, and wanted to build something similar in Las Vegas. Unfortunately, he ran out of money and was forced to seek financing from other sources, eventually partnering with Siegel. Bugsy Siegel, a notorious mobster, gradually assumed control of the hotel construction; as he did so, he overspent his budget several times over and then he too had to seek more money from his Mafia bosses.

By the time the hotel opened on December 26, 1946, it had cost $6 million. Comedian Jimmy Durante, Spanish bandleader Xavier Cugat, and singer Rose Marie were hired for the opening night, but were able to keep the showroom full for only two nights.[35] After that, attendance declined sharply, and the opening was a flop. Much of the hotel was unfinished and the formal atmosphere and the fancy attire of the dealers put off the local customers.

Siegel closed the hotel to finish building it and held a second opening on March 1, 1947. He also hired Maxine Lewis away from the Last Frontier to be his entertainment director. "He liked the shows I had, you know, and he used to try and get them from here. . . . He offered them more money, but they wouldn't leave." She remembered booking the Andrews Sisters for this second, more-successful opening. Even though Siegel knew he was now in trouble with his bosses, Lewis said that you would never have known that he was nervous about anything. "No, you never knew it."[36]

Bugsy Siegel was murdered in 1947 and a new Mafia owner, Gus Green-

baum, took over. Susan Berman's father, Dave, was one of the Mafia oper-
atives now in charge of the Flamingo. "Before Ben Siegel's body was cold,
Gus Greenbaum, Moe Sedway, and my father walked into the pit of the Flamingo, where they already worked, and said, 'We're in charge now.'" Singer
Rose Marie said, "We were told that Mr. Siegel went back to L.A. evidently
to try and get more money, and that's when he was killed." Entertainer Alan
King remembered, "I'll never forget how I was told that Benny Siegel was
killed. Somebody said to me, 'Benny took a cab.' That was the line. . . . See,
nobody ever died. They took them out, they were eighty-sixed."[37]

This was the darker side of life for the mob families who were building
their lives in Las Vegas:

> Vegas is not a woman's town. . . . The shadows of their husbands'
> former and present Mob lives were always hanging over them.
> Men died 'suddenly' in my dad's business—Ben Siegel, many
> others—would their man be next? Would their children be kid-
> napped? Would they be harmed? . . . No matter how successful
> my father became, when he was speaking at civic events, elected
> head of the Temple, honored by City of Hope and the Variety
> Club, somehow there was always the message that we were still
> a little different from other successful people in the nation, that
> we could only trust our own, that one has to make one's way out-
> side the structure of America as a whole, because even though the
> word never left my father's lips, we were Mob.[38]

This seemed to give the mobsters all the more reason to focus on
entertainment as escapism. Berman continues, "Most of the floor-show
stars came to our home to hang out with my dad. He loved entertainers,
especially Jimmy Durante and Jack Benny. . . . We were there for every
floorshow opening at a ringside table with a host of my dad's friends and
guests. . . . I can still remember how my heart stopped in anticipation when
I heard 'And now from the fabulous Flamingo Hotel, here's our lovely line
of dancers.' And the chorus girls would parade out in glory."[39]

After school, Berman would rush to the showroom to see the dancers rehearsing for a new floorshow every two weeks. She remembered the
house orchestra, the Tune Toppers.[40] Greenbaum made the Flamingo profitable and his success drew many other crime syndicate figures to Las Vegas

to build casinos in the 1940s and 1950s.[41] By the end of the 1940s, the resort hotels included the El Rancho, the Last Frontier, the Flamingo, and the Thunderbird, in addition to other smaller properties.[42]

The mob owners liked and respected the house musicians, and not just the big-name entertainers. Quite a few of the musicians referred to these older syndicate casino owners as "the boys." The musicians knew that the boys would often skim money off the top of their profits, and so not have enough to cover their bills. Casinos frequently went out of business. Las Vegas musician and contractor Johnny Haig remembered one entertainer at the Frontier, Victor Borge. Borge, who was paid $35,000 a week in the 1950s was packing the place and even had people sitting on the stage. Haig said that Borge would go to the cashier cage each afternoon and demand $5,000. "If they didn't have it, he wouldn't play."

Almost all of the musicians who worked for the boys enjoyed the experience, though they were still very careful. According to Johnny Haig, "They had two rules: You don't mess with their women or their money . . . , which was understood. [You were fine] as long as you were what they would call a 'stand up' guy. . . . I never signed a contract." The Mafia business owners never wrote things down, to avoid leaving a trail that could be used as evidence later, but they also wanted to be treated with respect like other businesspeople. E. Parry Thomas, the first banker to regularly lend money to casino owners in Las Vegas, kept no notes, calendars, or appointment books. He recalled similar experiences when dealing with the mob: "We did so many deals, especially in the early years, where you'd made a verbal agreement with someone on a loan or whatnot, and you'd look them in the eye and shake hands on it and that would be that. I learned that from the gamblers, because that's the way they operated. The most important thing in the world for those old-timer gamblers was their work. You had a lot of tinhorns you had to separate out, but the real honest-to-goodness gaming people—their word was their bond."[43]

It was, in some ways, a simpler time. Johnny Haig remembered a typical way that one casino owner used to work with him. This man "called me into his office and said, 'I got Isaac Hayes, Sammy Davis Jr., [and I need] a 42 piece orchestra, New Years' Eve. . . . How much is it going to cost me?'" Then, said Haig, "He just stared at me. I told him what the price was and he looked at me and said, 'Okay.' Negotiations were much simpler then. 'You're getting $90 a week. How about $100 a week?' 'Sounds good to me.'"

Casino owners recognized that big-name entertainers attracted customers and raised profits and all of the new resorts needed good local musicians to support the stars. Comedians such as Sophie Tucker, Milton Berle, and Joe E. Lewis, and musicians like pianist Liberace and singer Sammy Davis Jr., were just some of the stars who worked in Las Vegas during this period. Headliners who had previously shunned Las Vegas were suddenly interested. "Now they all wanted to play there," said Lewis.[44]

Still, it was difficult to keep the showrooms filled with big-name stars all the time. Because of this, talent bookers like Maxine Lewis were willing to give unproven acts a chance to work, something that rarely happened with the later corporate hotel owners, who rarely used unknown entertainers. Lewis said, "I was good with knowing talent. And so, acts that I knew had the talent. . . . I would give them the opportunity. . . . My judgment was right because then they would go on to higher things." She remembered booking Dean Martin and Jerry Lewis in 1949, "before they were tried and true."[45] And as a performer herself, Lewis made sure that her show people were given livable salaries. This, too, differed from the usual attitude of the later corporate owners who did not always reward talent or potential with fair wages.

An entertainer who drew big crowds to the casino could have several hotels competing for his or her services. The crime syndicate owners notoriously skimmed profits and concealed money, but they spared no expense on top-quality entertainment. Musician Don Hannah recalled that the syndicate was always willing for entertainment and food to take a loss as long as the owners made money in the casinos; the owners considered musical entertainment a necessity for attracting customers. No matter what happened, the owners never wanted to have a theater "dark" (closed). The entertainers and owners worked together to make sure that this never happened. As an example, one musician told of a casino owner who flew an entire band back from New York just to keep the showroom open when the scheduled entertainer became ill. Headliners would occasionally be asked to stay on to cover for other performers when necessary. The fact that the audience was getting a different show from the one they expected was not as important as keeping the showroom open to the owners.

The early casino owners were generous to their employees and seemed to be genuinely interested in their well-being. They inquired about family members, gave money to those who were struggling, and complimented musicians and performers on their talents. They paid double and triple fees for performers to entertain during off hours, and tipped heavily. Even Las Vegas town members gave the mob owners credit for keeping crime to a minimum. The word was out that if you were going to do something criminal, then you should stay away from Las Vegas. With the boys in control, there was little crime in the city, and they worked hard to make sure that it stayed that way. Former Stratosphere owner Bob Stupak noted, "It was like we had two police forces. We had the regular police . . . and we had the boys."[46] Musician Don Hannah remarked that the mob members were even known to take dead bodies to California just to avoid attaching any stigma to Las Vegas. According to writer Susan Berman, "The rule was, in fact, that nobody gets killed in Vegas. . . . What morons would rob the men who ran Murder, Inc.?"[47] Actress and performer Debbie Reynolds recalled, "No one got killed that wasn't supposed to, and we were never frightened of anything of that sort."[48]

Maxine Lewis never had any problems with the mob owners. "Believe it or not, they [the mob members] minded their own business and they never bothered me. They certainly treated me wonderfully. . . . They had no influence [on her bookings and] . . . they always left it up to me." Lewis remembered the early days of Las Vegas entertainment fondly. "I loved Vegas. . . . It was wonderful in those years. Nobody had the fun that we had, I'll tell you that. . . . Nobody!"[49]

Ed Von Tobel, longtime resident and business owner, remembered, "When the Eastern guys came and opened hotels and casinos in the Forties and Fifties, we were happy to see them. They brought business to town and became active in the Elks and Rotary Club like the rest of us. We didn't look down on them. This town has always been friendly to anyone that brings in business."[50]

The multitalented entertainment writer Bill Willard arrived in Las Vegas in 1949 and became the first entertainment editor of the morning edition of the *Las Vegas Sun*. He also reviewed shows and filed hard news about Las Vegas for the daily and weekly *Variety* magazines. From his correspondence, it is apparent that not everyone was pleased with the business methods of the mob hotel owners as time went on. In a letter to his bosses at *Variety* in April of 1951, Willard wrote, "The townspeople resent the gangster methods of the resort hotels and casinos. . . . Petitions are being prepared for circulation, in order that an anti-gambling bill might be introduced in the legislature next session."[51] Needless to say, this effort was unsuccessful.

The early owners were good to "their" people, but closed ranks to outsiders. Bill Willard wrote about his experiences as a show critic:

I admit I'm puzzled about motives behind many things here. The bosses are a secretive lot, given to banding together for their competitive, yet joint enterprises. Unless you happen to be a brownnoser or a member of that ilk, you are always on the outside looking in. I am neither. My business here, reporting and reviewing shows, and as a columnist for a local paper, has never received solid backing from the various bonifaces. They want full control, and definitely resent any criticism of their operations. Although Las Vegas is an important center for show business, not a single owner fully understands show business. Men like Jake Kozloff, Beldon Katleman [El Rancho Vegas], book talent, yet they know little about productions or presentations.[52]

Willard was also an early witness to the discrimination that arose in the 1930s and 1940s. During the early part of the century, there had been a limited tolerance in the attitudes of the whites toward other races. Though people refused to sell property to non-whites in so-called white neighborhoods, it was common for all races to do business together, and some non-whites were financially successful and respected. Block 16 was closed to non-whites, so the property owners on Block 17 took advantage of the opportunity and established bars and brothels that served them.

Over time, as the town grew, Las Vegas began to lose its frontier town quality. Unfortunately, many new residents brought their prejudices with them. A branch of the National Association for the Advancement of Colored People (NAACP) was established in Las Vegas in 1928, followed by the Colored Citizens' Labor and Protective Association in 1931. The latter group was formed specifically to lobby the Hoover Dam project managers to hire black workers. In spite of their efforts, the number of black workers in the Boulder Dam workforce remained woefully small.[53]

In the 1940s non-whites were mostly segregated in the west side of town, known as the Westside, and race relations were at an all-time low. Discrimination continued to worsen until even the downtown casinos closed their doors to non-whites. Major entertainers such as Sammy Davis Jr. and Lena Horne were forbidden to stay in the hotel rooms, eat in the restaurants, or gamble in the casinos where they worked. The situation was the same for Hispanic performers. Sammy Davis Jr. referred to the segregation as "the Las Vegas version of Tobacco Road."[54]

Some of the early casino owners, like some of the later corporate owners, were opposed to integration and even lobbied against it in 1939, using the argument that admitting blacks would be bad for business. This created more opportunities for black business owners, who filled the gap by building their own casinos on Jackson Street. Beginning in 1945 the Westside casinos included the Cotton Club, the El Morocco, the Brown Derby, the Elks Club, and the New Town Tavern, and non-white performers like Sammy Davis Jr. and Cab Calloway were welcomed.[55] Las Vegas, in spite of the numerous non-white entertainers headlining on the Strip, had become one of the most segregated places in the country by 1950.[56]

Not all of the mob owners thought the same way. Bugsy Siegel greatly admired the singer Lena Horne and hired her for the Flamingo reopening. He also provided her with accommodations at the Flamingo, making her the first black person to stay at a resort on the Strip, though she was not allowed into the casinos because he was "pressured by certain patrons to remember that Las Vegas was segregated."[57] Management also reportedly required that after she checked out the sheets be stripped off her bed and burned.

Abel Green, the New York *Variety* editor, wrote to Bill Willard in 1951 about the possibility of a hard news story on the discrimination in Las Vegas when he heard that entertainer Billy Daniels was angry about having to "cross the tracks" just to eat. "We don't want to make a federal case out of it, but there might be a yarn there."[58]

Around this same time, Willard was banned from reviewing the shows at the Last Frontier. Attempting to explain the ban to his editors, Willard mentioned several things that could have created the problem, but believed that one incident in particular was the most likely cause: an unpublished item about black entertainer Hazel Scott. Scott had a contract with the Last Frontier that guaranteed "full privileges," meaning that she could stay in the hotel, eat in the restaurants, and swim in the pool. In a phone call to Scott, Willard mentioned that he had been tipped that the pool was being "repainted" in order to prevent Scott from using it. Scott was "alarmed, thinking that the rumor was all over town." She immediately called the owner Jake Kozloff, who in turn questioned Willard about the conversation. Willard was honest and told him about the tip, but also indicated that he had no intention of using the item without checking it thoroughly. "O.K., I take your word," said Kozloff.[59]

After Scott did go for a swim, she told Willard that it had again been closed, this time for chlorination. "It was the longest chlorination job I've ever known for a swimming pool," she said, "Three days!" Willard wrote to his editors, "I'd be willing to put up a buck that the ban from the Last Frontier is because of the Hazel Scott incident, although it was never published. With Josephine Baker arriving on April 18 for a couple of weeks, Mr. K. just might be put on the spot. . . . Hazel has informed Baker about the management's disarming front. Josephine Baker will not only have full privileges of the hotel, but will see that the Negro residents come out from 'behind their iron curtain,' and attend her nightly soirees."[60] Eventually, Willard was allowed back in to the Last Frontier, but the discrimination issues continued for quite some time.

By the end of the decade, Las Vegas could boast an impressive list of entertainers who had appeared on the Strip: the Andrews Sisters, Louis Armstrong, Gene Austin, Vic Damone, Sammy Davis Jr., Delta Rhythm Boys, Jimmy Durante, Benny Goodman Orchestra, Mitzi Green, Lena Horne, Ink Spots, Spike Jones, Peggy Lee, Joe E. Lewis, Liberace, Rose Marie, Dean Martin and Jerry Lewis, Mills Brothers, Harry Richman, Danny Thomas, Sophie Tucker, Rudy Vallee, and the Paul Whiteman Orchestra were just some of famous performers from that time.[61] The stage was set was for the construction and entertainment boom of the 1950s.

NOTES

1. Moehring, *Resort City in the Sunbelt,* 21

2. Eugene P. Moehring and Michael S. Green, *Las Vegas: A Centennial History* (Reno: University of Nevada Press, 2005), viii.

3. "Local Notes," *Las Vegas Age,* December 21, 1907, http://digital.lvccld.org/lvccg/image/13022.pdf.

4. Ainlay and Gabaldon, *Las Vegas,* 29.

5. Moehring and Green, *Las Vegas,* 32.

6. "Local Notes," *Las Vegas Age,* August 21, 1909, http://digital.lvccld.org/lvccg/image/21125.pdf.

7. "Local Notes," *Las Vegas Age,* August 7, 1909, http://digital.lvccld.org/lvccg/image/20796.pdf.

8. Ainlay and Gabaldon, *Las Vegas,* 24.

9. Moehring and Green, *Las Vegas,* 67.

10. Eugene P. Moehring, *Resort City in the Sunbelt,* 2nd ed. (Reno: University of Nevada Press, 2000), 13.

11. Moehring and Green, *Las Vegas,* 61.

12. Ibid., 11.

13. Ibid., 82.

14. Moehring, *Resort City in the Sunbelt,* 18.

15. James Roman, *Chronicles of Old Las Vegas: Exposing Sin City's High Stakes History* (New York: Museyon, 2011), 52, 53.

16. Moehring, *Resort City in the Sunbelt,* 21.

17. Ibid.

18. Frank Wright, *Nevada Yesterdays: Short Looks at Las Vegas History* (Las Vegas: Stephens Press, 2005), 81.

19. Ibid.

20. "Story," Hotel El Rancho Vegas: The Strip's First Resort, virtual exhibit, Special Collections, UNLV Center for Gaming Research, Las Vegas, http://gaming.unlv.edu/ElRanchoVegas/story.html.

21. Lecture notes, Bill Willard to the Nevada Historical Society, "The Entertainment Industry's Role in Shaping Nevada's Image," 13, Bill Willard Collection, MS 2001-17 Special Collections, UNLV Libraries, University of Nevada, Las Vegas.

22. Larry Gragg, *Bright Light City: Las Vegas in Popular Culture* (Lawrence: University Press of Kansas, 2013), 116; "Entertainment," Hotel El Rancho Vegas: The Strip's First Resort, virtual exhibit, http://gaming.unlv.edu/ElRanchoVegas/entertainment.html.

23. David Fluke, 1947–1981 Notebooks, Collection 89–29, Folder 25, Special Collections, UNLV Libraries, University of Nevada, Las Vegas.

24. Moehring, *Resort City in the Sunbelt,* 44.

25. "Entertainment," Hotel El Rancho Vegas: The Strip's First Resort, virtual exhibit, http://gaming.unlv.edu/ElRanchoVegas/entertainmentheadliners.html

26. Maxine Lewis, "Oral History," February 20, 1987, Special Collections, UNLV Libraries, University of Nevada, Las Vegas.

27. David Fluke Collection, Box 1, Folder 23, "Frontier Hotel Spends 100G for Talent in a Year, Plans Expansion," *Billboard*, October 16, 1943, 5; Gragg, *Bright Light City*, 117.

28. Letter from Maxine Lewis to Brigham Townsend, Box 11, Folder 5, Bill Willard Collection, MS 2001-17.

29. Lewis, "Oral History," February 20, 1987.

30. Ibid.

31. Valerie J. Nelson, "Mary Kaye, 83: Singer Brought All-Night Lounge Acts to Las Vegas," *Los Angeles Times*, February 20, 2007.

32. Ainlay and Gabaldon, *Las Vegas*, 61, 99.

33. Susan Berman, *Lady Las Vegas: The Inside Story behind America's Neon Oasis* (New York: A&E Network and TV Books, 1996), 24.

34. Barbara Land and Myrick Land, *A Short History of Las Vegas* (Reno: University of Nevada Press, 1999), 95–96.

35. Roman, *Chronicles of Old Las Vegas*, 80.

36. Lewis, "Oral History," February 20, 1987.

37. Berman, *Lady Las Vegas*, 74 ("Before Ben Siegel's")," 73 ("We were told"), 74 ("I'll never forget").

38. Ibid., 26–27.

39. Ibid., 78.

40. Ibid., 221.

41. Land and Land, *A Short History of Las Vegas*, 100.

42. Knepp, *Las Vegas*, 32.

43. Jack Sheehan, *Quiet Kingmaker of Las Vegas: E. Parry Thomas* (Las Vegas: Stephens Press, 2009), 92–93.

44. Lewis, "Oral History," February 20, 1987.

45. Ibid.

46. Land and Land, *A Short History of Las Vegas*, 101.

47. Berman, *Lady Las Vegas*, 79.

48. Land and Land, *A Short History of Las Vegas*, 101.

49. Lewis, "Oral History," February 20, 1987.

50. Berman, *Lady Las Vegas*, 186.

51. Bill Willard Collection, MS 2001-17.

52. Box 9, Folder 2, Bill Willard Collection, MS 2001-17.

53. Ainlay and Gabaldon, *Las Vegas*, 117.

54. Ibid.

55. Roman, *Chronicles of Old Las Vegas*, 101–103.

56. Ainlay and Gabaldon, *Las Vegas*, 117.

57. James Roman, *Chronicles of Old Las Vegas: Exposing Sin City's High Stakes History*, (New York: Museyon, Inc., 2011), 110.

58. Box 9, Folder 2, Bill Willard Collection, MS 2001-17.

59. Ibid. ("alarmed," "O.K.").

60. Ibid. ("It was the longest," "I'd be willing").

61. Lecture notes, Bill Willard to the Nevada Historical Society, "The Entertainment Industry's Role in Shaping Nevada's Image," Bill Willard Collection, MS 2001-17.

CHAPTER TWO
....

1950–1960:
The Roaring Fifties

Everybody was building hotels on the Strip,
hammering and construction everywhere.

SUSAN BERMAN, Daughter of Mobster and
Flamingo Executive Dave Berman

The world was your oyster.

DAVE HAWLEY, Musician

$\mathcal{I}$N THE 1950S it became clear that tourism and defense spending would continue to lead to more growth in Las Vegas as the successes of the 1940s resorts spawned further expansion.[1] By 1951 the Thunderbird Hotel, the Desert Inn, and the Silver Slipper had joined the El Rancho, the New Frontier, and the Flamingo on the Strip. Then a number of new properties were built in quick succession: the Sahara (1952), the Sands (1952), the Royal Nevada (1955), the Riviera (1955), the Dunes (1955), the Hacienda (1956), the Tropicana (1957), and the Stardust (1958), in addition to off-Strip properties such as the Showboat (1954), the Fremont (1956), and the ground-breaking Moulin Rouge (1955). "Everybody was building hotels on the Strip, hammering and construction everywhere," said Susan Berman, who grew up in Las Vegas. "Between 1950 and 1958, I watched so many hotels go up. . . . Eastern Jewish and Italian mobsters financed the hotels as usual and installed their own front men."[2]

According to Nevada historian Hal Rothman,

The purchase of the El Cortez [in 1945] initiated a pattern; in every subsequent purchase or development of a resort, 'connected' illegal gamblers who became legal in Nevada and prominent local citizens joined together. Outside capital and some form of local respectability were closely linked. [This pattern of financing continued throughout the 1940s, 1950s, and 1960s.] Siegel led a generation to Las Vegas that included Gus Greenbaum, an Arizona bookmaker; David Berman, a veteran of ten years in Sing Sing and the former boss of the rackets in Minneapolis. . . . Israel "Icepick Willie" Alderman, who ran typical 1930s gaming roadhouses called 'carpet joints' in Minneapolis; Moe Sedway, a Siegel associate from Los Angeles; Morris B. 'Moe' Dalitz, associated with the Mayfield Road Gang in Cleveland; Jack Entratter of the Copacabana in New York and . . . countless other figures linked to the underworld and illegal gambling. . . . Nowhere else in the nation could illegal gamblers ply their trade, make piles of money, and become respectable citizens.[3]

The locals welcomed anyone who brought business to Las Vegas. Casino owner Bob Stupak remembered, "They might have been a little tarnished. . . . When they came here, they were automatically respected citizens, part of the community."[4]

Each new hotel-casino owner sought to have high-quality entertainment and hired the best local musicians available for their in-house orchestras. They also hired entertainment directors, dancers, stagehands, costumers, and everyone else needed to put on a first-rate show. The Thunderbird, finished in 1948, opened with entertainer Nat King Cole, though he was not allowed to gamble in the hotel because of his race.[5] Hal Broadus was the entertainment director there in the 1950s.[6] The Al Jahns Orchestra provided accompaniment for the stars in the Pow Wow Showroom in addition to music for dancing, and there was a chorus line called, appropriately, the Thunderbird Dancers.[7] The showroom enjoyed an early period of success, with patrons such as Howard Hughes and Wilbur Clark regularly reserving booths to watch the shows.[8] They witnessed performances by big-name entertainers such as jazz singer Ella Fitzgerald, who made her Las Vegas debut there in 1949.[9] More celebrities began to come to Las Vegas for the shows, which continued to proliferate.

Wilbur Clark opened the Desert Inn on April 24, 1950, and hired Edgar

Bergen with Charlie McCarthy, actress Vivian Blaine, and the Donn Arden
Dancers to entertain in the Painted Desert Showroom.[10] At that time Las
Vegas residents called it "the most brilliant social event in the history of the
Strip."[11] The Carlton Hayes Orchestra was the house band, providing music
for the showroom and dancing, and jazz trumpeter and singer Louis Armstrong was an early headliner there.[12] This hotel was also the first in Las
Vegas to feature Frank Sinatra.[13] The new hotel was dazzling, with a spectacular room for dancing on the third floor called the Sky Room, and individual thermostats to control the air temperature in each guest room.[14]

　　Like Billy Wilkerson of the Flamingo, Clark was able to finish the Desert Inn only with the help of mob financing, provided by Moe Dalitz and
his Cleveland associates. Mob operators who ran the clubs in Cleveland
asked Donn Arden, who went on to become one of the most successful producers in Las Vegas, to come to the Desert Inn. "I felt obliged to go. They
were 'the boys' and they paid well."[15] Las Vegas was still small enough for
the mob owners to maintain a personal management style, in spite of the
rapid growth. "The boys were gentlemen at all times to me and treated me
like a Queen," said singer Rose Marie. "It was like a family. You could go
to any of the hotels, and you didn't pay for anything. If you wanted to go to
the bar and get a couple of drinks and they knew you were working the Flamingo, you'd get no check." Comedian Shecky Greene agreed: "These guys
were great. They would protect you, they would take care of you. . . . It was
a wonderful bunch of people to work for."[16]

　　The mob owners were often the biggest fans of the stars they hired. Like
Bugsy Siegel, they loved entertainers, and most entertainers loved working
in Las Vegas. "They were great, great audiences," said comedian Red But-
tons. "You'd look forward to working, and the money was enormous. Four
weeks in Las Vegas could buy you a Third World country."[17] Beldon Katleman, who owned and operated the El Rancho Vegas, would provide gourmet buffets for his entertainers and personal guests. Las Vegas manager and
producer Matt Gregory remarked, "The buffets, I don't have to tell you
what they looked like, you know, the Beluga caviar and champagne—and
this was for the entertainers, you know, and he had the band, Joe E. [Lewis],
the whole thing. He was an incredible host. . . . His employees were very
gung-ho on Beldon. Those that worked with him, to this day . . . people will

say, 'Beldon was a prick.' They [his employees] say, 'Hold it. Maybe to you, but not to me.'"[18]

Most people who worked in the mob-run casinos and hotels were so pleased with their work environment that they turned a blind eye to the mob's more sinister side. "I worked with a lot of management and this is by no means an apology for the behavior of some of these men in the past, but you didn't need a contract," said performer Alan King. "All you had to do was shake hands with one of them and that was solid." Hollywood star Debbie Reynolds noted, "They didn't come near you as a woman, you know what I mean? You were like their family. It was a wonderful time, and they were great bosses. I miss that loyalty, that respect. I don't say I respect how they got the money. It's none of my business anyway."[19] Matt Gregory remarked, "The thing that turned Beldon [Katleman] off was pettiness, grubbiness, cheapness—even when he did terrible things, he did 'em with style."[20]

The musicians who worked here during this period felt respected and valued; the mob owners paid them well and treated them well. The high demand for their services was only part of the reason that good musicians in Las Vegas were so appreciated by the moneymen. The mobsters genuinely enjoyed and rewarded real talent, generously sharing the profits generated by the successful new shows.

At first, the practice of changing shows every two weeks continued, and the new competition made it more difficult for talent bookers like Maxine Lewis to find top name entertainers for their showrooms. Lewis looked for talent in Los Angeles, New York, San Francisco, and Chicago, but she learned that audiences "wanted to see stars, not untried acts."[21] This led the showroom bookers to Hollywood, and the practice of featuring movie stars to draw the customers in to their casinos.

In 1952 the Sahara opened as a 200-room resort with headliners Ray Bolger and Lisa Kirk and the Sa-Harem Dancers. Danny Thomas was the star attraction for the opening of the Sands, also in 1952.[22] Bill Willard wrote a long column in *Variety* magazine about the glamorous four-day opening of this new hotel, mentioning the numerous stars attending. His review praised the Donn Arden Dancers; the lighting, costume, and set designs; and specifically mentioned the orchestra: "Ray Sinatra has 13 men on the stand, and all are capable musicians, judging from the excellent background supplied," wrote Willard. "Sinatra knows how to wield a baton for soloists and after several more shows will have all cues and passages dovetailing for proper welded flow."[23] The practice of naming and reviewing the house orchestras continued until the 1970s, when most corporate owners stopped listing the orchestras in their programs.

Sinatra moved on to another hotel when Jack Entratter offered Antonio Morelli the position of music director for the Sands and gave him billing on the Sands' marquee. (Entratter had previously worked with Morelli at the New York Copacabana Club.) Morelli not only led a long and illustrious career as music director for the Sands, but also was a classically trained musician who worked tirelessly to bring culture to the city of Las Vegas with his Community Chorus and Symphony Orchestra. (He can be seen in the background of the Rat Pack show films of the 1960s.)[24]

The Hollywood stars kept coming and their salaries increased exponentially. In 1953 Marlene Dietrich received the largest paycheck to date for her Las Vegas debut—$30,000 per week. Ronald Reagan made his one and only appearance in Las Vegas at the Last Frontier in 1954. In 1955 Liberace was the opening entertainment for the Riviera, the first high-rise property on the Strip.[25] "The Riviera was a beautiful, big hotel, and the stage was wonderful. In those days we had a 20-piece orchestra," said Debbie Reynolds. "You didn't have the expenses that you have today. The hotel picked up a lot of those costs in those days. But not anymore. That's changed."[26]

Star salaries continued to climb astronomically as the casinos competed for talent, and the money only got bigger. It was a great time to be a headliner in Las Vegas. The stars had their pick of places to perform during "the lushest price war in U.S. entertainment history."[27]

Bill Willard, the inimitable Las Vegas entertainment writer for *Variety*, charted the rising costs of entertainment and the difficulty of finding stars for so many showrooms. When the Sands opened in 1952, Willard wrote,

To alleviate the current shortage of top name talent, Entratter [the Sands entertainment director] is planning to keep his attractions in for at least six weeks. This policy, if put into practice, will receive the acid test during summer months when Vegas jumps with heavy tourist traffic and turnover is constant. . . . If the idea works, other hotels may follow suit. Seven plush niteries going full blast 52 weeks and hiring acts practically in wholesale quantities can put a drain on the talent market quickly. The Sands' scheme should be a boon to many new acts seeking work, and booking for longer span will make the western trek worthwhile. Further, the multi-week pact will hasten the end of monopolistic practices on the part of bonifaces wishing to grab and hold certain big name acts to 18-month 'no-contracts-elsewhere-on-the-Strip' ball and chain."[28]

The rest of the country began to take notice. Historian Larry Gragg wrote, "The arrival of so much talent in Las Vegas attracted the attention of major magazines and newspapers. In 1953, the *Wall Street Journal, New York Times, Los Angeles Times, Variety, Saturday Evening Post, Life, Look,* and *Time,* among dozens of periodicals, published articles that noted the explosion of celebrities appearing in the showrooms."[29] By July of 1953 Willard was able to boast, "Never before in nitery [*sic*] history has such a high-priced collection of show biz gems been placed on display in such profusion." Visitors to Las Vegas that month could see Spike Jones at the Flamingo, Milton Berle at the Sands, Betty Hutton at the Desert Inn, Herb Shriner and the Mary Kaye Trio at the Last Frontier, Gale Storm at the Thunderbird, Vic Damone at the El Rancho, and Red Skelton at the Sahara. A bidding war had transpired for Red Skelton, who was offered a weekly contract of $25,000. Willard also noted, "Low estimate of the combined outlay comes to $160,000 per week, including supporting acts, dance lines, orchs., etc."[30]

The rest of the country was entranced by all of the hoopla. In 1955 Joe Schoenfeld, an editor of *Variety* magazine, wrote to Bill Willard, "With Vegas booming constantly from an entertainment standpoint, you are on the ground to get the news of important booking more quickly than anybody. We are very interested in this and we are particularly interested in salaries, provided they are accurate and not blown up by press agents."[31] In response, Willard was able to point out that the outlay for entertainment had gone from budgets of $8,000 per week in 1950 to budgets of $30,000 per week by 1955. He wrote, "Some of these terpsichorean epics alone set casinos back $30,000 per week, and outlay for headline talent, although in many instance ballooned by eager-beaver pressagentry [*sic*], has soared to ridiculous heights in the talent battle." The population of Las Vegas had also almost doubled since 1950: from 24,626 people to 44,750 by 1955.[32]

The casino owners were not worried about the focus on Las Vegas. According to Willard, "The gambling bosses of Las Vegas pay little attention. . . . Even the guys who are named periodically on lists and who squirmed before the Kefauver Committee seem unconcerned. Inside their bailiwick, which is Nevada and which gives them asylum of a sort, the gambler is made to feel secure. He is a business man and gambling is big business here."[33]

To alleviate the pressures of constantly searching for new talent and paying the competitive salaries of the stars, some entertainment directors established long-running shows featuring the house band, dancers, and singers. In 1955 the Dunes was one of the first hotels to do this with its "Magic Carpet Revues."[34] Another plan put forth by several of the hotel owners was to create one booking agency responsible for hiring all of the entertainment for the Strip. "The claim is, if it works, that bidding for top name acts via big salaries would cease," said Willard.[35] This did not come about. Star salaries continued to climb, and many of the hotels began featuring the elaborate shows called Las Vegas Spectaculars by the late 1950s.

Some of the largest of these were produced by Donn Arden at the Desert Inn and Harold Minsky at the Dunes. Minsky, part of a family dynasty that produced burlesque and vaudeville shows, was lured to Las Vegas from New York, where there was a crackdown on the so-called indecency of the Minsky productions and others like them. "Sure, I like this better than New York," said Minsky. "Here at the Dunes, we can stage a show on a decent budget to run four months at a whack, instead of having to put a new one together every week. We can pay our performers more and rehearse them better. We can mount the whole show more lavishly. What we're trying to put on is a full-scale big-time Broadway-type musical, but with a genuine Burlesque flavor. That's why we've got Pinky Lee as our star in this show."[36]

The fiercest competition came from Jack Entratter of the Sands Hotel, whose entertainment budget was much bigger than theirs.[37] Minsky responded to Entratter by putting the first topless showgirls onstage in 1956 for the production "Minsky Goes to Paris," and a new tradition was born.

Not to be outdone, in 1958 Arden brought the Paris production "Lido de Paris" to the Stardust. Although it was not the first French show in Las Vegas, it was produced on a much more spectacular scale than the others had been. This show (also topless) enjoyed an enormous success, running until 1991.[38] It required six hydraulic lifts to move props, musicians, and performers thirty feet below or ten feet above the stage.[39]

When it opened, the Stardust was the world's largest resort complex, with a thousand guest rooms.[40] It also contained the largest casino in Las Vegas. In addition to the "Lido" show, the showroom at the Stardust hosted singer Wayne Newton for ten years.[41] Eddie O'Neil and His Orchestra served as the house band.[42] Some musicians referred to O'Neil as "Full-Moon Eddie," because he was rumored to fire a band member every time there was a full moon.

Donn Arden went on to become the most prolific producer in Las Vegas, presenting shows such as "Hello America," "Hello Hollywood, Hello!," "Hallelujah Hollywood!," and "Jubilee!," which is still being performed today in Bally's showroom. These Vegas spectaculars came to be a staple on the Strip, and required bigger and bigger budgets as time went on. Arden's shows were easily recognizable by their "over-the-top costumes and sets, novelty acts, [and] special effects." His shows also had very specific requirements for his showgirls and dancers: the women had to be at least 5 feet 8 inches tall and have "small, firm breasts," while the men needed "tight and firm butts."[43] (Minsky had an even longer and more specific list of requirements for his showgirls.)

Arden became known as the Master of Disaster after he staged events such as the sinking of the Titanic and the 1906 San Francisco earthquake. He also created the "showgirl walk." "There's a certain way a girl can walk," said Arden in 1989, "particularly when you're going across the stage. By simply twisting the foot, it swings the pelvis forward, which is suggestive and sensual. If you twist right and swing that torso, you get a revolve going in there that's just right. It isn't the way a woman should walk, necessarily, unless she's a hooker. You're selling the pelvis; that's the Arden Walk."[44]

The competition was intense. Minsky remarked:

> All you have to do is ride up and down the Strip once and look at the signs to realize how tough the competition is here. Right now, we're competing with the Lido show at the Stardust, with Ed

Sullivan and Dan Dailey and Eddie Fisher and Rosemary Clooney and George Gobel and Milton Berle and Jack Benny, to name
just a few. Next month, there'll be a whole new team of stars coming in to take their places and draw fresh customer interest. You
can't compete with a lineup like that merely on a star basis. People
here are so used to stars they don't mean much anymore.[45]

After the opening of the "Lido" show at the Stardust, Minsky raised the
stakes again by featuring six nude "models." "Here in Vegas, you've got to
have gimmicks and you've got to keep them coming all the time."[46]

The long-running shows were very stable, but not as interesting as the
star room shows from a musician's point of view. The mind-numbing boredom of playing the same material night after night was rough on many
musicians, though these jobs were also well paid and usually long term,
much like working on Broadway. This type of long-term work exists only in
cities that attract large numbers of tourists, such as New York and Miami as
well as Las Vegas, so musicians were drawn from all over the world.

As the work began to multiply, great musicians with no obvious "bag-
gage" began to come to Las Vegas to work. One musician relates the story
of an entire band that quit a tour overnight so they could stay on in Las
Vegas and get jobs in the hotel bands. The opportunities seemed endless,
and the money was good. In addition to bandleaders O'Neil, Morelli, and
Sinatra, there were also orchestras led by Marvin Hamby, Bob Rite, Morris
Brand, Garwood Van, Ted Veslie, Lou Basil, Cee Davidson, and Al Jahns.[47]
The addition of so many new showrooms and lounges created a need for
numerous musicians, and the groups continued to expand as the budgets
got larger. In a review for the El Rancho Hotel that was then featuring Vic
Damone, Willard noted, "Bob Ellis [bandleader] has added three violins to
his 10 AFMers [members of the Musicians Union], giving a lush sound for
Damone's purring."[48]

Many musicians welcomed the chance to get off the road and settle
down in one place, to have some stability and permanence, secure in the
knowledge that the most popular entertainers and headliners would all
make their way to Las Vegas eventually. In an interview given around 1957,
Morelli noted, "It is safe to presume that, here in Las Vegas today, we have
the best organized presentation of musicians and music available in the

entertainment world. It is no secret that this did not come about by accident. These men and their families have been drawn here to the Las Vegas
economy from every metropolitan center in America, hopeful and ready to
continue in the chosen way of life in music."[49]

At first the musicians were the only casino employees who were not
working for tips, and they had to report all of their earnings to the IRS while
others were not doing so. Johnny Haig recalled, "Everybody was getting $1
an hour. Town ran on silver dollars. If you went anywhere, it was $1. Every
waitress, shill, and dealer earned $1 per hour, but they could have thrown
that all away because they could walk home leaning to one side from all
the silver dollar tips in their pockets." Over time the Las Vegas musicians
were able to get benefits that they did not have before, such as health care
and retirement pensions. New hotels meant new contracts, which attracted
musicians who were both talented and relatively stable.

With the success of "Lido de Paris," other hotels scrambled to find their
own "French" shows. Some of these included "Nouvelle Eve" at the El
Rancho in 1959 (which featured Dick Rice and His Orchestra, according
to a Las Vegas show program from that time), "Folies Bergere" at the Tropicana also in 1959, and "Casino de Paris" at the Dunes in 1963.[50] The downtown hotels moved away from the Western-style entertainment previously
favored there. The Fremont Hotel had opened in 1956 with the Jo Ann Jor-
don Trio in the Carnival Room lounge; later, it was the first downtown
casino to bring in star headliners, such as Wayne Newton, Kay Starr, and
Pat Boone, among others.[51]

The concept of a "Broadway West" in Las Vegas is an idea that has
recurred periodically since the 1950s, but has never really taken hold. Various shows have enjoyed profitable runs, but their success does not guaran-
tee the success of other Broadway productions. Nevertheless, hotels have
competed at different times to have the best Broadway show on their stage.
Several hotels claim to have brought the first Broadway show to Las Vegas.
In 1955 the Dunes presented a revue starring dancer Vera-Ellen called
"New York–Paris Paradise" and billed it as the first Broadway show to play
in Las Vegas.[52] The short-lived Royal Nevada presented an abbreviated version of the New York Broadway production "Guys and Dolls," also in 1955.
"My husband, Manny Frank, and I tied up the rights and cut the show to an

hour and a half," said singer Vivian Blaine, the first Adelaide in the original production. "We'll duplicate the costumes and sets of the New York run. I think it will start a trend of musicals in Las Vegas. 'Pajama Game' would be wonderful there."[53] The entertainment producers at the Thunderbird Hotel presented the Broadway show "Flower Drum Song" in 1961, initiating their own plan to become the Broadway of the West.[54] In response, the Riviera named itself the Broadway of the Desert, bringing in shows such as "Gypsy" with Ethel Merman.[55] By the late 1950s and during the 1960s, the Broadway shows that had played in Las Vegas included "A Funny Thing Happened on the Way to the Forum," "Bye Bye Birdie," "Anything Goes," "Fiddler on the Roof," "Sweet Charity," "South Pacific," and "Funny Girl."[56]

The lounges continued to proliferate, bringing in some of the most memorable performers in Las Vegas history. The legendary run of comic musicians Louis Prima and Keely Smith, with Sam Butera and the Witnesses, began in the Casbar Lounge at the Sahara Hotel in 1956.[57] The Mary Kaye Trio remained popular and continued to play in both the lounges and the showrooms. They received great reviews from Willard in *Variety*: "Tablers received a tremendous lift from the dynamic Mary Kaye Trio. Rocketing from in-the-dark opening measures of 'Lonesome Road' theme through tunes well spaced for comedy or seriouso [*sic*] effect, [the] act stops the show. Mary, brother Norman, and madman Frank Ross are great on vocal blends."[58] Other lounge entertainers included Harry James in the Flamingo Driftwood Lounge, as well as Gene Krupa and Artie Shaw in the same lounge, while the downtown lounges featured country music stars such as Ray Price and Patsy Cline.[59]

The lounges were much more freewheeling and "anything goes" than the main showrooms. Often the musicians and dancers from the star rooms and production shows would finish the night sitting in the audience of the lounges. Perennial lounge favorite Freddie Bell later recalled, "At night when you got off, you went to see the other acts. There was no competitiveness . . . in those days, everyone was on the way up. The town was building, and we were all growing with the town. It was like family. Performers were a family." Headlining entertainers were often persuaded to do an impromptu set after their own performances were over and the lounge performers kept their shows loose and fluid. According to Mary Kaye, "We never did the same act twice. We could put any song anywhere. They came back night after night, because they never knew what we were going to do, and we didn't either."[60]

Some of the livelier gatherings were found on the Westside of Las Vegas, where the black clubs were segregated. According to writer Earnest N. Bracy, some of the early black bars and clubs on the Westside included The New Town and Tavern, Cotton Club, El Morocco, and Ebony Clubs. Performers such as Harry Belafonte and Sarah Vaughan would often perform late-night shows in these clubs after they finished their Strip performances.[61]

Jazz musicians of all races intermingled on the Westside late into the night. Bill Trujillo, a talented woodwind doubler, flirted with the idea of coming permanently to Las Vegas for work in the early 1950s. At first, he said, "It was not my cup of tea. . . . It was very commercial. And I'm a jazz musician, my whole family are musicians." Trujillo, who is white, began to spend a lot of time in the Westside around H Street, a strictly black neighborhood at the time. Soon he felt at home. He fondly remembered, "The Brown Derby, the Louisiana Club, the Carver House. . . . I mean, it was jumpin'! That was even before the Moulin Rouge." (The Moulin Rouge opened in 1955.) He would go jam with his friends in the Westside after work because "They weren't even allowed on the Strip. . . . That was totally disgusting." Eventually, he moved in with some of his Westside friends. "It was fun. We were playing jazz and bebop tunes and it was wonderful."

Las Vegas was still segregated and it was rare to see white people anywhere on the Westside, unless they were entertainers. Famed singer and television personality Bob Bailey also remembered, "Musicians of every color would come to play jazz on Jackson Street [and the] races intermingled."[62]

In the 1950s many of the most popular entertainers on the Strip were black: Louis Armstrong, Pearl Bailey, Nat King Cole, Sammy Davis Jr., Billy Eckstine, Billie Holiday, and Eartha Kitt were just some of these performers. The April 15, 1954 edition of the city's first black newspaper, the *Las Vegas Voice*, pointed with pride to the success of the Bill Davis Trio on the Strip: "Bill Davis and his trio, now appearing at the Royal Room in Hollywood, did such a bang-up job at El Cortez Hotel that in less than three weeks they're due back for an engagement at the Last Frontier Hotel. Las Vegans recognize a good act when they see one."[63]

There was still resistance to the idea of integration on the Strip, however. In a 1954 editorial entitled "Progress!" the *Las Vegas Voice* was able to
report the following:

> On Monday, March 29, 1954 at a special meeting the Las Vegas
> Board of Commissioners, in a 4 to 1 vote, approved a zone variance
> for the Will Max Schwartz Associates, thereby paving the way for a
> resort hotel in West Las Vegas. It is extremely gratifying to the citi-
> zens of West Las Vegas to know that Mayor Baker and Commis-
> sioners Harris Sharp, Wendell Bunker and Reed Whipple believe
> in boosting the progress of our community. The Moulin Rouge is
> to be a resort hotel comparable in all aspects of the luxuriousness
> to the Strip Hotels located in Clark County on Highway 91.
>
> It is to be a 100-room hotel with a casino, bar, theater restau-
> rant and swimming pool. In addition it will be the first cosmopoli-
> tan hotel in the state of Nevada.
>
> It will be a distinct improvement for the area and provide the
> incentive for other investors to come into our community. This is
> the first real step in our development and the most important one,
> for it has opened the door and given us a much-needed shot of
> confidence.
>
> Our thanks.[64]

The Moulin Rouge, opened in 1955, was the first interracial hotel-casino
in Las Vegas. For the showroom of the Moulin Rouge, Clarence Robinson
created a show with black entertainers and brought in Bob Bailey to be
the coproducer and master of ceremonies. Benny Carter, "America's most
versatile bandleader," according to the hotel press release for the *Las Vegas
Sun,* was hired for the opening. He played trumpet, saxophone, and clarinet.[65] Another band that worked in the Moulin Rouge was Lionel Hampton
and his twelve-piece orchestra.[66]

The opening of this new interracial hotel galvanized the Westside residents, according to Alice Key, who was hired as the publicist: "There was a
tremendous amount of excitement because we finally had a place that we
could call our own. The place was jam-packed, people came all the way from
Los Angeles, and it was very important for the community. Black people
were earning and spending money and it made business good for everyone

else in the area. . . . What really fascinated us all when it was finished was the elegance that went into it. It was a truly beautiful hotel."[67] The entertainers for the Moulin Rouge were also enchanted. Dee Dee Jasmin, a seventeen-year-old dancer in the chorus line, said, "You just dream of going to Vegas with all the glitz and the glitter and the bright lights. When we arrived, we had our Sunday best on, believe me. The high-heel shoes on and the hats and the furs and everything. Then we saw this beautiful hotel. It said Moulin Rouge. Well, that lifted our spirits to no end. We saw the place where we were going to work. My God, it was breathtaking."[68]

Bob Bailey recalled, "Our public relations man Martin Black had the brilliant idea to try a third performance [of its 'Tropi Can Can' production show] at 2:15 A.M. for the entertainers and musicians in town who were just getting off work. . . . We tried it for a week, and discovered that was when the casino truly came to life."[69] In another interview, Bailey noted, "Entertainers congregate according to talent, not color. So they all wanted to see our show, and would come over and watch. And as the showgirls go, so go the players."[70] In general, most of the musicians and showgirls were opposed to segregation. One former showgirl, Ffolliott "Fluff" LeCoque, remarked, "For us, in the entertainment business, in show business, it [segregation] was shameful. It was just a crime, the way they [minorities] were being treated."[71]

The Moulin Rouge was temporarily successful and very popular with all races from the outset. The owners fought with each other, though, causing the hotel to go bankrupt after only seven months. Some would still argue that the Moulin Rouge failed because, according to some witnesses, the Strip owners, noticing that they were losing gamblers at night, forbid the showgirls and musicians from going to the Westside. Both Bob Bailey and Alice Key believed this was true. Key said, "The hotel owners on the Strip barred their girls from coming over after they got off work. Because of the late shows at the Moulin Rouge, you could practically shoot a cannon off along the Strip."[72] Others thought that the closure was due to bad management.

What the Moulin Rouge did prove, however, was that desegregation in the casinos was possible and this fact, combined with the civil rights movement of the 1960s, helped to eventually end segregation in Las Vegas.[73] By

1960 there were more than eleven thousand black residents in Las Vegas; in part, these residents filled the large number of service-sector jobs created by the resort industry. This population also put pressure on the casino owners to change. After a threatened mass march on the Strip in 1960, most resorts agreed to accept desegregation.[74] "It's money that has driven Vegas since her founding days in 1905," said longtime resident Susan Berman. "And there was no questioning the fact that black performers brought cash in by the bucketful. Eventually, even the most rigid racist policies had to bend to the reality of economics."[75]

Unfortunately, the successful integration of the Strip also led to the demise of the Westside hotels and casinos. According to writer James Roman, "Black entertainers and their entourages now stayed at the hotels that hired them; now their contracts even stipulated the number of hours they needed to *remain* in the hotels after the show."[76]

Though his was an exceptional success story, Johnny Haig's arrival and subsequent musical career in Las Vegas was in many ways typical of those musicians who came here during the 1950s. He started out as a trombone player and came to Las Vegas to work a steady hotel band job around 1955 after turning down an offer to play with the legendary Woody Herman in New York. At this time, construction of new hotel-casinos was at a record high, and virtually all of the new hotels had some connection to the mob.[77]

Eventually Haig replaced a trombone player at the Frontier Hotel. Haig remembered that the trombone player he replaced was perpetually late, making his entrance by running through the audience and climbing over the rail as the pit stage was rising. Understandably, this made the conductor nervous, so the tardy trombonist was fired and Haig got the job and worked there for many years until the hotel went bankrupt.

The next gig for Johnny Haig was with the Dunes Hotel as part of the first topless show in Las Vegas. The show was booked by Major Auterburn Riddle, who was hired in 1957 to make the Dunes more profitable, and debuted on January 10, 1957 under the title "Minsky Goes to Paris."[78] According to Haig, the show featured burlesque comedians and a twelve-piece band. Because it was a topless show, the job paid 50 percent more than the standard rate and ran three shows a night. By the time the band was on its third performance, he recalled, many of the showgirls were sitting in the audience with the high rollers. The show set an attendance record of 16,000 audience members in a single week. This hugely successful show was followed at the Dunes by "Vive les Girls" and the French spectacular "Casino de Paris," which ran there for more than twenty years.[79]

Woodwind doubler Dave Hawley was another musician who played for a topless show at the Dunes. He remembered his first encounter with a showgirl, recalling the big platforms that would come down from the ceiling, each adorned with an almost naked woman. Facing the platforms, and playing his part for the first time, he was completely unprepared for the sight. He said, "I played my baritone sax right into a rest. . . . Bonk! I was so embarrassed. I had never seen anything like it!"

Woodwind doubler Matt Saporita witnessed the growth of the entertainment industry through the 1950s. He said, with a twinkle in his eye, that he arrived in Las Vegas riding shotgun on a covered wagon with Al Capone. While that may not be exactly true, Saporita has been in Las Vegas a long time. He first came in the 1940s to Nellis Air Force Base (then the Las Vegas Army Air Corps Gunnery School) to play for the troops during World War II as part of a band that was touring the United States playing military bases. He said the band members wore zoot suits and had long watch chains. In 1945 he returned to Las Vegas to stay, and worked steadily as the resort industry grew during the 1950s.

Saporita also had a connection with a young Doc Severinsen, who was recognized early as a special talent among trumpet players in Las Vegas. Severinsen was first asked to play fourth trumpet with a Las Vegas–based band in 1942, the Ted Fio Rito Orchestra, at the age of fifteen. His parents thought he was too young to travel with the band, but the parents soon found a way they could agree to him going along: Saporita was paid $20.00 a week to room with Severinsen and look after him on the road. Saporita remarked he was probably chosen for this role because he did not drink or smoke and that he wrote his parents every day. While on the road, he made sure that Severinsen wrote home every day as well, and that he called his parents once a week. Saporita met his second wife, Marie, while on the boardwalk with Severinsen in Atlantic City, so he thought "it was a good trade."

Saporita was in the band the night there was a kitchen fire at the El

Rancho. His pit position, which was against the kitchen wall, kept getting hotter and hotter. Saporita passed the word up the section that there was a fire nearby. The word came back down to "shut up and keep playing." As the temperature in the pit rose, players took off their jackets and ties. Finally, the fire could no longer be ignored and the band was allowed to clear out.

By the mid 1950s it seemed that there were more jobs than musicians, so many began to play extra jobs. Some musicians would play four two-hour shifts a day: they played for a house band at 8:00 P.M. and 12:00 A.M. and for a lounge band at 10:00 P.M. and 2:00 A.M. String players would often take on strolling musician work between shows or even during the day. Since all the hotels had the same basic schedule, this was possible to do if the musician was energetic and motivated. Tommy Check, a percussionist who sometimes kept this schedule, said he found it hard to stay awake.

The best way to get a job on the Strip was to be referred by someone already working there. Contractors were always looking for musicians with excellent sight-reading ability and musicianship, but who also had easy personalities, who would not create stress for their colleagues. People who worked in such close proximity night after night, perhaps fighting the tedium of playing the same music all the time, did not want anyone in their midst who was difficult. No applications were needed—just the ability to perform well under pressure and not bother or annoy the others.

Audience members sometimes provided extra entertainment by heckling the performers or getting into fights among themselves. One musician recalled an incident at the Desert Inn at the end of the show after the curtain came down. Hearing a commotion in the audience, the musicians looked out to see two men fighting, but not for long. In the old days hotels had security "like you wouldn't believe," said musician Don Hannah, "A minimum of six feet tall. Those guys could see someone who was getting rowdy and take him out by the elbow." The mob owners prided themselves on keeping Las Vegas "clean."

What most of the musicians really miss about the old days are all the stars who came to Las Vegas. There were numerous casino showrooms that were "star policy" rooms, hosting popular artists who would typically have a two- to four-week engagement with the hotel. The orchestra musicians for the star rooms usually were members of a house band; otherwise, they were hired on an as-needed basis, unlike the musicians for the production shows, who usually worked the same show for years at a time. Many players had the opportunity to work both types of jobs over the course of their career.

Working in a star room, the musicians had the unique opportunity to observe famous singers, comedians, and other entertainers from behind the scenes. These encounters were often treasured memories. There were always those special performers who stood out for the players—not just for their talent or popular appeal, but because they were nice people. "The great percentage of acts I worked with, and I worked with just about all of them, were very good to me and the musicians," recalled Johnny Haig.

Frank Sinatra first performed in Las Vegas at the Desert Inn in 1951. Later, Sinatra performed twice nightly at the Sands, which opened in 1952. "Anytime he had a suggestion for the band, you listened, because he knew. He grew up in bands," said Hannah. Throughout the years, musicians continued to praise Sinatra. Violinist Patricia (Saarinen) Harrell said, "Frank Sinatra could hear anything that was wrong. . . . He would have been a great educator."

Horn player Beth Lano remarked, "Obviously, I loved playing for Frank Sinatra. It was my dream to play for him." Violinist Rebecca Ramsey also said that Sinatra's show was her favorite. "He was a great musician, and it was always a special, electric feeling in the air whenever he would walk into the room and you really felt like you were in the center of the musical universe whenever he was there. . . . He knew every part of the music, every part of his arrangements. He was always very gentlemanly and respectful." Added musician Sharon Street-Caldwell, "Sinatra liked to have a full 70-piece orchestra. I've never felt such charisma in my entire life as from this man. During rehearsal, he would just stand there and he was listening to every single person. He could tell who was in tune. . . . [His show was] the most amazing show I think I've ever played. . . . I could see what all the hype was about." Haig, who generally liked all the stars, said that Sinatra in particular was "a pleasure to work for." Even the musicians who never played for him remembered that Sinatra was always good to the band.

Another favorite from the 1950s and later was Sammy Davis Jr. "He was the guy who would send champagne to other acts on opening night, or invite a group of dancers out for Chinese food or for screening 35-mm prints of movies in his hotel suite," said Jerry Kurland, a Las Vegas tap dancer. "He cared for all the show kids, all of us who worked hard."[80] Patricia Harrell said, "We loved Sammy [Davis Jr.]. He'd bring in hush puppies; he'd put on music and dance." Sharon Street-Caldwell remembered Sammy Davis Jr. fondly as well. "Never held himself from the musicians, ever." He would go to the movies with the musicians sometimes after the show. He was "very personable, very, very nice."

Liberace was, in 1955, the highest-paid performer in Las Vegas, earning $50,000 a week at the Riviera.[81] By the time he opened the Las Vegas Hilton in 1972, he was getting $300,000 per week.[82] "He was called 'Mr. Showmanship. But more than that, he was a great friend. He was wonderful," recalled Debbie Reynolds.[83] The band members remembered him as a warm and witty person. Liberace continued to perform in Las Vegas until 1986. Other performers who appeared in the showrooms during the 1950s included the Andrews Sisters, Maurice Chevalier, Tommy and Jimmy Dorsey, Elvis, Judy Garland, Benny Goodman, Joel Grey, Betty Hutton, Gene Krupa, Don Rickles, Ginger Rogers, Artie Shaw, Dinah Shore, Red Skelton, and Esther Williams, among many others.[84]

When the shows finished up for the night, many of the musicians were not ready to go home because they were still wired from performing. Musicians described how everyone knew one another and that between their shows they would often go to different hotels to visit the other bands in the coffee shops. Sometimes they went to the hotel lounges, and other times they congregated at Chuck's House of Spirits to drink and socialize. Later, the Musicians Union provided a place for them to meet and play music.

Many of the musicians fondly remembered Chuck's House of Spirits, a liquor store that stood next the Desert Inn in the 1950s and 1960s. Chuck's served as the unofficial gathering place for all of the hotel musicians after work. Bassist Ed Boyer said that he was a regular there. "There was a bench outside where you could sit. And you'd drink your beer, or your bottle of gin . . . whatever the booze-du-jour was. What was really cool about it was that Chuck would let you run a tab." Haig added that many musicians would get a bottle and drink it in the parking lot. "Chuck was a nice guy, he knew the musicians; he knew who he could give a bottle to and who not to trust." Tom McDermott said, "He was amazing! A lot of the guys stayed in front of that place."

Because there was no place for so many people to sit inside, trombone player Ralph Pressler recalled that musicians often sat on or around their cars. "We sat on the curb, the sidewalk. Most of the stuff happened after work." He remembered sitting at Chuck's long enough to see the sun come up. "A lot of glare!" Trumpeter Tom Snelson remarked, "I really wonder how some of us are still alive. After working two production shows a night you weren't ready to go home . . . [so] you ended up hanging out a lot." Percussionist Howard Agster agreed, "At 4:00 A.M. there would still be about forty black suits outside at Chuck's House of Spirits." As Haig recalled, "All musicians would congregate there after the last shows. Even before the shows ended, everybody knew [what] had happened on the Strip that night."

"Lots of business was done," said Pressler "We'd sit and talk. We'd find out ahead of time who was available, who was getting fired or leaving. Live bulletin board." Musician Dave Hawley remembered a story that made it all the way to Miami the same night it happened. More often than not, the stories involved mishaps that occurred during a particular show. It was inevitable that things would not work perfectly all the time, and the stories of the mistakes provided the most interesting gossip. Haig noted, "We would go just to find out what happened that night. It was always something!"

Another popular early hangout was the Silver Slipper. Between shows Bill Trujillo enjoyed going there when he was not headed home to his family because "they had drinks for 35 cents and a good jazz band. It was a big hang." Another woodwind doubler, Sam Pisciotta, said that his friends would deliberately start false rumors for him to hear at the Silver Slipper bar.

All Las Vegas musicians have their stories and anecdotes, told and retold and embellished over time. These stories become part of the collective repertoire until it is hard to know which version is true. Some players, when recounting a particular event, had trouble remembering whether they were actually there or had just heard about it later. The hothouse working conditions of the Las Vegas hotel musicians and entertainers provided the perfect medium for gossip to flourish; the more social musicians helped the stories and gossip spread quickly. Like most musicians, Dave Hawley remembered those times fondly: "The world was your oyster. You saw people you knew everywhere." Bill Trujillo remarked, "I loved it, absolutely loved it. It was a small town." While the small town days of Las Vegas were numbered and the family atmosphere would not last forever, as Las Vegas headed into the 1960s it was riding high.

NOTES

1. Moehring and Green, *Las Vegas*, 132.

2. Berman, *Lady Las Vegas*, 91.

3. Hal Rothman, *The Making of Modern Nevada* (Reno: University of Nevada Press, 2010), 108, 107.

4. Berman, *Lady Las Vegas*, 93.

5. "Dreaming the Skyline: Thunderbird," UNLV Libraries Digital Collections, http:// digital.library.unlv.edu/skyline/hotel/thunderbird.

6. Box 49, Folder 1, Bill Willard Collection, MS 2001-17.

7. "Dreaming the Skyline: Thunderbird"

8. Moehring, *Resort City in the Sunbelt*, 50.

9. Knepp, *Las Vegas*, 276.

10. Moehring, *Resort City in the Sunbelt*, 74.

11. Hal Rothman, *The Making of Modern Nevada* (Reno: University of Nevada Press, 2010), 110.

12. Las Vegas Show Programs, Box 1, Folder R, Collection 93–28, Special Collections, UNLV Libraries, University of Nevada, Las Vegas; Box 49, Folder 1, Bill Willard Collection, MS 2001-17.

13. Knepp, *Las Vegas*, 276.

14. Moehring, *Resort City in the Sunbelt*, 74–75.

15. A. D. Hopkins and K. J. Evans, eds., *The First 100: Portraits of the Men and Women Who Shaped Las Vegas*, (Las Vegas: Huntington Press, 1999), 256.

16. Berman, *Lady Las Vegas*, 92.

17. Ibid., 107.

18. Box 38, Folder 8, Matt Gregory interview transcript, October 24, 1975, Bill Willard Collection, MS 2001-17.

19. Berman, *Lady Las Vegas*, 94 ("I worked with"), 95 ("They didn't come").

20. Box 38, Folder 8, Matt Gregory interview transcript, October 24, 1975, Bill Willard Collection, MS 2001-17.

21. Lewis, "Oral History," February 20, 1987.

22. Knepp, *Las Vegas*, 276.

23. Bill Willard, "5,500,000 Gamble and Gambol Spa Is Writ on The Sands of Las Vegas, Where a Preem Means Four Days," *Variety*, December 24, 1952, 45.

24. Antonio Morelli Papers, 2009–17, Special Collections, UNLV Libraries, University of Nevada, Las Vegas.

25. Knepp, *Las Vegas*, 276–277.

26. Berman, *Lady Las Vegas*, 106.

27. Casey Shawhan and James Bassett, "Costly Floor Shows Frost Las Vegas Gambling Cake," *Oakland Tribune*, July 21, 1953, D10 ("the lushest price war"); Gragg, *Bright Light City*, 120.

28. Willard, "5,500,000 Gamble and Gambol Spa," 45.

29. Gragg, *Bright Light City*, 120.

30. Bill Willard, "Vegas' New Year's Eve in July," *Variety*, July 22, 1953, 50 ("Never before," "Low estimate").

31. Box 9, Folder 2, Letter to Bill Willard from Joe Schoenfeld, Editor *Variety* magazine, June 20, 1955, Bill Willard Collection, MS 2001-17.

32. Bill Willard, "Vegas' $164,000,000 Question," *Variety*, July 13, 1955, 52 (budget data, "Some of these terpsichorean," population data).

33. Bill Willard, "Vaudeville: Nat'l Spotlight Feeds More Fuel to Vegas 3 G's— Gambling, Glam & Garble," *Variety*, January 14, 1953, 53.

34. Moehring, *Resort City in the Sunbelt*, 79.

35. Bill Willard, "Las Vegas Luck Riding Out Bad Time: 3 New Casino-Hotels Set to Bow," *Variety*, January 11, 1956, 66.

36. Thomas R. Fuller, "Life Begins for Harold," *Sir Knight*, vol. 1, no. 5, 12, Box 1, Folder 19, Minsky's Burlesque Collection, MS 87–97, Special Collections, UNLV Libraries, University of Nevada, Las Vegas.

37. "American Experience, Las Vegas: An Unconventional History, People and Events, PBS," Public Broadcasting Service, http://www.pbs.org/wgbh/amex/lasvegas/peopleevents/p_entertainers.html.

38. "Lido at the Stardust," UNLV Libraries Digital Collections, http://digital.library.unlv.edu/collections/showgirls/lido-stardust.

39. Moehring and Green, *Las Vegas*, 137.

40. Knepp, *Las Vegas*, 277.

41. Roman, *Chronicles of Old Las Vegas*, 57.

42. "La Nouvelle Eve" program, Box 1, Folder L, Las Vegas Show Programs Collection, MS 93-28.

43. Hopkins and Evans, *The First 100*, 255–256.

44. Ibid., 255–256.

45. Fuller, "Life Begins for Harold."

46. Ibid.

47. Box 2, Folder 13, Antonio Morelli Papers, 2009-17.

48. Willard, "Vegas' New Year's Eve in July," 50.

49. Box 2, Folder 13, Antonio Morelli Papers, 2009-17.

50. "Lido at the Stardust."

51. Moehring, *Resort City in the Sunbelt*, 82.

52. Knepp, *Las Vegas*, 277.

53. "Nevada Show for Guys, Dolls," *The Times-News*, Hendersonville, NC, June 24, 1955, http://news.google.com/newspapers?nid=1665&dat=19550624&id=gvQZAAAAIBAJ &sjid=XSMEAAAAIBAJ&pg=4252,8303574.

54. Knepp, *Las Vegas*, 277.

55. "Riviera" programs, Box 2, Folder R, Las Vegas Show Programs Collection, MS 93-28.

56. Knepp, *Las Vegas*, 146–147.

57. Ibid., 277.

58. Willard, "Vegas' New Year's Eve in July," 1, 50.

59. Weatherford, Mike, *Cult Vegas: The Weirdest! The Wildest! The Swingin'est Town on Earth!* (Las Vegas: Huntington Press, 2001), 66.

60. Ibid., 64 ("At night when you"), 48 ("We never did").

61. Earnest N. Bracey, *The Moulin Rouge and Black Rights in Las Vegas: A History of the First Racially Integrated Hotel-Casino* (Jefferson, NC: McFarland, 2009), 27.

62. William H. "Bob" Bailey, *Looking Up! Finding My Voice in Las Vegas* (Las Vegas: Stephens Press, 2009), 111.

63. *Las Vegas Voice*, April 15, 1954, 3, Box 1, Folder 16, Alice Key Papers, MS 95–47, Special Collections, UNLV Libraries, University of Nevada, Las Vegas.

64. Ibid.

65. Bailey, *Looking Up!*, 106.

66. Roman, *Chronicles of Old Las Vegas*, 205.

67. Michael Paskevich, "Publicist Fondly Recalls Casino's Heyday," *Las Vegas Review-Journal*, 2E.

68. Berman, *Lady Las Vegas*, 115.

69. Bailey, *Looking Up!*, 109.

70. Hopkins and Evans, *The First 100*, 205.

71. Berman, *Lady Las Vegas*, 113.

72. Paskevich, "Publicist Fondly Recalls Casino's Heyday."

73. Ainlay and Gabaldon, *Las Vegas*, 118.

74. Moehring and Green. *Las Vegas*, 197.

75. Berman, *Lady Las Vegas*, 115.

76. Roman, *Chronicles of Old Las Vegas*, 104.

77. Ainlay and Gabaldon, *Las Vegas*, 104.

78. "History of the Dunes / Bellagio," *A2Z Las Vegas Visitors Guide*, http://www.a2zlasvegas.com/hotels/history/h-bellagio.html.

79. Moehring, *Resort City in the Sunbelt*, 80.

80. Weatherford, *Cult Vegas*, 38.

81. Quentin Parker, Paula Munier, and Susan Reynolds, *The Sordid Secrets of Las Vegas* (Avon, MA: Adams Media, 2011), 162.

82. Hopkins and Evans, *The First 100*, 248.

83. Berman, *Lady Las Vegas*, 107.

84. Knepp, *Las Vegas*, 67–134.

CHAPTER THREE

1960–1970:
Prosperous and Thriving

To me, it was like being a kid in the candy shop.

RALPH PRESSLER, Musician

It was a looser time. Nobody was worried about their job.

TOM McDERMOTT, Musician

*M*UCH HAS BEEN WRITTEN about what was probably the most famous show in Las Vegas history: "The Summit at the Sands." This gathering on one stage of Frank Sinatra, Sammy Davis Jr., Dean Martin, Peter Lawford, and Joey Bishop is without a doubt the most iconic event in all of Las Vegas entertainment. It was the hippest of all hipster events, a show so popular that large numbers of people were turned away every night. When people think of Las Vegas entertainment, they usually conjure up images of the Rat Pack performing and partying, and Las Vegas works hard to capitalize on those memories today.

Though all the performers returned to play in Las Vegas both together and separately, there was something very special about their first group appearance in the Copa Room at the Sands Hotel from January 20 to February 16, 1960. "The air in the Sands crackled," said Las Vegas business magnate Steve Wynn. "The electricity in the building that afternoon was beyond belief. There is no parallel to it today. The lights go out. The band plays the music, and announcer's voice says 'Welcome to the Sand's Copa Room.' And without another word, the curtain opens and Frank Sinatra walks out, with no introduction."[1] Las Vegas entertainment columnist Ralph Pearl recalled, "Of the more than ten thousand shows I've seen in

Las Vegas, there's no question [that this was] the most exciting night in a showroom during those twenty years."[2]

Frank Sinatra had first appeared in Las Vegas at Wilbur Clark's Desert Inn in 1951.[3] He established a fourteen-year relationship with the Sands Hotel after he performed there in 1953. When Sinatra decided to film the original *Ocean's 11* in Las Vegas, he arranged for the Rat Pack to perform at night in the showroom. Later, Sinatra expressed great satisfaction with the results: "There's little doubt that Las Vegas is the Show Business capital of the world today and I'm convinced that it's the people who live and work here—as well as the stars—who help to make it that. I'm sure that Dino, Sammy, Pete, Joey, and all the guys and gals from our Copa show and the film appreciate it."[4] And Sinatra was good for business in Las Vegas. Lounge singer Sonny King remarked, "He was actually the king of Las Vegas, because the minute he stepped in town, money was here. He drew all the big money people. Every celebrity in Hollywood would come to Las Vegas to see him, one night or another."[5]

The year 1960 was a heady time for Las Vegas; it is impossible to overstate how important Sinatra was in creating this most lasting impression of Las Vegas entertainment. *Las Vegas Review-Journal* columnist Forrest Duke wrote, "The Las Vegas Chamber of Commerce ought to give one of the town's best boosters, Frank Sinatra, a special citation (a case of Jack Daniels, maybe?) for instigating the filming here of 'Ocean's Eleven.' Not only will the picture give our town a fantastic amount of good publicity, but it will give extra employment to many local entertainers."[6]

On opening night the show started with the CopaGirl Dancers, then Sinatra took the stage for twenty minutes. "That was a great opening act!" cracked comedian Joey Bishop, who was the next performer.[7] Peter Lawford and Sammy Davis Jr. did some dancing and Dean Martin blundered around with a drink in one hand, playing his usual part of the "happy drunk."[8] Throughout the night the friends kidded and heckled each other as they performed, to the delight of the audience. The rest of the run continued in much the same way, with each show seeming more outrageously fun, as the group filmed during the day, performed in the showroom in the evening, and spent the wee hours of the morning hanging out together in the lounge and spa. As word spread about the special show, more and more people called in favors to be able to get in to see it. Entertainment writers from all over the country flew in to write about the phenomenon. They had been primed by the ads placed in the newspapers and entertainment guides: "Opening Wednesday—Jack Entratter presents Star-light, Star-bright—Which Star Shines Tonight? It's a guessing game, and you'll be the winner at the show-of-shows any night . . . every night! Yes, there's magic in the Sands air. Frank Sinatra, Sammy Davis Jr., Dean Martin, and Peter Lawford! A galaxy of great stars . . . one-two-three-or all four on stage at once! It's a Jack Entratter special and it *is* special, even for the Sands. That's Jan. 20–Feb. 16 in the fabulous Sands Copa Room, America's No. 1 Nightclub!"[9]

"Mr. Entratter, sir, you have a 'gasser' on your hands. The only possible topper to this show is booking the Civil War and its original cast and we hear you're working on that," wrote *Las Vegas Review-Journal* columnist Les Devor. "Batten down the hatches and get ready for a real blow. . . . Sinatra is back at the Sands."[10] Each new show reviewer tried to top the others, heaping praise (and prose) on the performances.

The Rat Pack continued to play in Las Vegas in various combinations after the movie wrapped, sometimes popping by unannounced. The Sands publicists put teasers on their marquee: "Dean Martin, Maybe Frank, Maybe Sammy."[11] One surprise appearance by Sinatra occurred after a particularly difficult time for the singer. On December 8, 1963, just two weeks after the assassination of President John F. Kennedy, Frank Sinatra Jr. was kidnapped from Lake Tahoe, where he was just beginning his own singing career. The FBI advised Sinatra to pay the $240,000 ransom fee, which he did on December 10, and the agents were able to track the money and catch the kidnappers.[12] Jack Entratter stayed with Sinatra in Reno until Sinatra Jr. was returned to him. Sinatra celebrated the end of "the most harrowing and also joyful week" of his life by making an unannounced appearance at the Sands, bringing his girlfriend, actress Jill St. John, along with Dean Martin and Yul Brynner. Sinatra and Martin joined the scheduled performers Sammy Davis Jr. and Danny Thomas, and were welcomed with a standing ovation by the many celebrities in the audience. Casino and hotel guests crowded around to express their relief. "Well, it's quite a thing for a parent to go through," said Sinatra. "Let's say I'm glad it's over."[13]

Sinatra continued to remain loyal to entertainment director and hotel manager Jack Entratter, who was equally loyal to Sinatra. "Sinatra's allegiance to Jack Entratter was because Jack stood by him through all his troubles," according to singer Freddie Bell. "Jack stood by him when Frank was down and out [before Sinatra was back on top]."[14]

Sinatra's success seemed to make him believe he was untouchable, and he had relationships with the mob owners that are difficult for researchers to untangle. It is not clear how close he was to various mob figures, but J. Edgar Hoover and the FBI were keeping a close watch on his activities. Sinatra enjoyed a number of special privileges at the Sands, including the use of the presidential suite with a private swimming pool and unlimited gambling credits.[15] Numerous sources report that Sinatra collected his winnings, but rarely, if ever, paid his losses; a few others report that he was actually acting as a shill.[16]

Some of the hotel staff grew tired of his antics and demands: it was not uncommon for Sinatra and his entourage to have food fights or to trash their rooms. Sinatra felt entitled at the Sands, where he briefly owned a small percent interest, and he was likely encouraged in those feelings by the mob owners who loved his singing, his persona, and the money his appearances always brought in to the hotel. His bad behavior would catch up to him later, but for the time being Sinatra could do as he wished.

Though the Rat Pack show was a phenomenon, it was not the only exciting attraction in town at that time. Throughout the 1960s, Las Vegas entertainment was an embarrassment of riches. Las Vegas *Variety* writer Bill Willard was kept very busy. Willard recalled that he would stay up all night in the lounges, go home to write his stories, then sleep through the afternoon until it was time to go out again. "I miss the camaraderie, the close-knit feeling of trust that we had even with the toughest of hoods in the 50s and 60s," recalled Willard in 1976. "I don't like what has happened to Las Vegas since the take over of the corporations. The mood, the feeling in those years, was fun. . . . You look at the hardness and the crassness of it now and you see what's happening to our entertainment scene. I think they're [corporations are] ruining it. They've got a real wrecking concern moving."[17]

Still, the list of stars who performed in Las Vegas during the 1960s was long, full of some of the most popular stars of the day. It was not uncommon for the headliners to perform at more than one hotel, though showroom bookers had their stable of regular acts. At the Flamingo Hotel some of the performers included Ray Charles, Rosemary Clooney, Bill Cosby, Bobby Darin, Duke Ellington, Robert Goulet, Lionel Hampton, Harry James, the Supremes, and Sarah Vaughan.[18] The orchestra was conducted by Johnnie Spence for at least a part of the 1960s, and the hotel was considered a good place to hear jazz music.[19]

The Riviera performers, backed by the local Jack Cathcart Orchestra and the Ray Sinatra Orchestra, included Louis Armstrong, Tony Bennett, Harry Belafonte, George Burns, Marlene Dietrich, Duke Ellington, Ella Fitzgerald, Betty Grable, Shecky Greene, Johnny Mathis, Lionel Hampton, Debbie Reynolds, and Barbra Streisand. At the Sahara, you could see entertainers like Count Basie, Shirley Bassey, Victor Borge, Johnny Carson, Rosemary Clooney, Connie Francis, Judy Garland, Robert Goulet, Louis Prima, and Don Rickles. The Louis Basil Orchestra was one group that provided accompaniment during this decade. The Sands Hotel, home of the Antonio Morelli Orchestra and the CopaGirl Dancers, featured Carol Burnett, Diahann Carroll, Chubby Checker, Nat King Cole, Vic Damone, Eydie Gormé, Lena Horne, Quincy Jones, Jerry Lewis, Bob Newhart, Richard Pryor, Buddy Rich, the Righteous Brothers, Doc Severinsen, and Mel Tormé.[20]

The Desert Inn regularly featured string ensembles, most often in the lounge or gourmet restaurants. They had a regular string ensemble, made up of glamorous young women on the violins with a male rhythm section. Sasha Semenoff and his Romantic Strings was another ensemble that played in the lounge in the early 1960s. Semenoff was a highly trained classical musician who came to Las Vegas for a two-week engagement in 1959 and then stayed on, eventually moving to various other hotels, including the Dunes, the Sands, and the Hilton.[21] Some of the other showroom and lounge performers were Milton Berle, Sid Caesar, Jimmy Durante, Eddie Fisher, Goldie Hawn, Danny Kaye, Guy Lombardo, and Andy Williams. The Desert Inn also featured some Vegas spectaculars, including Donn Arden's "Hello America" and "Pzazz '68." They were backed by the Carlton Hayes Orchestra during at least part of the 1960s.

The Dunes remained focused primarily on their restaurants and production shows such as "Vive les Girls" and "Casino de Paris," backed at different times by Earl Green and his twenty-one-piece orchestra or Bill Reddie and Orchestra.[22] The new six-ton electronic stage, known as the Octuramic, cost $250,000 and was capable of moving "up, down, sideways, and into the audience like a multi-fingered octopus."[23] The Sinbad Cocktail Lounge was billed as "The Swingin'est Lounge in Town!"[24] There were a few stars that worked at the Dunes, including Tony Bennett, Carol Channing, Al Hirt, Eleanor Powell, Dan Rowan and Dick Martin, and Rip Taylor.[25]

In 1962 Selma Matthews became the first female producer and director for a large production show in Las Vegas; the show was "Gotta Get to Vegas!," and was performed onstage in the Arabian Room of the Dunes Hotel. The *Las Vegas Review-Journal* article writer who publicized the show referred to her several times as the "lady-producer," and noted, "She comes to work in a pair of pants and all of the men who are assisting her in staging this show take direction from her as if she were a football coach." The overall tone of the column makes it clear that the writer thought the Dunes was taking a risk. Her assistants were said to have reported to the newspaper that the producer "knows the business."[26]

At the Tropicana customers could see shows with Louis Armstrong, Dave Brubeck, Maynard Ferguson, Benny Goodman, Gene Krupa, Guy Lombardo, and Si Zentner.[27] Many of these performers worked in the famous Blue Room, a venue mostly for jazz. In the main showroom, the French production "Folies Bergere" continued to be successful, under the direction of Nat Brandwynne and His Orchestra.[28] The Mary Kaye Trio first played the lounge at the Tropicana in May of 1962, and notably recorded a live album while in residence.[29]

The Frontier also featured some stars during the 1960s: Sid Caesar, Bill Cosby, Vic Damone, Bobby Darin, Jimmy Durante, Harry James, Peggy Lee, Jim Nabors, Wayne Newton, and Jerry Vale.[30] Bill Miller had been brought in as the entertainment director in 1959 and the Freddie Martin Orchestra most likely still performed there in the early part of the 1960s. I have been unable to find any orchestras listed on the photos of the hotel sign or programs from that time, which I suspect is because the Frontier was focusing on its Frontier Village and not as much on entertainment.

This decade was a great time to be a musician in the Las Vegas hotels.

The 1960s also saw the creation of a special Las Vegas group: the relief band. The function of a relief band was to substitute for the regular hotel band once a week so the house players could have a night off. In the days before corporate-run casinos, the syndicate casino owners refused to have a night when a showroom was dark, or closed. These owners considered the showroom entertainment paramount to attracting and retaining customers. To get the regular hotel band to come in on their night off, though, the management had to pay double scale, so the relief bands played the extra day, rotating through the hotels on different nights.

Johnny Haig spent the 1960s in a relief band led by Jack Eglash. By 1970 Haig had the opportunity to take over the management of the Eglash relief band, which he continued to run for seventeen years.[31] Eventually there were three relief bands in Las Vegas, their creation made necessary by the demands of the syndicate casino owners.

A good relief band could, in those days, work six or seven nights a week, filling in at numerous hotels. Many of the musicians considered the positions in relief bands some of the best ones to have. This type of group needed players who were able to sight-read a different show every night with little to no rehearsal. Because of the challenges, this type of work also paid more than the standard hotel bands. Las Vegas attracted many top musicians who were up to this kind of challenge, and who thrived on it. The relief bands were "the best of the best," Johnny Haig said. "The musicians are my product. The better the guys I have in there, the better the product."

A relief band player needed to be focused as well as talented. The musician had to remember which hotel he or she was playing on which night, where to park at each hotel, how to get to the various bandstands, what to wear for each show, and the show times. Woodwind doubler Dave Hawley, who was a member of Lew Elias's relief band, said, "You really had to stay organized to remember where you were going that night, what instruments, what doubles were needed. It was different for every show. But, I don't want to overlook how much fun it was!" The relief band musician who combined work with drinking was liable to make some mistakes. Johnny Haig recalled a particular trombone player who was also a heavy drinker. After imbibing a few too many between shows, the trombonist took a seat onstage at the Desert Inn. Gradually, he began to notice that he did not see any familiar faces.

The problem was that the rest of his band was at the Sahara. Embarrassed, the trombonist packed up and relocated to the correct stage. The relief band jobs disappeared after the 1989 musicians strike, in part because the corporate owners did not care if the showroom was dark for a night.

At the height of the mob entertainment era, not only did the showrooms have no dark nights, but there might even be a third show offered at 2:00 A.M. Most of the hotels were running the same schedule so the regular show times usually did not vary that much: 8:00 P.M. and 12:00 A.M. were typical. The bands and orchestras would normally play from 8:00 P.M. until 9:30 P.M. or so, then go on break until midnight.

The Las Vegas Musicians Union had an office with a rehearsal hall and a bar. Musicians went there after work, still keyed up after their last shows. Many would go to the union to see their friends, drink, or find out the gossip for the night. Sometimes friends would still be drinking and/or playing their instruments at 10:00 the next morning.

The after-show gatherings also had a more practical purpose. If you were new in town and wanted to work your way into the hotel bands, the union was the place to do it. "Kicks" bands (a group of musicians who play together "for kicks"), made up of working Strip musicians and those who aspired to land a position, played all night long. Contractors could hear new players or seasoned players who wanted a change. The band members could also preview a newcomer. At night the union building was the place where many of the musicians networked.

It is a testament to the high quality of the musicians who now flocked to Las Vegas that in 1960 one kicks band, made up of fifteen all-star players from various Strip hotels, won first place in both the Western and national divisions of the annual Musicians Union New Dance Bands competition. Under the direction of thirty-five-year old tenor saxophone player Jimmy Cook of the Thunderbird Hotel, the band members were Eddie Butterfield, Bob Enevoldsen, Carl Fontana, Austin Goodman, Bill Hodges, Bob Lawson, Charlie Loper, Charles McClean, Tom Montgomery, Al Porcino, Carson Smith, Bob Steed, Charles Walt, and Eddie Wied. They won $20,000 worth of new instruments, a recording contract, a two-week engagement at the Flamingo, a national tour, and an appearance on a national television show taped in New York.[32]

Composer, arranger, and musician Don Hannah remembered the bands and orchestras as tightly closed shops with jobs almost handed down from father to son. When Hannah was asked to audition to replace the bass player in the Flamingo house band, he was told that the hardest part of the job was turning the pages for the show. So to audition Hannah sight-read the bass part and the old bassist turned pages for him. "I lost four pounds that day, but I got the job!" In addition to playing for the stars, the Flamingo musicians also recorded albums with several of them: Bobby Darin recorded *The Curtain Falls: Live at the Flamingo* and Tom Jones recorded *Tom Jones Live in Las Vegas* there.[33]

Trombonist Ralph Pressler came to Las Vegas in the 1960s. He remembered working with old-time vaudevillians at the Frontier. "Remember the phrase, 'Get the hook?' There was a need for it sometimes!" Stagehands would sometimes have to pull a particularly long-winded performer off the stage. Pressler worked on the Strip for almost twenty-one years. "To me, it was like being a kid in the candy shop."

According to musician Dave Hawley, there were around 850 musicians working in the showrooms during the early 1960s. The town of Las Vegas had a population of about a hundred thousand people at that time, making the ratio of musicians to population much higher than it is today, when Las Vegas has a population of over 2 million. The musicians formed a tight-knit community of friends and colleagues who looked out for each other.

Of course, some people did go home between shows, to relax and perhaps see their families. Bassist Ed Boyer said he liked to go home and watch television. Bill Trujillo wanted to spend as much time with his wife and family as he could. When his son got into baseball, he would try to see the games between shows. Ralph Pressler remarked, "That whole era back then was really neat . . . because there were so many musicians working full-time, being able to keep their significant others or their spouses at home, raise kids and send them to college." There were perks for working the showrooms: musicians were often able to go to any of the other shows for free if they were working on the Strip. Pressler continued, "If our parents [or other relatives] came to town . . . you could get just about anybody in to see a show."

One very special institution was The Musicians' Wives Club, chartered in February of 1964 for wives of musicians and female musicians. They were part of a national organization, with the stated purposes of promoting friendship among all musicians and their families, improving the image of musicians, working for the betterment of their community, encouraging young musicians, and providing opportunities for music education.[34] The Las Vegas chapter was especially active throughout the 1960s. Through their efforts, they provided music scholarships to high school and University of Nevada, Las Vegas (UNLV) students, planted trees, and assisted Child Haven (an organization that serves abused and neglected children), various senior citizen programs, the Welfare Kitchen, needy families, local youth groups, widows of musicians, and dependent children.[35] They sponsored successful fundraisers, including an annual celebrity auction and cocktail party, "Jazz in the Park" concerts, and spring family picnics. Their monthly newsletter reported a crowd of two thousand for the jazz concerts.[36] Some of the celebrities who donated items for the auctions included Tony Bennett, Jack Benny, Tony Curtis, Vic Damone, Jimmy Durante, Billy Eckstine, Harry James, Frankie Laine, Patti Page, Louis Prima, and Henny Youngman. Phyllis Diller was one of the auctioneers, and Bobby Rydell sang at a function.[37]

The success of these activities inspired the club members, many of whom were musicians or dancers themselves, to write five original shows that included timely skits and production numbers. These shows did not start until 10:15 P.M. so that working musicians could participate in between their Strip gigs.[38] Percussionist Howard Agster remembered that the Musicians' Wives Club was very influential with hiring, and that they helped their husbands get jobs.

Most of the musicians continued to support civil rights. One of the first activities of the Musicians' Wives Club was to sponsor a talk hosted by civil rights activist Bob Bailey entitled "Human Rights—Women's Rights, Especially in Southern Nevada."[39] After a threatened mass march on the Strip in 1960, most resorts had agreed to accept desegregation. According to historians Moehring and Green, "By 1960, thanks to the growth of the resort industry and the thousands of low-paying service-sector jobs it created, the number of black Las Vegans had swelled to more than eleven thousand in the metropolitan area, more than enough of a base to support effective protests."[40] Writer Hal Rothman agreed: "The combination of necessary labor and celebrity performers gave the African American community influence that it lacked in most other American cities."[41]

With so many musicians and their families in town, it was inevitable that the cultural options would expand. A cursory look at the professional and amateur groups in Las Vegas during the 1960s provides astonishing evidence of a vibrant and thriving arts community. The instrumental groups included the Las Vegas Boulevard Hotel Symphonists, the Las Vegas Brass Sextet, Las Vegas Civic Orchestra, the Las Vegas Jazz Septet, the Las Vegas Junior Symphony Orchestra, the Las Vegas Percussion Quartet, the Las Vegas Philharmonic (different from the current Las Vegas Philharmonic that was launched in 1998), the Las Vegas Pops Concert Orchestra, the Las Vegas Symphonic Society Orchestra, the Las Vegas Wind Symphony, the Las Vegas Youth Band, the Musical Arts Workshop of Las Vegas, the New Jazz Orchestra, the Promenade Orchestra Pops, and the Southern Nevada Festival Orchestra. In addition, there were regular chamber music matinees and Sunday music matinees, the Musical Arts Chorale, and numerous choral ensembles of various sizes.

The syndicate owners supported these efforts, often providing the venue for various concerts or contributing financially to the organizations. One hotel orchestra leader who was also a composer, Bill Reddie, premiered his *"Symphony No. 1"* with a seventy-five-piece orchestra in the Arabian Room of the Dunes Hotel. Reddie was a highly trained classical musician whose parents were string musicians with the Chicago Symphony Orchestra.[42] The *Las Vegas Review-Journal* printed an article about the symphony premiere, as well as several photographs, including one where Reddie and flutist Phil Cenicola were joined by Major Riddle, president of the Dunes Hotel.[43] Columnist Les Devor wrote about the event:

> It's very gratifying to see the manner in which the whole Strip, including hotel bosses, employees, and show people have gotten behind the support of the forthcoming Symphony Concert to be presented in the Arabian Room of the Dunes Hotel on Sunday, January 31, at 3 P.M. An all-out effort is being launched with the help of local radio, TV stations, and newspapers cooperating to make this the biggest musical event of the year. . . . Bill Reddie . . . will conduct the 75-piece orchestra composed entirely of

local musicians. The concert will be sponsored by the American Federation of Musicians Local 369 with all proceeds going to the music fund of Nevada Southern. . . . Let's all show our appreciation for our local musicians and help train future ones at Nevada Southern by attending this symphony concert.[44]

The Dunes Hotel's Major Riddle allowed a benefit performance of "Casino de Paris" in 1968 after acrobat Diego Alfredo Reyes was permanently paralyzed in a car accident. According to Forrest Duke, "Riddle and the other generous execs at the Dunes are sponsoring the entire benefit."[45]

Another important concert, the "Five Stages of Jazz," was held on May 10, 1961 and showcased many top jazz musicians such as the All Star Band featuring Tommy Turk and Tommy Lewis, Lionel Hampton and His Orchestra, Vido Musso, Henri Rose and Bobby Stevens, and Charlie Teagarden and His Dixieland Band. The groups were gathered from the six Strip hotels and downtown casinos where they were featured. "Las Vegas is the home of some of the greatest musicians in the entire nation," said Local 369 president Jack Foy. "And it is hoped that this concert will introduce many of them to local residents. . . . We are certainly grateful to the Flamingo Hotel for allowing this to be presented on their beautiful grounds and we hope that the Five Stages of Jazz can become an annual event."[46] The concert was presented free of charge to the public, with the Musicians Union trust fund providing the pay for the musicians.

In 1962 the Las Vegas Convention Center hosted both Eugene Ormandy with the Philadelphia Orchestra and the first Las Vegas Jazz Festival.[47] In 1969 Antonio Morelli conducted the Las Vegas Pops Orchestra in "A Musical Portrait of Nevada," presented at the Sands Hotel where he was the house orchestra leader. The *Las Vegas Review-Journal* noted that more than two thousand people attended the concert.[48]

It is difficult to imagine that level of support for classical and jazz music on the Las Vegas Strip today. Las Vegas cultural life was decimated after the failed strike of 1989, after which the majority of musicians left town; this loss becomes clear when comparing the levels of musical activity from that time to this. The loss of all that talent had a domino effect—not just on Strip hotel entertainment, but also on the city's cultural groups. Though the music scene has managed to rebuild itself over time, it has certainly not reached the quantity or arguably the quality of what it was. The Las Vegas Philharmonic Orchestra today has a regular audience average of about 1,400, with Las Vegas metropolitan area population figures at about 2 million. In other words, it would appear that a much smaller percentage of the total population attends the classical concerts today than those who attended performances in the 1960s on the Strip. While there are a number of factors that have contributed to this state of affairs, it is clear that the changed ownership of the casinos had a devastating effect on musical life in Las Vegas.

Even as the 1989 strike was ongoing, musicians tried to make clear the repercussions of firing so many musicians at once. Denis Applenan, a percussionist from the "Folies" show band, when asked what he thought would happen, replied, "We're all going to leave town is what's going to happen. What's going to happen when they try to have an opera? The symphony orchestra is going to go down the toilet. There won't be any jazz in the park because there won't be any jazz players to play it. The way they're going, they're going to drive all the musicians out of town. We can't play the fun things if we don't play the bread and butter gigs. Those of us who play in the house orchestras also support the arts. These hotels, by getting rid of us, are going to destroy the pool of creative musicians in this town."[49] He was right.

In the 1960s, however, times were still good. And it was not just the showrooms that were popular: the lounges were also hot. "In those days there were no nightclubs or sports bars where employees could go," said performer Freddie Bell. "They would all come into the lounge—showgirls, pit bosses. The 5:00 A.M. show would be packed. The Sands would serve Chinese food." The showroom headliners would often gather in one lounge or another and stay there all night, listening to the bands and singers. The Sinatra-led Rat Pack was notorious for doing just that, sometimes performing impromptu. The lounge performers fed on the energy of their audiences and remember those years as a good time. "We always had fun," said Claude Trenier, front man for the Treniers. "That's what I liked about the lounge."[50] The entertainment was continuous in the lounges, and for many years could be enjoyed for nothing more than the cost of a drink.

The Mary Kaye Trio continued to be popular. Louis Prima and Keeley Smith were wildly successful until their divorce in October of 1961. The separation of this famous duo was front-page news in the *Las Vegas Review-Journal*, which closely followed the activities of the lounge performers.[51]

In 1963 *Las Vegas Review-Journal* columnist Murray Hertz wrote,

> The trend toward larger lounges filled with more powerhouse entertainment continues to swell like an ever-filling balloon, almost ready to burst, but never quite doing so. Where does it end? The lounges keep getting bigger, the entertainment more spectacular. . . . The biggest names in show business are now playing Las Vegas lounges—and at capacity business too. Outfits like Louis Prima, Shecky Greene, Henny Youngman, Kay Stevens, Ben Blue, Harry James, Vaughn Monroe, Sarah Vaughan, Della Reese, Louis Jordon, and I don't know how many others are examples. One lounge even has a complete French Revue, while the main room boasts a hit musical comedy. Fantastic, isn't it? . . . The importance of this type of entertainment cannot be underestimated. Some lounges hold as many as 300 persons and have facilities for 200 persons to stand. . . . They usually turn over three shows a night for the principals, which accounts for almost 1,500 people in one night. Then, there's the secondary acts. . . . Persons have easier access to the gambling tables while in a lounge, and there are some hotels that feel that gambling action is important.[52]

A 1964 show schedule lists typical activity in the lounges during the week of April 9. The Desert Inn Lady Luck Lounge featured Pinky Lee, Davis and Reese, and the Lilting Strings, among others. The Silver Slipper Gay 90's lounge showcased Charlie Teagarden's Jazz Group. The Driftwood Lounge at the Flamingo Hotel presented Della Reese and Cleopatra's Nymphs of the Nile, among others. The Starlight Lounge at the Riviera hosted Johnny Diamond and the Diamonds, the Betty Ayres Sparkling Strings, and the Hal Iverson Quartet. The Casbar Lounge at the Sahara Hotel still featured Louis Prima, but with his new singer Gia Mione. The Sands Copa Lounge hosted Martin Denny, the Stardust Lounge at the Stardust Hotel presented The Four Aces, and the Thunderbird lounge presented the Brothers Castro and the Treniers. The Dunes' Persian Room was home to the revue "Vive les Girls," while the Tropicana Showcase Lounge hosted Perez Prado.[53]

By now, there were minimums in most of the main showrooms and many of the hotel owners wondered whether there should be minimums in the lounges, due to the rising costs of hiring stars. According to writer Murray Hertz, "Las Vegas entertainment directors, already losing hair over the tremendous competition for big name acts in their lounges, are now wondering how they're going to handle the tremendous increase in costs brought about by the competitive situation." The Dunes was the first to require a $3 minimum, but it did so because the main showroom was under repair. The Dunes' press agent, Less Fisher, remarked, "It's only temporary. . . . One of the purposes of a lounge is to make it easy for the gamblers to wander in and out to the tables. The minimum is a stop gap to this very thing." Dave Victorson of the Thunderbird Hotel disagreed, remarking that establishing minimums was inevitable: "The high cost of entertainment will force us to do just that." Henry Dunn of the Tropicana countered, "The purpose of the lounge is to lead people into the hotels. If you impose a compulsory amount of money that they should spend, then you defeat your purpose. I am presently operating my lounge without a minimum and it is breaking even therefore serving the purpose for which it was intended. I also think that a minimum would hurt the reputation that Las Vegas has as being the best entertainment bargain in the world. This is one of our biggest selling points. I won't say that we are going to have minimums in our lounges. . . . I just say we shouldn't!"[54]

With so many people in the showrooms and lounges, money flowed freely to the casino workers. Sahara worker Autumn Burns recalled, "It was fabulous, the players were great. We used to make a fortune on tips. . . . We lived on tips. . . . We were up all night at the tables, slept all day. I got to know the entertainers, the hotel owners."[55] The mob owners and their front men often passed money to workers who needed it. Corinne Entratter, wife of Sands front man Jack Entratter, remembered, "He never went around that he didn't always have at least $6,000 in one pocket, and the other pocket he had about a thousand dollars. I said, 'Jack, why don't you keep your money in one pocket?' He said, 'Oh no I have to have two pockets, one to give away, and one for my own use.' Many times if a cocktail waitress or a busboy, if they had trouble and they couldn't make their house payment or if they had a son or daughter in the hospital, or a mother, Jack always paid for everything."[56]

Moe Dalitz, the mob owner who had first stepped in with money for Wilbur Clark's Desert Inn, was considered a community supporter. Along with Allard Roen and Merv Adelson, he built Sunrise Hospital, the Las Vegas Country Club, and the Boulevard Mall. According to *Las Vegas Sun* writers Ed Koch and Mary Manning, Dalitz "helped charitable causes, often reaching into his own pocket to buy uniforms for local youth sports teams. He won many civic awards in Las Vegas for giving back to the community."[57]

Las Vegas hotel musicians also became used to seeing large amounts of money change hands around them. Johnny Haig remembered a particular night when a couple came to hear the band, as they were thinking of hiring his group for a private party. Haig met them before the show and asked how they were doing. "Jammed up," was the reply from the man, meaning that he was losing money. Haig introduced the couple to the showroom maître d' and asked him to take care of them. Throughout the show, Haig noticed that the man would disappear and reappear. After the show was over, the maître d' said, "Johnny, send me all the people you can!" As it turned out, the man had won $25,000 in the casino; after that, he tipped the maître d' $100 every time he came back into the showroom. Tipping the maître d' for good seats, as well as some other types of tipping, disappeared when the casino ownership changed. So did the open-handed generosity of the hotel owners.

The mob owners would try anything to keep people in their hotels, having a good time and spending money without a care. "The key to a hotel here is Vegas is, first, you've got to get something to draw people in," said Bill Miller, entertainment promoter for the Frontier and the Sahara. "Second, you've got to make them stay there. Once they walk out the door, you don't have a shot at them. That's when they found out the lounges would stop people."[58]

Working as part of a hotel lounge act brought its own special challenges. Bassist Tom McDermott remembered playing for entertainer Ray Anthony at the Desert Inn Lounge. Anthony had matching suits, ties, everything down to the socks and shoes for the musicians to wear. McDermott's shoes were huge and had to be stuffed with tissue just so he could keep them on. Another musician actually did not get this lounge job because the suit would not fit him. McDermott, who was doing both the production show and the lounge act in the hotel at this time, remembered having to run back and forth between the lounge and the showroom. One night he forgot to change his socks and said that Ray Anthony noticed it immediately. Just trying to get to each location could also be a challenge. McDermott called the back hallways of the Desert Inn "the catacombs." He remarked, "If you got lost, you could be down there a week." McDermott also noted that the music was often more difficult than in the main showrooms. "I had the illusion that if you could get into the main room those were the most, the best venues, the most talented people . . . but that wasn't true, the hard stuff was in the lounges."

Word spread about the money and work in Las Vegas, and musicians arrived from all over the country to fill the showroom and lounge bands. Dave Hawley remembered that the first thing he did when he got to Las Vegas was to look up everyone from his hometown. He found a friend working at the Dunes Hotel, and he was able to sit with the Dunes Hotel band and meet the musicians. When his friend needed some time off, Hawley was hired to play baritone saxophone as his friend's substitute. Just like Don Hannah, Hawley auditioned by sitting in on a show: in other words, sight-reading an actual performance with the band. Hawley described this, his first job in town in 1966: "It was such a thrill, a big show, a lot of notes, you are really working hard. . . . I didn't even own a baritone [saxophone] when I took the job. On the road I played alto [saxophone]. Once you work one thing in this town and you do a good job on that, then . . . well, you are a baritone player."

Pianist Ronnie Simone never forgot his first visit to Las Vegas in 1959. He arrived at 9:00 P.M. and immediately saw a show featuring twelve strolling mandolins, a piano, guitar, harp, and bass. At midnight, twelve strolling violins replaced these players. He heard "a fabulous two piano group" and ate a free chuck wagon dinner that started at midnight. "I'm right out of New York City. . . . I cannot believe this. . . . These people are eating free and there's music all night. . . . There were no time clocks. I had a few drinks, next thing I know, I'm finally leaving there at 6:00 in the morning and the sun is out and it's the next day. . . . That was my introduction to Las Vegas! I really soaked it up. . . . I don't think I slept more than eight hours [during his visit]."

Simone decided to come back and work in Las Vegas someday, which he did with great success in the 1960s. He was just one example of the new type of musician who began to work in Las Vegas during this time. According to Tom McDermott, Ronnie Simone was "world class. . . . [There are] not enough accolades to talk about that guy. He's met them all, played for them all." Johnny Haig said this about Simone: "He was like the number one person they called. . . . [He] could sit down and play anything in any key at any time, and read anything."

Bill Trujillo, who lived on the Westside in the 1950s, left Las Vegas to tour with Woody Herman and then continued touring with various other road bands, eventually heading to Europe with a jazz quintet. After his return, he played with jazz great Stan Kenton's band for two years, also on the road, but then he decided that the touring life was not for him. "You get home, and the kids don't know you." He returned to Las Vegas when he got an offer of a steady job at the New Frontier (the Frontier Hotel, remodeled and under new management). He remembered the show was "Holiday in Japan" and that he played the rehearsals still unsure if he actually had the job. Finally, he asked the bandleader whether he was hired, and he told Trujillo, "You play pretty good kid. . . . Yeah, you got the job."

Trujillo stayed with one group for a few years until he got the inevitable phone call offering more money to move to a new band. With so many hotels needing musicians, the players who were at the top of the field could count on having opportunities to jump ship. Trujillo made the move to the "Lido" show at the Flamingo. "Same music every night. I didn't like it, but it was a job. I had a nice family life. . . . It was just a normal family life." To keep his interest in the music going, Trujillo memorized the entire show. "I made a project out of it." He thought, "If I do this, I won't go stale."

In 1968 trombonist Ken Hanlon moved to Las Vegas to have the chance to play music full time. He had been teaching and had a young daughter, but said, "I didn't want to hang up my horn." Hanlon also remembered that there was "no such thing as overtime on contract in those days." Once, when opening a new show, he went to work on Christmas Eve at 2:00 P.M. and did not finish rehearsing until 7:00 A.M. on Christmas morning. After a few hours of sleep, he was back at rehearsal from 3:00 P.M. until 8:00 P.M. It was not the musicians who needed the rehearsals, however, but the showgirls. Some of them seemed to have trouble remembering the walking choreography. The musicians would play the show music, then, from the back of the showroom, the choreographer would yell something like, "No, no, no, how many times have I told you? You go right!" After a collective groan from the musicians in the pit, the show music would start up again from the beginning.

Sometimes, musicians could work two different shows in two different locations if the timing worked out. Hanlon remembered having trouble only once. His first show, with a comedian at the Landmark Hotel, ended late because the comedian refused to quit until he had the audience laughing. Unfortunately for Hanlon, the comedian kept going until 9:55 P.M. "I grab my trombone, grab my gig bag from backstage. I'm running across the parking lot trying to jam my trombone into my gig bag. I drove seventy miles an hour down Paradise [Road]" to get to the 10:00 P.M. show at the Flamingo. "I wasn't the only guy that ever happened to." He said they held the curtain for him.

Musician Matt Saporita remembered the time he showed up to work only to find that the electricity was out for the entire hotel because one of his band mates had backed into a significant power pole. He also remembered an incident at the Flamingo when the curtain going up caught hold of the band's bass player, lifting both player and bass up to the rafters. In a similar story, Bill Trujillo recalled the curtain catching a bass and the player refusing to let go of the expensive instrument. The musicians were yelling, "Just let it go!" and the bass player was yelling back, "No, no, man, I'm not going to let go!" So Trujillo grabbed the bass players' legs and another musician grabbed Trujillo's legs until all three musicians were going up with the bass and the curtain.

Curtain incidents continued to be a problem. D. Gause, a musician who came to Las Vegas later, remembered a trombone at Caesars Palace that became hooked in the curtain and went up, minus the trombone player. A similar incident involved a Japanese trombonist, who began screaming as he watched his trombone being lifted quickly thirty feet above his head. Those with instruments that had protruding parts had to watch them closely.

When Ronnie Simone helped open a new show, Donn Arden's "Hello

America," an extra percussionist was hired who was "not the quickest," according to Simone. It was the job of this percussionist to hit a gong that signaled the showgirls to start coming out from the wings. The conductor had practiced this repeatedly with the percussionist and finally said, "When I cue you, you hit this!" Everyone was nervous about the opening and Simone remembered that there were "all these fights going on." When the premiere began at last, the percussion player was ready. Unfortunately, he was so ready that he mistook the clarinet cue for *his* cue and hit the gong eight pages too early. "Next thing you know, the showgirls, who are not ready, they hear it, 'Oh, that's our cue!' So they start coming out from the wings, they crash into the set. Bang! Things are falling. . . . Donn Arden almost had a stroke sitting there! These are things . . . you gotta be there!"

Simone believed that the boys were some of the best people for whom he worked. He said, "They knew how to run a casino, [but] you did not say 'no' to the boys!" On one particular night, Simone got a call from his boss wondering where he was. Though it was Simone's night off, the boss wanted him to come to the casino right away. He had some big-time gamblers that he wanted to entertain. "Minnesota Fats, Jimmy the Greek, plus some others." Simone stayed until 2:00 A.M., making big tips the entire time. For the next two years Simone worked seven nights a week for a week and a half's pay.

Even during the freewheeling days of mob-owned casinos, musicians were subject to intense pressure and stress. Performing is both mentally and physically taxing, and can only go on for set amounts of time before the players must take a break. While all working musicians experience a certain amount of pressure, working in the Las Vegas casinos called for special skills not always needed by other musicians. For example, most orchestra and band musicians know the repertoire very well and come to the first rehearsal well prepared. Once a concert has been performed, the repertoire changes, which keeps things interesting for the musicians. In the Las Vegas star rooms, the show book might not arrive until just before the first rehearsal and the music was often difficult. Musicians working these shows needed to possess excellent sight-reading ability and strong technical skills. Long-running shows were, and in many ways still are, even more difficult than the shows that change quickly: musicians in these productions must endure the same material every night, sometimes for years on end, without losing focus. Only Broadway shows, production shows, or touring musicals present the same type of challenge.

Las Vegas hotel musicians typically performed an 8:oo P.M. show for about an hour and a half, then were on break until the midnight show. This break was necessary for all the performers, both physically and mentally, to prepare themselves for the next show. It was especially important for brass players, though. Playing a brass instrument such as trumpet or trombone requires the use of strong lip muscles (called "chops" by the players), and these muscles tire and weaken after repeated use. The players used the downtime to rest their chops and usually could not practice between shows even if they wanted to—and most did not. Brass players who played their instruments on break might start missing notes on the next show and get fired.

Some musicians, typically rhythm section members or string players, were able to work lounges in between shows, but many players took advantage of the downtime to relax in the hotel coffee shops. Like Chuck's House of Spirits, the hotel coffee shops were clearinghouses for gossip. They also served as a place for musicians to read, network, or even play cards and games. Quite a few of these musicians became skillful in something other than music to help pass the time.

Johnny Haig said, "I went into the coffee shop every night and played chess. That became a big thing. Chess players that came to town, they knew we were playing . . . [and] waitresses wouldn't bother us. I became a real fanatic, entered tournaments. I was studying books, studying other games." Some of the musicians from other hotels would come over just to see the chess matches. There could be three or four chess games going at once. Haig became so proficient that he eventually achieved the status of master. Woodwind doubler Sam Pisciotta also recalled playing chess. In addition, Pisciotta liked to visit the other hotel coffee shops to see his friends or read lengthy novels such as *War and Peace*.

Ed Boyer remembered a trumpet player who would make homemade Italian sausage and who took orders for sausage during the week. Eventually this side business became so successful that the sausage maker opened an Italian deli, and soon had two more. "My side industry was photography," said Boyer. He did shoots with some of the musicians and photographed the

Musicians Union conventions, including the hundredth anniversary of the union in 1996.

Dave Hawley knew a trumpet player from the Stardust who was also a barber and would cut hair between shows for the band. "I had a regular appointment," Hawley added. Tom McDermott remembered that guitarist Joe Lano would work on cars between shows. McDermott said, "[He] could change your transmission then he would go play something that couldn't be played on the guitar. . . . He's always been my mentor, he's like an encyclopedia."

The pressure for constant perfection could be difficult to handle, especially for those musical high-wire artists, the trumpet players. Dave Hawley recounted, "Those shows on the Strip were murderous for trumpet players. A lot of great players came and blew their lips out. . . . Arrangers would want higher and higher and louder and louder. Some great guys came and lasted so long but just couldn't last any longer."

Other brass instrument players had similar problems. Hannah often served in a double capacity for the bands—tuba and bass—which was not unusual in earlier days. For one show, his first entrance on tuba called for some very high notes. Hannah started the show on bass and only had a few seconds to grab the tuba and play these notes. The tuba, sitting on the bandstand for so long, was always stone cold, which made it very difficult to play. Inevitably, Hannah's first entrance was a clam. (A "clam" is what brass players call a note that comes out on the wrong pitch.) Hannah recalled one clam that "went as far as the Boulder Dam!" Musicians do not like to be foiled by equipment issues. Frustrated, Hannah realized that he needed a way to warm up his tuba before he had to play it. So, he rigged up an old hair dryer to keep warm air blowing on his tuba. This creative solution kept the tuba warm and ready to play, and he never had to fear his first tuba entrance again.

Most musicians remembered the work was more interesting in the earlier days before the corporations took over the hotels. Don Hannah recalled, "One entertainer might get sick, and another from up the street would come in, and musicians would sight-read the act. A lot of fun; you were out there on the edge." Tom McDermott said, "The guys who were writing these early shows . . . the bass parts looked like violin parts . . . so there was a big hunt for guys who could read."

The production shows brought in guaranteed money but were not much fun for the musicians. Some of them turned to drugs or alcohol, or fell asleep on the job. During the "swinging sixties," many people, and not just the musicians, were interested in pushing the boundaries of social customs and relaxing social taboos. Tom McDermott said, "It was a looser time. Nobody was worried about their job. . . . More than one trombone player has been held up by someone on each side." He recalled a particularly boring production number when he "kind of fell over into the saxophone player's lap. . . . He said, 'Wake up!'"

There were various other ways that the musicians dealt with the tedium. Dave Hawley remembered playing at the Riviera the day Neil Armstrong walked on the moon. The lead trumpet player had a small television on his stand so he could watch the moonwalk that took place during the show. Hawley recalled that there was "a glow" in the trumpet section all night. At the Sahara Hotel, Hawley recalled band members with earphones listening to the World Series as they played the show. "Sometimes they would forget and cheer for their team!"

While the building spree of the 1950s had not continued into the 1960s, there were a few new properties in town: Caesar's Palace on the Strip, inaugurated on August 5, 1966, and built with money from the Teamsters Central States Pension Fund; the Four Queens on Fremont Street, also opened in 1966. The 1,500-room International, at that time the largest hotel in the world, was built by Kirk Kerkorian and opened on July 4, 1969. Barbra Streisand was the attraction for the main room of the International, with Peggy Lee in the lounge, though the rooms were still unfinished.[59]

Caesar's Palace was a game changer; many consider this to be the first major resort on the Strip. Its Circus Maximus Showroom seated eight hundred and featured Andy Williams for the gala opening.[60] The Ritz Brothers were the first entertainers in the hotel lounge, Nero's Nook, that seated 250. "You absolutely couldn't get in to see us during that opening week," remembered Harry Ritz. "It was the biggest opening event I have ever seen. We did everything on stage that you could think. We were originally signed for 28 weeks and stayed for over two years. At the time we were the highest paid lounge act ever. We received $12,500 per week, two suites at the hotel and other complimentary items."[61] Other performers at Caesars Palace in the 1960s included Woody Allen, Petula Clark, Tony Curtis, José Feliciano, Bob Fosse, Judy Garland, Dizzy Gillespie, Andy Griffith, Don Knotts, Mickey Rooney, an Ed Sullivan Show production, Tiny Tim, and Andy Williams.

A 1967 program for Caesars Palace listed Nat Brandwynne as the maestro for the forty-piece Circus Maximus Orchestra. Brandwynne came to Las Vegas from New York City where he conducted at the Waldorf Astoria for twenty-five years, as well as opening the Stork Club, the Pierre, and the Copacabana.[62] Dave Victorson was the entertainment director responsible for bringing in the big-name stars.

Tony Bennett celebrated his twentieth anniversary in show business at Caesars Palace on June 27, 1968, sharing the bill with Buddy Rich and his fifteen-piece orchestra.[63] Tony Bennett was a hands-down favorite of just about every Las Vegas musician who worked with him. Dave Hawley said, "Tony was great . . . [and] he liked us. Some people put up with us, some people really liked us." Trombone player Dick McGee added, "Tony Bennett would hang around and talk to the band afterwards." Ralph Pressler also named Tony Bennett as a favorite, "not only because of his ability to sing and interpret . . . [but also because he had] neat arrangements. The band really got a chance to dig in. Very approachable backstage, very nice, very humble, easy to talk to." Johnny Haig cherished one special memento from Tony Bennett: "I have a picture of me sitting in front of a 100-piece orchestra with Tony Bennett singing to me during a rehearsal!" Bennett was exceptionally loyal to the musicians, and still is.

George Burns was another entertainer the musicians remembered fondly. Don Hannah pointed out how supportive Burns was of other entertainers and said that Burns helped bring people like Ann Margaret or Bobby Darin to Las Vegas. Johnny Haig, whose band played for Burns' ninety-fifth, ninety-sixth, and ninety-seventh birthday bashes said, "He was a joy; he loved everybody in show business." Haig remembered that Burns would always watch the opening act, sitting in the wings in his bathrobe, smoking his cigar. He also remembered how Burns used to call him "Kid." "You're the only person in this hotel who can call *me* Kid!," Haig said he told Burns. He added, "I was on CBS 60 *Minutes* with him [most likely in 1988]."

Many people liked Jerry Lewis. Dave Hawley said, "Jerry Lewis loves the musicians." Johnny Haig added, "Jerry Lewis was great to musicians. Always insisted on a big orchestra." Haig remembered one time in particular when Lewis wanted to add two French horns to his show, but the syndicate owner was resistant, asking, "What are French horns?" The owner eventually relented, though, and allowed Lewis to hire the musicians. Later, as Haig was rehearsing for the show, the owner walked in and shouted, "Hey Jerry, show me the two French horns." Lewis had the two French horn players stand up, then the owner "waved at them and walked out," according to Haig.

Ronnie Simone also liked Ann Margaret. "She was delightful . . . [and] she was sweet." Bassist Ed Boyer said that Sarah Vaughan would "hang out between sets. Everybody loved her. The Thunderbird [Hotel] was a hip store in those days." Trombonist Ken Hanlon added, "The band was blown away. To play for Sarah Vaughn was like going to heaven." Don Hannah had his own favorites. "Jack Benny, what a treat! Harry Belafonte. Hair-raising, the man was so good." Other musicians liked Julie Andrews because she had a great ear, and of course many loved the voice of singer Robert Goulet.

Dave Hawley remembered liking Roy Clark when he was working for the Frontier. Clark had first come to Las Vegas in 1960 as part of a band, but he soon became a headliner himself. Clark had a trailer backstage and liked to have the musicians come back and visit between the shows. He even kept a bowl of peanuts or other snacks around for visitors. Hawley remembered, "The whole feeling of the show was good even if you didn't like country music. He was just one of the people, just a regular guy, and he was a real warm, interesting person to know."

Some of the stars were prima donnas. Ronnie Simone once filled in for Burt Bacharach, who was playing piano for Marlene Dietrich at the time. Because Bacharach improvised and did not write down what he was doing, Simone had to learn the music by listening to performance tapes. Everything went smoothly until Simone had his first day off and was helping a friend. "For some reason, they tracked me down. 'Get down to the Riviera.' Marlene refused to rehearse with the relief guy. . . . Being a pianist, many times I had to rehearse between shows. . . . I can't tell you the times I had to stay behind and they would want me to rehearse a certain number, play an audition for a new singer." Simone found that his least favorite performers were those who were not solid musically and needed him to cover for them. One popular entertainer "couldn't feel time. . . . He would drop beats, add beats [lose his rhythm and get ahead or behind the piano player]. Oh my God!" Another singer would "milk" the audience, said Simone, rolling his eyes. She would complain every night that her throat was "bad" and then ask the audience, "Should I continue?" knowing that they would beg her to keep singing and forgive any mistakes. Many singers did experience trouble if they were not used to the dry desert climate; the musicians called it "Vegas throat." Still, most singers would not share this information with the audience or use it as an excuse. Over time, however, the bad memories tended to fade and most of the players enjoyed being onstage with the big-name headliners and talented entertainers. "You remember the good ones, not the pains in the butt!" said Sam Pisciotta.

A major favorite of the musicians, Frank Sinatra, made his move to Caesars Palace following an extreme falling out with the Sands management after Howard Hughes purchased the hotel. The eccentric billion-aire Hughes had arrived in Las Vegas in 1966, while Sinatra was still very much at home in the Sands. Forrest Duke, entertainment writer for both the *Las Vegas Review-Journal* and *Variety* magazine, noted a typical three-week engagement there of "Dean Martin and His Friends," which included Sinatra and Joey Bishop, as a "ring-a-ding gasser." The Rat Pack still drew a crowd with their onstage banter and showmanship. One clever gag had Sinatra and Bishop pretending that Martin was missing; while one performed onstage, the other acted as though he was searching for the absent singer backstage and in the audience. Finally, Martin appeared with a drink in hand saying, "I heard Dean Martin being announced—you know how crazy I am about him, so I went out and sat in the audience!"[64]

Howard Hughes, after a secretive late-night arrival in 1966, checked into the Desert Inn ninth-floor suite. Already exhibiting signs of mental illness, Hughes created more concern for his sanity when he bought the Desert Inn simply because he did not want to leave the hotel. He continued to buy Las Vegas properties one after the other in a major spending spree: the Sands, the Castaways, and the Frontier.[65]

Hughes's first purchase was approved by county officials in "less than five minutes." District Attorney George Franklin remarked, "This is the best way to improve the image of gambling in Nevada by licensing an industrialist of his stature. It will be an asset and a blessing." Las Vegas lawyer and Gaming Commission Chairman George Dickerson noted, "I can think of no one who can enhance the image of Nevada gambling more than Howard Hughes. He has been successful in every business venture he has ever conducted. . . . These men [Del E. Webb and William Harrah] have shown that gambling is like any other business and that a businessman can use time-tested practices to show a profit."[66]

Soon after Hughes purchased the Desert Inn, speculation ran rampant about how he would change the casino business. Rumors reached New York *Variety* editor Abel Green, who quickly put reporter Bill Willard on the task. "This might be a story you can best ferret out for yourself," wrote Green. "No. 1, there are recurrent rumors that the Hughes assault may phase out gambling in the not-so-many-years to come. This is hard to believe. . . . Anyway, write it exclusively for us, and maybe you can get a local savvy lowdown by some of the other operators. Ask Jack Entratter, for example, what he thinks."[67]

One change happened rather quickly: after his purchase of the Sands, Hughes installed new management who would no longer look the other way when Frank Sinatra suffered gambling losses and refused to pay up. When the casino cut off his credit, Sinatra reacted with fury, eventually getting involved in a brawl with hotel security and management. *Las Vegas Review-Journal* writer Don Digilio reported,

> Singer Tony Bennett left his heart in San Francisco and Frank Sinatra left his teeth—at least two of them—in Las Vegas. . . . Sinatra parted company with both the Sands and his teeth Monday morning in the Garden Room of the Sands Hotel that was described by witnesses as a nightmare. It was Carl Cohen, vice-president of the Sands, who finally halted Sinatra's wild weekend. The Sands executive bloodied the singer's nose and knocked his teeth out after Sinatra tipped a table over on him in the Garden Room of the hotel. Cohen will not talk about the incident, but a battery of witnesses, hailing Cohen as a hero, have come to the front to speak for the Sands exec and against Sinatra.[68]

One waiter at the hotel said, "Sinatra had been going wild at the hotel all morning. I am told he even set fire to his room. . . . Obviously, I can't give my name, but boy, did he [Sinatra] have it coming." A security guard said, "Sinatra was yelling at Cohen because Carl had cut his credit off." A floor-man reported that Sinatra had yanked all the telephone jacks out of the hotel switchboard. He said, "I don't have anything to say about it but if I did, I would have got rid of Sinatra long ago." A bellman noted that Sinatra had taken a baggage cart and driven it through a plate glass window. "Why should he be allowed to act like a wild animal?"[69]

The musicians respected Sinatra probably more than any other headliner, but they knew he had a temper. Ronnie Simone had a memorable personal encounter with Sinatra while playing for Juliet Prowse during her first Las Vegas show in the 1960s. Prowse had started dating Sinatra, probably during the making of the film *Can-Can*. After rehearsing with her frequently, Simone had gotten to know her a little bit. One night, she asked if he would escort her into the Riviera lounge to hear Buddy Greco perform. Simone was happy to oblige. "I walk in with her, the maître d' just gives us a look and he gives us a great table. It can't be ten minutes after, Frank Sinatra comes in with his whole entourage, and I mean ENTOURAGE. Next thing you know, he sends the maître d' over. . . . They want to check me out! I realized what happened: they [Prowse and Sinatra] had some kind of spat or argument or something. I was what they call a 'beard' that night. I was looking at Sinatra and those guys trying to say, 'Hey, I'm just passing through! There's absolutely nothing here!'"

Sinatra announced his new contract with Caesars Palace and hinted that his Rat Pack might soon follow suit and leave the Sands. His public statement was diplomatic, but he was quoted as saying, "I built this hotel from a sand pile and before I'm through that is what it will be again." One source countered, "The casino just didn't think it would be a good idea to let Sinatra run up a big tab."[70]

This was one of the first harbingers of the changes to come. The Mafia owners were being outspent and were under increasing pressure from the Nevada Gaming Commission to clean up their act or leave town. According to Hughes's chief executive of Nevada operations, "The places he [Hughes] bought were the places that were in trouble with the federal government.

And the owners, for the most part, were very anxious to get rid of them." Soon, Hughes owned several major businesses in addition to the casinos, and he began to have enormous power and influence in the state. Ultimately, he spent over $300 million on his Las Vegas properties.[71] And it was his investment in Las Vegas that gave a new legitimacy to the town, something the state politicians and many townspeople desperately wanted.

"In a strange way, Howard Hughes resembled the gangsters he replaced more than the corporate America that revered him," wrote historian Hal Rothman. "Hughes was a confirmed risk-taker who flaunted rules all of his life; he was beholden to no one, and even more important, owed no one." In other important ways, however, Hughes was much different. For one thing, Hughes was adamantly opposed to unions. The mob owners had maintained close relations with their unionized employees, even secretly bringing out "food and cold drinks to the strikers in the Downtown Strike of 1967, hiding from their own security." Hughes worked very hard to break the union in his hotels, and the corporate investors that came after him followed suit. Rothman wrote, "The onset of the corporate era altered the tacit labor arrangement. Unionization worked because gaming made the hotels so consistently profitable, and the union's ability to produce labor contributed to their success. The Corporate Gaming Act of 1967 and its amended version in 1969 allowed corporations with pre-existing assumptions about labor-management relationships to own hotels. . . . Quickly the familiarity between management and labor diminished. The handshake contracts soon disappeared. All the documents bore signatures."[72]

Hughes was also notoriously racist. In a time when the worst discrimination issues had been resolved in Las Vegas, Hughes came in with a strong bias. According to his longtime aide Robert Maheu, Hughes made his position very clear: "Now I [Hughes] have never made my views known on this subject. And I certainly would not say these things in public. However, I can summarize my attitude about employing more Negroes very simply — I think it is a wonderful idea for somebody else, somewhere else." He also cancelled the Howard Hughes Open, a new tennis tournament that he had created, when he learned that Arthur Ashe was scheduled to play.[73]

There were worries that Hughes's new management teams would change the character of entertainment in Las Vegas to something more

G-rated. Howard Hughes was surrounded by a tight circle of employees, sometimes nicknamed "the Mormon Mafia," and these men were known to interfere when they thought something was offensive. One musician remembered a secretary for Hughes who previewed a show rehearsal. The secretary told the production manager that not only could they not do a top-less show, but they had to remove one song: "Hate You." He said, "You're not singing that in this show. This is a family show!" The song he was refer-ring to was "Hey Jude." This incident was in many ways typical of the per-ceived micromanagement by the Hughes Corporation and the new style of casino owners who followed him.

Hughes's success drew other corporate owners to Las Vegas; after they had bought or built properties, they began to examine every part of the casino industry for both legality and potential profit. Hughes eventually left Las Vegas, as secretly as he had arrived, but not without leaving a last-ing mark on the town. According to Las Vegas history writers Thomas Ain-lay Jr. and Judy Dixon Gabaldon, "When he [Hughes] left, it had become a corporate town—a newly opened playground for millionaires."[74] And the changes that the corporate owners made were not good for the local musi-cians. Ed Boyer noted, "I think Howard Hughes was the downfall, proba-bly. . . . They brought in the bean counters."

Initially, the entertainment industry ran the way it always had. Wayne Newton signed a two-year contract with the Frontier Hotel and was paid $50,000 a week; Frank Sinatra Jr. also performed there with the Harry James Band.[75] In addition to the headliners, lounge acts, and revues, the late 1960s saw a large number of Broadway musicals on the Strip. In 1966 the Riviera featured "Hello Dolly," and in 1967 it presented "That Certain Girl," "Any-thing Goes," "High Button Shoes," and the "Ziegfeld Follies." Caesars Pal-ace followed with "Mame" and "Sweet Charity" in 1968.[76]

The revues, however, were becoming more and more risqué (some thought more sleazy), and many of the hotels used the sex angle to attract customers, publishing racy advertisements. Even "serious" cultural writers sometimes used the sexy reputation of Las Vegas as a hook. In 1963 Bill Willard received a request from a New York publication to write an article on Las Vegas entertainment; he wanted to write about all the new cultural offerings, but it soon became clear that the publication owners expected something more exotic. His editor wrote, "Since we are both striving for national publicity of the cultural side of L.V. let's compromise with them. If you could get a few spicy semi-nudes . . . that have not been published, we would have a good chance to tell the story of art and culture in Las Vegas."[77]

The trajectory of the "sleaze factor" progression is clearly visible in the history of one type of revue, the ice show. According to Everett McGowan, he produced and directed the first ice show in Las Vegas in 1941 at the El Rancho Hotel, where Garwood Van was the orchestra director.[78] In 1957 the El Cortez presented "Rhythm on Ice." The Frontier featured "Carnival on Ice" and "Rhapsody on Ice" in the early 1960s. These shows were wholesome compared to what was to come. The Thunderbird Hotel came out with "Ecstasy on Ice" in 1959, followed by "Scandals on Ice" in 1961. By 1965 the Mint was producing "She-Bang Follies '65," and the Four Queens produced "Ice-A-Go-Go" in 1967. The Aladdin topped them all with their 1967 show "Nudes on Ice." After this, where was there left to go?

Topless female bands, as it happened. In August of 1967 Aladdin entertainment director Dick Kanellis hired the Ladybirds, billed as "the world's only authentic All-Girl Topless Band." This novelty act, "all competent musicians," first garnered a following in San Francisco.[79] Don Digilio, with his tongue firmly in his cheek, wrote a column about the group for the *Las Vegas Review-Journal*:

> Just why the girls play with their blouses off is a mystery to me. I mean I'm not knocking the idea, I just wonder if it helps them play in tune or something. . . . I'd like to make a few suggestions as to what songs they should play during their act. What about opening with the number, "Hey, Look Me Over," and then follow that with the very popular song, "With These Hands." . . . How about the group singing a snappy version of "Baby It's Cold Outside." . . . Well, I hope the Aladdin Hotel, Kanellis and the girls in the band don't get upset over this column. You see, it is just something I had to get off my chest.[80]

Not everyone was laughing, however. The union musicians were outraged over the perceived insult to the profession and wanted no part of the gig, ordering sixteen members out of the hotel and lounge after the first show. "We feel we are trying to make the image of the musicians in this town a good one," said George Beedy, representing the union view. "The girls can go on in any capacity but not with instruments or as musicians unless they are dressed differently. We will not honor the union contracts and are pulling out Las Vegas musicians."[81] When the hotel officials contacted the national union office, however, the local musicians were told to return to the showroom.

There was a shift in the type of entertainment being booked in the hotels as the 1960s ended. Las Vegas entertainment lost some of its luster, according to entertainment writer Mike Weatherford. The major stars of the 1940s and 1950s began to retire, die, or lose their popularity, and the production shows were becoming cheesier and even less classy.[82] Sinatra could still fill the town, but there were few sure bets other than him.

One well-known pop singer brought the spotlight back to Las Vegas: Elvis Presley. "They were standing in line at six in the morning waiting to see Elvis, hoping that maybe somebody wouldn't show," said Bill Miller, entertainment director for the International Hotel. "There was never an empty seat for Elvis Presley. It was just unbelievable." Joe Guercio, long-time musical director for Elvis at the International, said, "It will never be again; I don't care how big the star is. It was another world. You can't get that going again."[83]

Elvis made his Las Vegas debut in 1956, but the rock-and-roll singer was not a hit on the Strip at that time, although he was very popular with teenagers around the country. Susan Berman thought Elvis would be a success in Las Vegas: "I watched Elvis do 'Don't Be Cruel' then called my father saying, 'He's a hit, hire him, can I meet him?'"[84] Bill Willard was not impressed, however, and in his review said, "For the teen-agers, the long tall Memphis lad is a whiz; for the average Vegas spender or show-goer, a bore. His musical sound with a combo of three is uncouth, matching to a great extent the lyrical content of his nonsensical songs."[85]

When he returned to Vegas in 1969, Elvis and his manager "Colonel" Tom Parker presented Elvis differently. This time Elvis and his five-piece band were supplemented by a thirty-five-piece orchestra under the direction of Joe Guercio and two soul and gospel groups, bringing the total number of performers onstage to fifty. According to writer K. J. Evans, "In

Las Vegas and elsewhere, he would never again perform without at least a 30-piece orchestra and a legion of backup singers."[86]

This time, Las Vegas embraced Elvis with enthusiasm if not love, and Parker quickly brokered a deal to have Elvis perform four weeks twice a year for the next five years at an astounding $125,000 per week salary. Evans wrote, "Showrooms at the time were expected to lose money . . . but by the time Elvis concluded his first month-long engagement, the showroom had generated more than $2 million. It was the first time that a Las Vegas resort ever had profited from an entertainer."[87]

Elvis, like many of the hotel band musicians, suffered from the boredom of doing the same show night after night. One of Presley's entourage, Lamar Fike, pointed out the physical difficulties of headlining a show of this kind: "Do you realize what kind of hell four weeks is? That's a marathon — nearly 60 performances. And Elvis had such a high-energy show that when he would do an honest hour and 15 minutes twice a night, he was so tired he was cross-eyed. That's why he took all that stuff to keep him going."[88]

Percussionist Tommy Check, who performed with Elvis, thought he was a total gentleman, though he noted that Elvis seemed like "a little boy with more money who didn't understand his success." He added that Elvis liked to sing gospel at night after the shows. Elvis also relieved the tedium by trying to stump the band. In response, Guercio "ordered oversize stands and separated the charts with cardboard tabs for quick access."[89] Unfortunately, Elvis also staved off his boredom with pills and food, and he died prematurely in 1977.

By 1969 the Las Vegas Musicians Union membership exceeded 1,400.[90] In spite of the gradual exodus of mob owners and the arrival of corporate ones, most musicians did not see the clouds gathering on the horizon. There was more than enough work to go around, and with Elvis in town Las Vegas entertainment was once again in the national spotlight. The heyday of hipness was already over, though, and the changes made by corporate owners in the 1970s and 1980s would turn Las Vegas entertainment into the frequent punchline of a joke: "Vegas is where entertainers go to die." The heyday was over.

NOTES

1. Roman, *Chronicles of Old Las Vegas*, 143.

2. Gragg, *Bright Light City*, 149.

3. Hopkins and Evans, *The First* 100, 221.

4. Ken Hansen, "Ocean's 11 Cast's Sands Perfect Success," *Las Vegas Review-Journal*, February 6, 1960.

5. Hopkins and Evans, *The First* 100, 222.

6. Forrest Duke, "Salute to Sinatra," *Las Vegas Review-Journal*, January 19, 1960.

7. Les Devor, "Vegas Vagaries," *Las Vegas Review-Journal*, January 21, 1960.

8. Gragg, *Bright Light City*, 149.

9. Advertisement, *Las Vegas Review-Journal*, January 19, 1960.

10. Devor, "Vegas Vagaries" January 21, 1960.

11. "Dean Martin, Maybe Frank Maybe Sammy," (1963?) 0027 0051, Sands marquee, Sands Hotel Collection, Special Collections, UNLV Libraries, University of Nevada, Las Vegas.

12. "A Byte Out of History: The Kidnapping of Frank Sinatra, Jr.," http://www.fbi.gov/news/stories/2013/december/the-kidnapping-of-frank-sinatra-jr/the-kidnapping-of-frank-sinatra-jr.

13. James Bacon, "Unexpected Hotel Appearance: Frank Surprises Vegas," *Las Vegas Review-Journal*, December 16, 1963.

14. Weatherford, *Cult Vegas*, 13.

15. Gragg, *Bright Light City*, 153.

16. Weatherford, *Cult Vegas*, 15.

17. Bill Willard interview by Mark Tan, MS 089 Mark Tan, Box 1, Folder 84, 1976, Special Collections, Nevada State Museum, Las Vegas. (All interviews cited in the notes can be found at Special Collections, Nevada State Museum, Las Vegas, unless otherwise indicated.)

18. Index to *Las Vegas Review-Journal*, Special Collections, Nevada State Museum, Las Vegas. (All indexes can be found at Special Collections, Nevada State Museum, Las Vegas, unless otherwise indicated.)

19. "The Fabulous Flamingo Hotel History from the 1960s–1980s," http://classiclasvegas.squarespace.com/a-brief-history-of-the-strip/?currentPage=8.

20. Index to *Las Vegas Review-Journal*.

21. Box 20, Folder 11, Dunes Hotel Collection, MS 93-08/2010-14.

22. Box 5, Folder 2, Dunes Hotel Collection, MS 93-08/2010-14; Las Vegas Show Programs Collection, MS 93-28.

23. Solomon, "Jack Cortez' Fabulous Las Vegas Magazine."

24. Las Vegas Show Programs Collection, MS 93-28.

25. Index to *Las Vegas Review-Journal*.

26. "'Gotta Get to Vegas!' Opens at Dunes Tonight," *Las Vegas Review-Journal*, October 19, 1962 (both quotes).

27. Index to *Las Vegas Review-Journal*.

28. "The Tropicana Hotel History: Miami Comes to the Las Vegas Strip," http://classiclasvegas.squarespace.com/a-brief-history-of-the-strip/2008/3/23/the-tropicana-hotel-history-miami-comes-to-the-las-vegas-str.html.

29. "The Tropicana Hotel History: The Tiffany of the Strip," http://classiclasvegas.squarespace.com/a-brief-history-of-the-strip/?currentPage=29.

30. Index to *Las Vegas Review-Journal*.

31. Mike Weatherford, "Bandleader Johnny Haig Dies of Cancer," *Las Vegas Review Journal*, August 8, 2007.

32. "Cook's Crew: Vegas Band Captures U.S. Crown," *Las Vegas Review-Journal*, November 23, 1960.

33. "The Fabulous Flamingo Hotel History from the 1960s–1980s," http://classiclasvegas.squarespace.com/a-brief-history-of-the-strip/2007/11/24/the-fabulous-flamingo-hotel-history-from-the-1960s-1980s.html.

34. Musicians' Wives Collection, MS 2004–13, Box 1, Notebook 3, Special Collections, UNLV Libraries, University of Nevada, Las Vegas.

35. Musicians' Wives Collection, MS 2004–13, Box 1, Notebook 2.

36. Between Shows Newsletter, June 1969, Musicians' Wives Collection, MS 2004-13m Box 1, Notebook 1.

37. Musicians' Wives Collection, MS 2004–13, Box 1, Notebook 1.

38. Musicians' Wives Collection, MS 2004–13, Box 1, Notebook 2.

39. Musicians' Wives Collection, MS 2004–13, Box 1, Notebook 3.

40. Moehring and Green, *Las Vegas*, 197.

41. Rothman, *The Making of Modern Nevada*, 119.

42. "Bill Reddie's Original Work to Highlight Sunday Program," *Las Vegas Review-Journal*, January 17, 1960.

43. "Symphony Concert Will Benefit NSU [Nevada Southern University]," *Las Vegas Review-Journal*, January 17, 1960.

44. Les Devor, "Vegas Vagaries," *Las Vegas Review-Journal*, January 21, 1960.

45. Forrest Duke, "Dunes Benefit Show for Injured Performer," *Las Vegas Review-Journal*, July 10, 1968.

46. "First Jazz Concert on Set on Saturday," *Las Vegas Review-Journal*, May 10, 1961.

47. "Jazz and Jim Crow," Editorial, *Las Vegas Review-Journal*, May 21, 1962.

48. Florena Lee Jones, "Bravos Still Echo," *Las Vegas Review-Journal*, March 16, 1969.

49. David Reeves, "Musicians on the Brink," *Las Vegas Sun*, June 16, 1989.

50. Weatherford, *Cult Vegas*, 46 ("In those days," "We always had fun").

51. Colin MacKinlay, "Divorce Decreed Here: Louie, Keeley Split," *Las Vegas Review-Journal*, October 4, 1961.

52. Murray Hertz, "Lounges Boast Biggest Names in Business," *Las Vegas Review-Journal*, July 5, 1963.

53. "Las Vegas," April 9, 1964, 6, Box 1, Folder 4, Wingy Manone Collection, MS 2001-28, Special Collections, UNLV Libraries, University of Nevada, Las Vegas.

54. Murray Hertz, "Minimums in Lounges Next for Las Vegas???," *Las Vegas Review-Journal*, November 5, 1963 (all quotes).

55. Berman, *Lady Las Vegas*, 191.

56. Paul Joncich, "The Life and Times of a Casino Boss' Wife," http://klas.dsys1.worldnow.com/story/24664463/the-life-and-times-of-a-casino-bosses

57. Ed Koch and Mary Manning, "Mob Ties," *Las Vegas Sun*, May 15, 2008, http://www.lasvegassun.com/news/2008/may/15/mob-ties/.

58. Weatherford, *Cult Vegas*, 47.

59. Deirdre Coakley with Hank Greenspun, Gary C. Gerard, and the staff of the *Las Vegas Sun*. *The Day the MGM Grand Hotel Burned*. (Seacaucus, NJ: Lyle Stuart, 1982), 30.

60. Las Vegas Caesars Palace—Opening Week," http://classiclasvegas.squarespace.com/a-brief-history-of-the-strip/2008/7/20/las-vegas-caesars-palace-opening-week.html.

61. "Las Vegas Caesars Palace—Opening Week," http://classiclasvegas.squarespace.com/a-brief-history-of-the-strip/2008/7/20/las-vegas-caesars-palace-opening-week.html.

62. Caesars Palace program "Sweet Charity with Juliet Prowse," 1967, Las Vegas Show Programs Collection, MS 93-28.

63. Press release from Ron Amos, Public Relations for Caesars Palace, Box 9, Folder 7, Bill Willard Collection, MS 2001-17.

64. Forrest Duke, "Martin, Sinatra, Bishop in Ring-a-Ding Gasser," *Las Vegas Review-Journal*, April 15, 1966.

65. Ainlay and Gabaldon, *Las Vegas*, 125.

66. "Hughes Takes DI Reins," *Las Vegas Review-Journal*, April 1, 1967 (all quotes).

67. Letter to Bill Willard from Abel Green, December 5, 1967, Bill Willard Collection, MS 2001-17.

68. Don Digilio, "Sinatra Loses Teeth in Strip Hotel Brawl," *Las Vegas Review-Journal*, September 12, 1967.

69. Ibid. (all quotes).

70. Don Digilio, "Angry Sinatra Quits at Sands," *Las Vegas Review-Journal*, September 11, 1967 ("I built this hotel," "The casino just").

71. Corey Levitan, "Top Ten Scandals," *Las Vegas Review-Journal*, March 2, 2008 ("The places he [Hughes] bought").

72. Rothman, *The Making of Modern Nevada*, 128 ("In a strange way,"), 134 ("food and cold"), 135 ("The onset of the corporate").

73. Greg Niemann, *Las Vegas Legends: What Happened in Vegas* (San Diego, CA: Sunbelt Publications, Inc., 2011), 109 ("Now I have," cancellation of Hughes Open).

74. Ainlay and Gabaldon, *Las Vegas*, 127.

75. "Frontier Hotel History," http://classiclasvegas.squarespace.com/display/ShowJournal?moduleId=1093544&currentPage=5.

76. Las Vegas Show Programs Collection, MS 93-28.

77. Letter from Helen Grant to Bill Willard, March 1, 1963, Bill Willard collection, MS 2001-17.

78. Letter from Everett McGowan to Bill Willard, 1967, Bill Willard Collection, MS 2001-17.

79. *Las Vegas Review-Journal*, August 18, 1967 (photograph).

80. Don Digilio, "The Aladdin Comes to the Front," *Las Vegas Review-Journal*, August 17, 1967.

81. William Spaniel, "Bosoms Bug Musicians," *Las Vegas Review-Journal*, August 20, 1967.

82. Hopkins and Evans, *The First 100*, 299.

83. Berman, *Lady Las Vegas*, 110 ("They were standing"), 130 ("It will never").

84. Ibid., 108.

85. Weatherford, *Cult Vegas*, 119.

86. Hopkins and Evans, *The First 100*, 301.

87. Ibid., 301.

88. Roman, *Chronicles of Old Las Vegas*, 180.

89. Weatherford, *Cult Vegas*, 133.

90. Musicians' Wives Collection, MS 2004–13, Box 1, Notebook 2.

·································

CHAPTER FOUR

1970–1980:
Gone with the Bosses of Old

Howard Hughes saved Vegas and then he destroyed it.[1]
BILL MILLER, Entertainment Director

There's a price tag to growth too, and
with growth comes more control.[2]
ROBERT MAHEU, Howard Hughes Executive

Y THE END OF THE 1960s, and in spite of the continued presence of the Rat Pack and the wild success of Elvis, Las Vegas
was no longer at the forefront of the entertainment business.
Las Vegas lost its cachet for a number of reasons. For one, the music industry itself had undergone a major shift away from big bands and crooners
toward rock-and-roll bands. Though this shift started in the 1950s and 1960s
in the rest of the country, the hotel entertainment directors did not really
notice because their audiences were older; it was the younger generation
that favored the rock bands like the Beatles and the Rolling Stones. By the
1970s it was clear that the old-style singers were for an old-style crowd, and
that the young adults who had come of age during the beginnings of the
rock-and-roll era were not interested in their parents' music. Yet the Las
Vegas hotels did not change their style, preferring to cater to the older,
more-reliable crowd. "Vegas is not geared towards young audiences," noted
Mark Tan, writer for *The Hollywood Reporter* and author of the *Vegas Visitor*
columns on entertainment.[3]

Tan interviewed longtime Las Vegas writer Bill Willard in 1976. Willard
thought that the younger audiences were running away from most Strip

entertainment as fast as possible: "I don't think Vegas is still as important for performers as it was back in its real heyday, when Vegas really meant you had arrived, because we have a schism, a split in the performing arts when that devil rock and roll came in. . . . Vegas is regarded by some large segments of the music world as probably the lowest of all places to play, they can't find enough vile adjectives. . . . They're [the entertainment directors] employing the geriatrics to play to geriatrics. They don't want to give up the older people because they come back."[4]

The Woodstock generation of "sex, drugs, and rock-and-roll" placed a premium on youth and freedom and were not interested their parents' music; Frank Sinatra and others like him had little appeal for them. "The audiences have changed," said Tony Bennett. Now, the corporate owners had to look for other ways to draw tourists to their hotels. Bennett continued, "In the very beginning, it was definitely the whole night club set that made this town . . . now, it's just very organized. Big conventions that come in, golf tournaments, giant excuses to be here."[5]

Another factor that contributed to the downslide of Las Vegas entertainment in popular culture was the proliferation of television. Willard remarked, "Audiences that come here now are not impressed because they can get anything they want on T.V. They don't have enthusiasm for live entertainment, it's a whole different thing. . . . I see the whole thing as being almost unpredictable, what the audiences are going to pay their money for and be satisfied. Things are so ephemeral now. A T.V. star is made and broken in one season."[6] Mark Tan agreed: "Now, they're [the audiences] T.V. watchers and a lot of them don't even know who they're seeing part of the time. . . . It's part of a package or tour."[7]

One of the biggest changes in Las Vegas entertainment in the 1970s was the gradual disappearance of the all-night lounges. As Howard Hughes and the other corporate entities began to take over the ownership of Las Vegas Strip hotels, they were able to invest much more money than the mob owners had been able to do. At the same time, though, they were determined to control all costs and to make every part of their hotels profitable because they had stockholders to answer to. With six hotels under Hughes management in a short amount of time, Tan believed that the hotels began to become much more similar to each other, and to be almost indistinguishable. And managers were making spending cuts in every area, including entertainment. In 1976 Mark Tan remarked, "In a matter of a year it seems everything was cut to the bone. Restaurants closed, lounges closed, and all of a sudden restaurants became like bus stations up and down the Strip." And, as the lounges closed, Las Vegas continued to lose its former glamour. Hollywood stars were no longer visiting Las Vegas in large numbers. When asked why, the stars told Tan, "There's nothing to come out for. . . . There are no lounges anymore."[8] Many people really missed the lounges. Once the lounges disappeared, the all-night gatherings with visiting Hollywood stars and the Strip entertainers also went away. "In those days everybody hung out together after the second show, they would get together in the lounges or coffee shops, but you don't find that much going on any more," said Tony Bennett. "It was different than it is now [in 1976]. Everybody sticks in their own hotel, whereas even 10 years ago, everybody was running to see everybody else, and dropping in to see the other shows and they would get together at 3 o'clock in the morning in the coffee shops."[9] Liberace recalled, "There was a time when the lounge shows were almost as important as the main room attractions. Many great stars were born in the lounges—people like Shecky Greene and Sarah Vaughan. It was so much fun then to be able to do your shows and then go out and see these performers in the lounges."[10]

Mark Tan, who arrived in Las Vegas during the 1960s, said,

> When I got here the lounges were booming. . . . Every hotel in town had something going almost 24 hours a day. In '68 and '69, the lounges started disappearing. Once Caesars closed 'Nero's Nook' . . . all the other hotels followed suit. . . . There used to be a show here called 'Vive les Girls,' you could go there any night of the week at 2:30 in the morning and see everybody in town. . . . Every star in town went to see that show. Or you could go see Don Rickles at the Sahara, or Shecky Greene at the Riviera, Totie Fields in the lounges, Johnny Ray, Della Reese. . . . It was more fun. There was more to do from midnight to 6 in the morning than any other time of the day.[11]

Bill Willard was unhappy with the new direction of Las Vegas. He recalled that the lounges and showrooms were originally loss leaders and were not expected to make a profit. "The casino had to do it and did," he said. "This is where the whole thing is turned around now. When you have every little nook and cranny of your hotel trying to make the money and make a profit, then you come into a totally different concept for Las Vegas."[12] Forrest Duke, another Las Vegas writer for *Variety* magazine, also expressed concern: "When some genius at the Sahara with a slide rule decided that every square inch of the building had to make a profit and decided to put in a Keno Lounge, they literally tore the thing [the lounge] out. I went there to the last show and people were in tears. As soon as the curtain went down they started banging back there and working with jackhammers."[13]

While the showrooms focused on big-name stars and large production shows, the lounges had been more experimental. Tony Bennett, speaking of the old owners, noted, "They'd put anybody in. I think they had more flexibility, the pressure was less."[14] The loss of this important performance venue meant that entertainment directors were less willing and/or able to take a chance on untried performers, even when the old-style performers began to seem stale to the younger audiences. "There's no place left where a Don Rickles could be discovered in Florida and brought into Vegas," said Bill Willard. "Those guys can't leave Florida and can't leave New York because nobody wants them. You'd think the three or four entertainment directors that are left and the hotel executives would take their heads out of the sand, get out there and beat the bushes and see where the talent is." Willard agreed that without the lounges, the hotels were simply afraid to try new acts: "It's the bottom line. They will go for what will be tried and true productions. . . . I agree with the statement that what Vegas needs is more showmen and less accountants and more people with greater vision who are not so entrenched in the old 'This has done it and always will do it.'"[15]

In a column for *The Hollywood Reporter*, Mark Tan remarked on the lack of visionary entertainment directors. "The hotels, like the movie studios of yesteryear, are no longer into discovering, grooming, presenting, and guiding new stars. Those necessary tasks fall to the managers, if existent, the agents, if interested, and the individual entertainment directors, if aware."[16] Even some of the entertainment directors themselves were disturbed by the lack of professional guidance for untried talent. Stan Irwin, the Sahara Hotel's director of entertainment, promotion and publicity, advertising, and public relations, noted, "There are many acts that are going out now that are just being booked, and someone should have the knowledge of how to produce them because there are a lot of good performers who, unfortunately, have been ill produced and thrown on the stage."[17]

So, why did the new Las Vegas hotel management close the lounges? Mark Tan said that it was primarily a financial decision. He remarked, "The official reason from what the hotel people have said is because of the high cost of their performers and the shows in there and they weren't making any money. Up until the late 60s making money in the lounges was not important. . . . It was a place to go and hang out. . . . Most of the lounges didn't even have a minimum. You could just go in and have whatever you wanted and stay as long as you wanted and there was a lot of in and out traffic."[18]

Norman Kaye, member of the popular Mary Kaye Trio, knew that the Las Vegas lounges were instrumental to his group's success. Still, he could see the management's side. He said, "I think economics is the reason for the demise of the lounges. So much per square foot, the return of the entertainer, if he's tremendous like Shecky Greene in a lounge, the money they're paying him still does not mediate the return of the people buying those drinks. It's strictly a mathematical problem."[19]

Reporter Phil Solomon saw the writing on the wall in 1971, and predicted that rising costs would drive some entertainment out of business. He wrote, "Show business is gradually losing ground. It is depressing. Fewer stars are being developed and the overall product is not the same as it was a few years ago. . . . Large production shows are a thing of the past due to the high cost. . . . The only spectaculars that seem to draw are the French nudie shows but how long will they continue if costs keep rising?"[20]

The growth of Las Vegas was another major factor in the changes most were noticing: everything was bigger. Corporations were able to build larger hotels and to add to the hotels that they bought. The population of Las Vegas grew as more people came to work in the hotels and others came to provide services for the hotel employees. And as everything grew, it was inevitable that the small-town feeling of the past could not last. "It's gotten bigger, more people," said Mark Tan. "The main change is that it's lost that personal touch. Before when you went into a hotel, you knew the dealers, the maître d's, the waitresses."[21] Las Vegas was becoming more impersonal. Stan Irwin added, "The feeling, at that time [before the corporations], was that whatever was good for Las Vegas was good for all the hotels. Whatever was good for one hotel was good for all the hotels, and whatever was good for the hotel was good for Las Vegas. This meant we had a spirit regarding our city, we weren't stockholders who never lived there, so we cared about Las Vegas."[22]

Growth begat more growth in order to keep the new investors happy. In a 1976 article in *Variety* magazine, Bill Willard wrote, "It took a lot of bodies, hearts, heads, minds, and sweat but Vegas resorts now pay off in very high rates of return on invested capital. This has consistently surpassed returns in many other industries and businesses as casinos' compounded growth rate has been over 10% per year for the past 10 years. All that expansion, that 'grow or die' concept, must have new financial shots or the gambling biz will get the chills on investment and net profits."[23]

The new managers used extensive data analysis, customer surveys, and various other tools to pinpoint every possible way to make a profit, making deeper and deeper cuts in their budgets while expanding their investments and passing those costs along to the tourists. Willard compared the new management to the old bosses: "Back in the old days you couldn't, or wouldn't dare clutter up the boss' mind with such trivia. He unerringly knew exactly where the bottom line was and where the line formed. . . . In those days, the price was right and $50 could guarantee fun in the showrooms for two, with something to spare for the slots. . . . Where's the Vegas bargain you've been hearing about for all those years? Gone with the bosses of old."[24]

The disappointment and disillusionment with the new direction of Las Vegas was palpable. Joe Delaney, critic and columnist for the *Las Vegas Sun* stated, "We've grown faster than the capacity of our executives, the elected and appointed officials in the government and the hotel executives, to keep up with. Our nature was casino owned/controlled until the coming of Hughes and corporations in the 60s. Suddenly, the direction shifted from casino to corporation/hotel. . . . I think it has been to our detriment, long range. . . . I really am not a doom-sayer but I have great misgivings. Our type of entity, the casino/entertainment/resort complex is built on personalities. . . . A situation was created that dehumanized and made this a cold place. We became another place and we had been a very special place."[25]

To illustrate, Delaney told of a 1940s casino boss who sent an intoxi-
cated gambler to sleep on the couch of a hotel employee rather than have
him continue to lose his money while drinking. The gambler later told Delaney, "The pit boss felt that he was probably going to get my money anyway
but he'd rather not take it when I wasn't in proper condition. He wanted
me to be full strength to defend my money." Delaney explained, "That was
the kind of thing that went on in our town then, but it no longer does. We
have become very cold. . . . The efficiency expert and the computer operator caused the greatest problem here because now it's 'Get them in, clean
them out, and send them out.' We have such a constant fresh supply of
tourists, conventioneers, etc. . . . we forget that what built the business and
made it so attractive in the first place was repeaters."[26]

Forrest Duke, who wrote for the *Las Vegas Sun* and the *Las Vegas
Review-Journal* in addition to *Variety* magazine, said, "It's [Las Vegas] become downright unfriendly. . . . These people should know that their livelihood depends on the people coming back. . . . In those early days people
were friendlier because it was a small town atmosphere and because they
knew that they needed those people to come back."[27]

With all hotel and casino costs now so closely scrutinized, it was not
long before the special comps and perks for the stars stopped. The mob owners had been very generous with the entertainers. Tony Bennett remarked,
"Everybody was comped in those days."[28] Norman Kaye recalled how much
he enjoyed working for the mob owners. "It was a tremendous amount of
fun, it was really, I wouldn't say a wild town per se, but it was really a great
town to be in. The bosses did anything they wanted to, they did it the way
they wanted to, they could afford to be what they wanted to. They took care
of the performers well because the performers did draw."[29]

The corporate owners stopped the fringe benefits for the stars. The gravy
train was over. More importantly, the headliners were no longer handled
with as much respect or care. Most of the stars would have continued to
visit the other hotels after their own shows if they had been treated better.
"I know from talking to performers themselves that they are not treated as
well when they go visit other hotels," said Mark Tan. "There was a time if you
were working at hotel A, you could go to any hotel in town and see a friend
who was working or go into the restaurant and you were automatically a

guest of the hotel and that doesn't happen anymore. The performers themselves are treated just like another customer."[30]

Joe Delaney put the blame on Howard Hughes for the new impersonal
relations, but he also noted that there was one hotel owner who knew how
to make the stars feel special: William Harrah. Harrah was an important
figure in northern Nevada and was responsible for a number of casino innovations that were adopted in Las Vegas and elsewhere. He opened his first
full casino in 1946 in Reno and built a second property at Lake Tahoe in
1959. According to writer Steve Friess, Harrah "installed the first casino car-
peting, hired the first female dealers and offered the first gaming lessons to
customers." He also invented the Keno runner position and was the first to
use an "eye in the sky," at that time simply a place above the casino where
the security could view the action through a one-way glass.[31] Joe Delaney
thought that Bill Harrah was able to get performers to come to Reno and
Lake Tahoe, even while offering less money, because he liked and respected
the stars: "There used to be a personal relationship with the people who ran
the hotels and the performers. The only one who treats them like that now
is Harrah and performers will work for less money at Harrah's than they
will work in Vegas because of that star treatment everyone gets whether it's
an opening or a closing act." Delaney sarcastically advised, "My suggestion is for the corporations to find some human beings to put in as liaisons
with the entertainment to create a more harmonious, more family-like relationship. They would be wise to go up and analyze the Harrah situation.
He certainly has maintained it with all the changes, they went public and
there has been no change in the relationship between him and the performers. . . . The bread cast upon the waters always returns a thousand fold."[32]
Ironically, the powerful and influential William Harrah was also the person
who ultimately was convinced to support the Corporate Gaming Act, which
changed the way most Las Vegas hotel owners operated.[33]

Some stars were no longer interested in performing on the Strip. In an
article for *The Hollywood Reporter*, Mark Tan wrote, "A little temper, a little
temperament, and a lot of loss of communication is the irritant between a
couple of very top name Strip stars and their current Strip hotel headquarters. Rumor is that several 'biggies' are balking at Strip dates until the hotel

can be taught to treat them better than acts dropping in for a couple of nights 'casual.'"[34]

It was not only the stars that suffered a comedown. Entertainment writers and reporters were now expected to pay their own way when reviewing shows. And, they were also treated impersonally. Joe Delaney remarked on the changes after the corporate owners began taking over: "For one thing, back in those early days, newsmen had like a carte blanche, they [the mob owners] were very friendly to us. I couldn't pick up a tab, buy a drink, and now it's just the other way around. In the Hughes Hotel, I have to pay my way if I'll be reviewing a show. [His company, *Variety*, actually paid.] It was probably an ego thing but in those days you walked in and it was 'Hey, how are you?' All the fellas in the pit knew you and now I know very few of them and I'm sure they don't know me. It's just very impersonal."[35]

Even the hotel guests were being treated differently. Joe Delaney told of a new phenomenon: overbooking in the hotels. By overbooking the hotel owners hoped to maximize their capacities, ensuring that as many rooms as possible were occupied; they were gambling on the chance that some people would not show up. If everyone who reserved rooms did appear, the later arrivals were sent to a different hotel, often a motel, a practice that created a great deal of ill will. "The hotels are overbooking and walking them down the street to a motel," said Joe Delaney. "When someone who comes here and thinks they're staying at a hotel and find that they're staying at 'Motel Z,' that's a turn off. They're never happy after that. We want to get every last dime, not last dollar but dime. The old attitude was never that."[36]

Bill Willard also thought that the corporate managers were creating ill will by letting the quality of their entertainment deteriorate, and he named the Hughes organization's entertainment director Walter Kane as part of the problem. "I notice on some nights [Kane] may come in and look at what's going on but he doesn't have that producer's touch. In many cases, he's seeing it [the show] for the first time himself. He wasn't there early for rehearsal making sure they didn't go overtime. The control has to be put back into the hands of the people who should have it." Willard predicted, "I think . . . they're going to have to get used to rotten shows and a bad bargain in Las Vegas . . . but it's the only game in town."[37]

Writing five years earlier in 1971, Mark Tan had been more hopeful and tried to put a positive spin on all the changes taking place. "All that talk about Vegas' 'corporate coldness' certainly doesn't apply to Hughes Hotels entertainment overseer Walter Kane, the most affable and accessible talent buyer in town. Walter makes it his business to meet and greet every performer in every Hughes hotel and attends every mainroom and lounge opening to congratulate and encourage talent. Kane's contagious congeniality has made a big difference in charming stars into the Hughes line-up!"[38]

As time went by, Tan became much less positive about the corporate management when he saw how things were really going to go. Many of the Mark Tan interviews included in this chapter come from what appears to be material Tan gathered for a book that he never finished. Tan conducted at least ninety interviews in 1976 and 1977 with entertainers, writers, showgirls, and other Las Vegas workers, and asked each person how he or she thought Las Vegas had changed. Their responses were consistent and overwhelmingly negative. "Vegas was a lot different in those days [before the corporations], it wasn't commercial," said Suzanne Vegas, an entertainment writer and featured exotic singer/dancer/actress in a typical interview with Tan. "I remember the great big free buffets, free food, free drinks, they had all these things for the gamblers. The corporations weren't much in power at the time and a lot more consideration was given to the customer."[39] She noted the same changes that everyone else did: not as many big-name lounge attractions and not as many all-night gatherings.

Bill Willard was also gathering material for a book that was meant to be a collaborative project with German artist Thomas Gribbohm. Though that project fell through, to Willard's intense annoyance, he kept the interviews that he conducted from about 1975 well into the 1980s for another book that he planned to call *Alas Vegas*. The notes for the introduction were mainly sad and reflective; he pined for what had been lost. His interview subjects also gave dark predictions for the future of Las Vegas. One example was comedian and musician Pete Barbutti. When asked what he would do if he had a hotel, he replied, "I would very seriously have the casino have more of a say in the operation of the hotel which they had in the old days. Because if the casino says to you 'we had a great night last night' . . . it really should not matter that the coffee shop or gift shop lost money, or the showroom.

I don't think you need a 12 year old kid that just got here out of CalPoly with a computer to say we can get them here, we can get them there, because you can't."[40]

By the time Mark Tan was doing his interviews, there was already nostalgia for the old days and the mob owners. It is still a Las Vegas cliché to say, "Things were better when the mob ran the town." That saying was in response first to the changes that Howard Hughes was making, and then later to the corporate owners who followed him. The earlier days, particularly the 1950s and 1960s, were held up as the model, when people had the most fun in town. Tracy Heberling, a showgirl at the Stardust Hotel, remarked, "The 60s, it was a wonderful time to be here, the early 60s. It was fun. It was still an adventure, and it was a great place to be. And looking back on it, we all feel that we did have the best of it, definitely the best of it working in the shows. It was really something to be a 'Lido Girl' in those days."[41]

Heberling was a performer in the first "Lido de Paris" show that was imported from Europe, and the European dancers really did not know what to expect from the mob owners. "We don't have gangsters in England," she said. "So really none of us had a thought about a town run by gangsters. It was an American thing. . . . It was what you saw in the movies." Heberling and her colleagues were not bothered by the mob owners or their associates. She continued, "Everybody was very nice to us. . . . You could leave your door unlocked, your car unlocked. Everybody felt safe. You could walk the streets safely."[42]

Joe Delaney was another of the many people who said they felt no fear dealing with the mob management. His sentiments were like those expressed by many of the hotel musicians, stars, and other show people: "I have never been in close communion with the so called syndicate operators, though working in the entertainment business I knew that they were behind some of the people I had to deal with: night club operators, record distributors, etc. I would say that—by and large—that if you were not associated with them in their endeavor, the relationship was a straight legitimate business relationship. If one of the people involved in that area gave their word it was solid as the Rock of Gibraltar."[43] Heberling said, "You know, for all the talk of gangsters and mobsters and everything like that, it was a time of innocence."[44]

It is possible to argue that the loss of innocence that Heberling described was a very real phenomenon, one that many people attributed to the corporate take-overs. Though the shows from the 1960s had pushed the limits, it seemed that many 1970s productions crossed the line from mild titillation to outright sleaze, presumably in an effort to attract more tourists. As entertainment became more sexualized, Las Vegas began to develop a reputation for tastelessness, a far cry from its previous status as the hip home of the Rat Pack, jazz clubs, and popular lounge entertainment. The advertisements for shows were noticeably lewd. More tourists began to come to Las Vegas for sexual thrills. "William," a male prostitute interviewed by Mark Tan, described the changes that he was witnessing in Las Vegas during the 1970s. "There's a lot more demand for this kind of service," he said. "There are a lot more people who are getting into orgies, 3 ways . . . particularly married people. . . . I think they consider it part of their fling in Las Vegas. . . . There's really a big market for it."[45]

It is, of course, somewhat disingenuous to suggest that mob-run Las Vegas was somehow more pure than corporate-run Las Vegas. There were those people, even some show people, whose dealings with the mob were not "innocent." Kathy Saxe, a former showgirl, remembered a chorine from the Flamingo who was murdered, most likely by her mob boyfriend or because of him. Saxe thought the woman had a so-called "juice job," in which a person was hired based on their connections, not their qualifications.[46] There were a number of juice jobs, many of those for mob friends or girlfriends, and those jobs often came with strings attached.

Johnny Haig, because of his work as a contractor, was one of the few musicians who had direct encounters with the mob managers and front men, and some of these experiences were nerve-wracking. One incident in particular stood out for him: a close encounter with Frank "Lefty" Rosenthal. Mr. Rosenthal, as he liked to be called, was with the Chicago Outfit who took over the Stardust Hotel, as well as some other hotels. After the Nevada Gaming Board denied him a gambling license in 1976, Rosenthal's official title was changed from floor manager to entertainment director, though he secretly continued to run the hotel just as he had before. In order to keep up appearances, Rosenthal came in every day as the hotel orchestra rehearsed and starred in an unintentionally humorous local television talk show where he interviewed various entertainers.

Haig remembered that Rosenthal sat in the audience of the Stardust "Lido" show every night, a show that worked with a "click track." The drummer, piano player, bass player, and conductor all wore headsets in which they heard voices in one ear and the beat (or click) in the other. In this way, the tempo or time of the music was always the same and really could not change. Large production shows often found a click track useful, especially to keep the tempos the same for the dancers.

One night, midway through the production, Haig received a phone call. "Mr. Rosenthal wants to see you downstairs." Haig immediately began to worry and wondered what could be wrong. He knew that a phone call like that could only mean trouble. "It isn't to tell me I have beautiful brown eyes or that I'm doing a wonderful job," he said. One of the hazards of working for the boys meant that meetings of this type could be frightening.

Haig continued, "I came downstairs. Two big guys, with the little choreographer 'Rocky,' flanked Haig. Mr. Rosenthal looked at me and said, 'Are you the band guy? What was wrong with the band? Tempos are confused.' I said, 'I thought that was one of the best shows we ever played.' The two guys look at me like 'What? How dare you?'" Haig tried to explain about the click track, but it was clear that he was not making himself understood. Finally, Rosenthal told Haig, who was leading the relief band, to come hear the regular house band the following week to learn what his relief band was doing wrong.

During the break between shows, Haig borrowed a production tape from a dancer and quickly found the problem: a guitar solo that was written with a "fuzz tone, very evil sounding thing" had been played by the regular band guitarist using a "wa-wa" tone. Haig told his guitar player to make the switch and that seemed to resolve the "tempo" issue. At the next show Haig got a call from one of the assistants, stating, "Mr. Rosenthal said you don't have to come in [to hear the regular band]." Haig was immensely relieved. "Things like that would happen all the time," he remembered.

Howard Hughes had no understanding of how the mob owners conducted business, according to his long-time aide Robert Maheu. Maheu recalled that Hughes nearly lost the Desert Inn deal when one of his lawyers tried to make changes to the agreement after Maheu had shaken hands with Moe Dalitz in front of the owners, the usual way in which the mob owners conducted business with no contracts. A very concerned Maheu offered Hughes his resignation, remarking, "I'm not going to be involved with any-one in Las Vegas or elsewhere who doesn't understand a handshake deal. It's that simple."[47] Once Hughes understood the situation, the deal went forward as planned and Maheu kept his position.

Though he was unnerved by this close call, Maheu respected the mob owners and front men. "I don't care what other people say, I have never met a better group of people than the so called old-timers in Las Vegas," said Maheu. "They give you their word, you can go to bed with it, and they'll stick to it. . . . They care about their families. They care about the com-munity. They've made some great, great contributions to this city."[48] For example, Moe Dalitz got a $1 million loan from Jimmy Hoffa in order to help build Sunrise Hospital, an important medical facility still in Las Vegas. Writer Greg Niemann noted, "Hoffa cut a deal with his union members in Las Vegas, their employers, and Sunrise Hospital where a fund was estab-lished to provide medical services for union members. Dalitz would later secure Teamster funding for numerous civic improvements in Las Vegas."[49]

In spite of his support of the previous hotel owners, Maheu thought that Las Vegas was fortunate that Howard Hughes came along when he did to provide a sorely needed influx of money. Maheu noted, "Things were depressed when Hughes arrived, there's no doubt about it. . . . Apartments had been overbuilt, the commercial facilities had been overbuilt, and it needed a shot in the arm."[50]

He also related the copious press attention to the news that Hughes was buying property in Las Vegas. "People seem to forget the attendant public-ity. It was phenomenal all over the world." Hughes was welcomed with immense relief from the city and state government, and many residents as well. In order for Las Vegas to grow, it had to find sources of financ-ing other than mob money. Hughes would bring respectability along with his money. "But there's a price tag to growth too," said Maheu, "and with growth comes more control."[51] Kathy Saxe embraced the changes: "Growth is good. I think it's up to us natives as individuals not to be swallowed in it."[52]

Interviewed in 1977, longtime Las Vegas choreographer and producer Matt Gregory said he, too, was initially positive when the "so-called legitimate businessmen came to Las Vegas, but they were the most hypocritical bunch of bastards you ever saw in your life. . . . Vegas should be the Disneyland of escapism, not some sleazy little carnival; it should be top drawer in every way. . . . They're [the corporate decision makers] raping and pillaging the concept of Vegas."[53]

Corporate manager Dick Lane, entertainment director at the Hilton Hotel in 1975, denied that the showroom of the hotel had ever been a moneymaker. "I can't find any figures to substantiate that," he said, though this was the very theater known to be profitable when Elvis was in residence. He continued, "I don't know exactly, I've only been here for two years and then I've been able to pick up figures for awhile, but at no time, from what I've seen, was it really a going concern as far as being a valuable asset, a contributor financially to our operations." In other words, no loss leader, however popular, was considered a "valuable asset." Granted, Lane was in a difficult position as an entertainment operator for a corporate hotel. "You have to take in consideration that those to whom you have to go to get the money have to be convinced," Lane said. "Quite naturally, they are not of an artistic nature, most of the fellows. . . . You really have to make a sale on it, which is as it should be. But still, you're talking about a lot of money. You're talking about a long time commitment and if it doesn't work, you've got a problem."[54]

In spite of the numerous budget-cutting operations beginning in the 1970s, most of the Las Vegas hotel musicians did not immediately feel the impact. Aside from the loss of a number of lounges, the nuts and bolts of the entertainment industry remained unchanged by the corporate owners; there were still mob owners in town that operated in the old way. The hotel bands, orchestras, and local groups continued to back the headliners and provide entertainment in the restaurants. The Strip hotel musicians and other backstage workers were still considered among the best in their field, making it a great place for headliners to play. Tony Bennett respected all the local people with whom he worked in Las Vegas:

There isn't any deal that you can't have if you're a performer to make sure the job is done right. The sound, the carpenters, the lights, the orchestras, the whole Strip—there isn't one bad organization on the Strip. They're all great, great fans because they come from all the ex-bands like Woody Herman, Harry James. . . . They came to settle down here because it has the highest scale that musicians are paid in the world. They love settling down here and living in the sun and going in and playing a show, and they're all magnificent musicians.[55]

The changes taking place were not immediately noticeable to the general show-going public either. In 1971 Mark Tan wrote, "It's been just one of those Las Vegas weeks, with 11 openings in four days, and as usual, celebrities joined flocks of visitors to see their favorites, including Elvis at the Hilton, Marty Allen and John Rowles at the Flamingo, Paul Anka and Joey Heatherton at Caesars, and David Frost at the Riviera."[56] In another article that year, Tan noted that well-known headliner Debbie Reynolds had set a new attendance record at the Desert Inn. He wrote, "Debbie Reynolds had the largest opening night crowd in the 21-year history of the Desert Inn. Miss Reynolds is expected to break the Desert Inn four-week attendance mark, which she set last March, when she concludes her engagement Aug. 23."[57] Other entertainers in town that year included Kay Ballard, Phyllis Diller, Mike Douglas, Jimmy Durante, Joan Rivers, Rip Taylor, and the Sun Spots.[58]

In the early 1970s Elvis was already showing signs of weariness with his Las Vegas show, but he remained enormously popular when he came to town. In a review for *The Hollywood Reporter*, Mark Tan wrote,

As performances go, Elvis Presley's at the Las Vegas Hilton is sloppy, hurriedly rehearsed, mundanely lit, poorly amplified, occasionally monotonous, often silly, and haphazardly coordinated. Elvis looked drawn, tired, and noticeably heavier—weight-wise, not musically—than in his last Vegas appearance. He wasn't in his strongest voice, his costume of studded white slacks and vest with black satin high collar and scarf was not his sexiest or most flattering. And do you know what? The packed to over-capacity audience—the first 2000 of the usual 120,000 he'll draw for his month-long engagement—positively couldn't have cared less about any pros, cons, or comparisons. They absolutely loved, honored, and obeyed his every whim with screams, shrieks, whistles and dashes to the stage apron whenever Elvis decided to wander downstage to kiss, touch, or wipe his brow amidst the adoring throng.[59]

In 1972 other headliners included Paul Anka, Jack Benny, Glen Campbell, Mac Davis, Sammy Davis Jr., Don Ho, the Mills Brothers, Liza Minnelli, Patti Page, Joan Rivers, Siegfried and Roy (who at that time were in the "Lido" show), Sonny and Cher, and Steve and Eydie.[60]

An April 1974 entertainment calendar gives a comprehensive view of the performers and orchestras in town at that time. In the Aladdin's Bagdad Theater, the production was "This Is Burlesque '74," while the Sinbad lounge was hosting the Vagabonds, brought in by entertainment director Mitch De Wood. The Caesars Palace Circus Maximus showroom remained devoted to headliners, with Andy Williams, Petula Clark, and Alan King all set to star there, accompanied by the Nat Brandwynne Orchestra. Their small lounge, Cleopatra's Barge, featured Don Cherry and Bruce Wescott, and their entertainment director was Sid Gathrid. For the Desert Inn Crystal Room, entertainment director Walter Kane hired Bobbie Gentry and Debbie Reynolds, but no longer had lounge entertainment. The headliners were backed by the Carlton Hayes Orchestra.

The Dunes Hotel continued with the still-popular "Casino de Paris '74." By now, some version of the show had been running at the hotel since 1964. In 1970 publicity director Lee Fisher presented an analysis of the production's business to date. The show attracted 2,049,014 people between 1964 and 1969, an average of 341,502 audience members each year. While the numbers had fallen off in 1970, Fisher was confident that "Casino de Paris" was still popular enough to continue. He wrote, "Casino de Paris, doing 290,000 a year or, about 5,575 a week—is not too far away from being high on the local hit parade—even in 1970. . . . A shot-in-the-arm of only 3000 more people a week, or 450 a night, would push it back into the big hit class." Fisher recommended that the show continue and thought that it was enough of a tourist draw without adding major star headliners. He wrote, "I don't think there is much chance that the Dunes is about to switch to a big-star, big-name policy . . . and since the main showroom attraction is so vital to the successful operation of a LV resort hotel, the time has come to make a decision as to the direction and policy which will be governing from now on. . . . Experience has taught us in Las Vegas that the hotel that has a 'high demand' show, will fill its rooms, its casino, its public space, etc."[61] In 1974 the orchestra was led by Earl Green, while the Russ Morgan Orchestra provided entertainment for their restaurant, Top of the Strip. Longtime Vegas showman Frederic Apcar was their entertainment director.

In the Flamingo Room of the Flamingo Hotel, various stars were expected: Sandler and Young, Leslie Uggams, Marty Allen, and Gladys Knight and the Pips. In the casino's lounge, audiences could watch the Mills Brothers, the Kim Sisters, and Paul Revere and the Raiders, all brought in by entertainment director Dick Lane and backed by the Earl Lowden Orchestra.

The Frontier Hotel, now a Howard Hughes property, featured Milton Berle, Robert Goulet, Wayne Newton, and Roy Clark in the Frontier Music Hall, while the Winner's Circle Lounge hosted Johnny Vanelli and Frank Ricci. In addition to working at the Desert Inn, Hughes employee Walter Kane also served as entertainment director for the Frontier, as well as for several other hotels. The Al Alvarez Orchestra accompanied the headliners.

The Hacienda Azure Room presented "Spice on Ice," yet another risqué ice show, and offered no other entertainment options. The Hilton/ International showroom hosted Tony Bennett, Glen Campbell, and Johnny Cash, while the lounge featured the Kim Sisters and Louis Prima, with entertainment director Dick Lane in charge and Joe Guercio still conducting his orchestra there. MGM's entertainment director, Bernie Rothkopf, brought Shecky Greene and the Jackson Five to the main showroom and Lou Rawls and Jackie Gayle to the Lion's Den lounge. The Tommy Moses Orchestra provided the support.

In the Riviera's Versailles Theater, the headliners were Don Rickles, Engelbert Humperdinck, Joel Grey, and the Supremes, most of them accompanied by the Jack Cathcart Orchestra or the Dick Palombi Orchestra. Entertainment director Harvey Silbert had no other venue to fill at the Riviera.

Featured entertainers in the Sahara Congo Showroom were Buddy Hackett, Johnny Mathis, Jim Nabors, and Rowan and Martin, all supported by the Jack Eglash Orchestra, while the lounge, the Casbar Theatre, offered a variety of different bands booked by entertainment director Arvid Nelson. The Sands entertainment director, once again Walter Kane, hired Wayne

Newton and Bob Newhart for the Copa Room, the former playground of the Rat Pack. In the Regency Lounge, the performers were Bob Curtola and Sonny King.

The Stardust continued with its successful production show "Lido de Paris" in the Café Continental main room, while the Starlight Lounge hosted "Barc Touch of Venus," Rip Taylor, and an Irish showband. At the time of these lounge shows, the entertainment director was listed as Moe Lewis; this job would become Frank Rosenthal's soon afterward.

The Thunderbird Continental Theatre featured Cyd Charisse, Tony Martin, and Keely Smith, while the lounge presented Dave Burton and Dianne Eddington for an indefinite run. The entertainment director here was Sid Gathrid, who also served in that capacity for Caesars Palace, and the house orchestra was conducted by Joe Mazzu. The Thunderbird owners were beginning to experiment with their star room entertainment. In 1976 Mark Tan noted, "The Thunderbird's on again, off again star policy is on again with the first showroom offering . . . starring Rodney Dangerfield and Dick Roman."[62] The Tropicana Superstar Theater was listed as dark, while the restaurant continued with "Folies Bergere," with Alan Lee as the entertainment director.

One can glean from this listing that by 1974 the lounges had been removed from the Desert Inn, the Dunes, the Hacienda, and the Riviera Hotels. Caesars Palace closed its very popular lounge Nero's Nook, only to replace it later with the smaller Cleopatra's Barge. Mark Tan was already writing about these changes back in 1971: "As tipped here months ago, the Dunes Hotel will shutter its Persian room lounge this month to make way for still another Keno parlor. Apparently neither the Riviera nor the Dunes is willing to learn from the mistake made by Caesars Palace when it closed its enormously successful Nero's Nook to make a Chinese bingo room. Contrary to hotel thinking, Keno is no more popular now than it was when players marked cards and played from anywhere and everywhere in the hotel. The Keno parlors now in existence — seating from 20–200 players — are rarely if ever more than one-fourth occupied."[63]

The loss of the lounges cost some musicians their jobs and made the competition for main room work more intense. Though most did not realize it, this was only a harbinger of things to come.

NOTES

1. Interview with Harry Merenda, KNPR *Vegas I Remember* transcripts, Box 1, Folder 19, MS 063.

2. Interview with Bob Maheu, KNPR *Vegas I Remember* transcripts, Box 1, Folder 18, MS 063.

3. Interview with Mark Tan by "J. R.," 1976, Box 1, Folder 74, Mark Tan Collection, MS 089. The Mark Tan interview was part of a series of over 100 interviews that were later published as Mark Tan's *All-Star Turn-About Quiz Book* (Los Angeles: Price/Stern/Sloan, 1977).

4. Interview with Bill Willard by Mark Tan, 1976, Box 1, Folder 84, Mark Tan Collection, MS 089.

5. Interview with Tony Bennett by Mark Tan, May 22, 1976, Box 1, Folder 6, Mark Tan Collection, MS 089.

6. Interview with Bill Willard by Mark Tan, 1976, Box 1, Folder 84, Mark Tan Collection, MS 089.

7. Interview with Mark Tan by "J. R.," 1976, Box 1, Folder 74, Mark Tan Collection, MS 089.

8. Ibid. ("In a matter of," "There's nothing").

9. Interview with Tony Bennett by Mark Tan, May 22, 1976, Box 1, Folder 6, Mark Tan Collection, MS 089.

10. Interview with Liberace by Mark Tan, June 18, 1976, Box 1, Folder 45, Mark Tan Collection, MS 089.

11. Interview with Mark Tan by "J. R.," 1976, Box 1, Folder 74, Mark Tan Collection, MS 089.

12. Interview with Bill Willard by Mark Tan, 1976, Box 1, Folder 84, Mark Tan Collection, MS 089.

13. Interview with Forrest Duke by Mark Tan, January 30, 1977, Box 1, Folder 22, Mark Tan Collection, MS 089.

14. Interview with Tony Bennett by Mark Tan, May 22, 1976, Box 1, Folder 6, Mark Tan Collection, MS 089.

15. Interview with Bill Willard by Mark Tan, 1976, Box 1, Folder 84 ("There's no place," "Those guys can't," "It's the bottom").

16. Mark Tan, "Inside Las Vegas," *The Hollywood Reporter*, April 1974, Las Vegas insert, Box 2, Folder 3, Mark Tan Collection, MS 089.

17. Interview with Stan Irwin by Mark Tan, June 1, 1976, Box 1, Folder 36, Mark Tan Collection, MS 089.

18. Interview with Mark Tan by "J. R.," 1976, Box 1, Folder 74, Mark Tan Collection, MS 089.

19. Interview with Norman Kaye by Mark Tan, November 20, 1976, Box 1, Folder 38, Mark Tan Collection, MS 089.

20. Phil Solomon, "Lights of Las Vegas," *Jack Cortez' Fabulous Las Vegas Magazine*, June 15, 1971, Box 5, Folder 6, Dunes Hotel Collection, MS 93-08.

21. Interview with Mark Tan by "J. R.," 1976, Box 1, Folder 74, Mark Tan Collection, MS 089.

22. Interview with Stan Irwin by Mark Tan, June 1, 1976, Box 1, Folder 36, Mark Tan Collection, MS 089.

23. Bill Willard, "Computer Colorless Sub for Old-Time Vegas Boss," *Variety*, October 26, 1976.

24. Ibid.

25. Interview with Joe Delaney by Mark Tan, November 14, 1976, Box 1, Folder 19, Mark Tan Collection, MS 089.

26. Ibid. ("The pit boss," "That was the kind").

27. Interview with Forrest Duke by Mark Tan, January 30, 1977, Box 1, Folder 22, Mark Tan Collection, MS 089.

28. Interview with Tony Bennett by Mark Tan, May 22, 1976, Box 1, Folder 6, Mark Tan Collection, MS 089.

29. Interview with Norman Kaye by Mark Tan, November 20, 1976, Box 1, Folder 38, Mark Tan Collection, MS 089.

30. Interview with Mark Tan by "J. R.," 1976, Box 1, Folder 74, Mark Tan Collection, MS 089.

31. Steve Friess, "The Quiet Storm: Bill Harrah's Impact on Gaming," August 2011, *Desert Companion*, http://knpr.org/desert-companion/quiet-storm-bill-harrahs-impact-gaming.

32. Interview with Joe Delaney by Mark Tan, November 14, 1976, Box 1, Folder 19, Mark Tan Collection, MS 089 ("There used to," "My suggestion is").

33. Friess, "The Quiet Storm."

34. Mark Tan, *The Hollywood Reporter*, February 23, 1976, Box 2, Folder 26, Mark Tan Collection, MS 089.

35. Interview with Joe Delaney by Mark Tan, November 14, 1976, Box 1, Folder 19, Mark Tan Collection, MS 089.

36. Ibid.

37. Interview with Bill Willard by Mark Tan, 1976, Box 1, Folder 84 ("I notice on," "I think").

38. Mark Tan, "Las Vegas Life," *The Hollywood Reporter*, April 12, 1971, Box 2, Folder 1, Mark Tan Collection, MS 089.

39. Interview with Suzanne Vegas by Mark Tan, 1977, Box 1, Folder 79, Mark Tan Collection, MS 089.

40. Interview with Pete Barbutti by Bill Willard, Bill Willard Collection, MS 2001-17.

41. Interview with Tracy Heberling, KNPR *Vegas I Remember* transcripts, Box 1, MS 063.

42. Ibid.

43. Interview with Joe Delaney by Mark Tan, November 14, 1976, Box 1, Folder 19, Mark Tan Collection, MS 089.

44. Interview with Heberling, KNPR *Vegas I Remember* transcripts, Box 1, MS 063.

45. Interview with "William," male prostitute, by Mark Tan, 1977, Box 1, Folder 83, Mark Tan Collection, MS 089.

46. Interview with Kathy Saxe, KNPR *Vegas I Remember* transcripts, Box 1, MS 063.

47. Interview with Bob Maheu, KNPR *Vegas I Remember* transcripts, Box 1, Folder 18, MS 063.

48. Ibid.

49. Niemann, *Las Vegas Legends*, 84.

50. Interview with Bob Maheu, KNPR *Vegas I Remember* transcripts, Box 1, Folder 18, MS 063.

51. Ibid. ("People seem to," "But there's a").

52. Interview with Kathy Saxe, KNPR *Vegas I Remember* transcripts, Box 1, MS 063.

53. Jane Ann Morrison, "From the El Rancho to Atlantic City," *Nevadan*, June 19, 1977.

54. Interview with Dick Lane by Bill Willard, October 31, 1975, Bill Willard Collection, MS 2001-17 (all quotes).

55. Interview with Tony Bennett by Mark Tan, May 22, 1976, Box 1, Folder 6, Mark Tan Collection, MS 089.

56. Mark Tan, "Las Vegas," *The Hollywood Reporter*, August 19, 1971, Box 2, Folder 1, Mark Tan Collection, MS 089.

57. Mark Tan, "Debbie Reynolds Sets Record at Desert Inn," *The Hollywood Reporter*, August 3, 1971, Box 2, Folder 1, Mark Tan Collection, MS 089.

58. Mark Tan, "Las Vegas Life," *The Hollywood Reporter*, August 5, 1971, Box 2, Folder 1, Mark Tan Collection, MS 089.

59. Mark Tan, "Uninspired Elvis Delights in Vegas," *The Hollywood Reporter*, August 12, 1971, Box 2, Folder 2, Mark Tan Collection, MS 089.

60. Box 2, Folder 2, Mark Tan Collection, MS 089.

61. Lee Fisher, "Analysis of Casino de Paris by Lee Fisher of the Dunes Hotel, 1970," Box 5, Folder 5, Dunes Hotel Collection (all quotes).

62. Mark Tan, "Las Vegas Life," *The Hollywood Reporter*, February 6, 1976, Box 2, Folder 26, Mark Tan Collection, MS 089.

63. Ibid.

CHAPTER FIVE

1970–1980:
"Must Be Good"

Just remember, guys—you're only as good as your last solo!
UNKNOWN LAS VEGAS MUSICIAN

You've got to know what key you're in. You don't rehearse, ever.
REBECCA RAMSEY, Musician

There is always somebody better.
DAVE HAWLEY, Musician

HE REPUTATION OF LAS VEGAS for supplying musicians with an endless number of gigs persisted even as the work dwindled. Musicians around the country were still making their way to Las Vegas seeking steady jobs, decent pay, and show business opportunities. The competition became stiffer, but there were fewer jobs to go around. The union began requiring new musicians to complete a six-week residency in Las Vegas before allowing them to accept work, and getting started was generally more difficult for most of the newcomers. The union later raised the residency requirement to three months.

The quality of the musicians grew even higher than it had been in the 1960s, and hotel musicians were no longer embarrassed to say they worked in Las Vegas. In fact, awards were established just for the house bands in the Annual Las Vegas Entertainment Awards, which were sponsored by the 1,500-member Academy of Variety and Cabaret Artists.

One award was for the orchestra of the year in a main room. In 1976 the contenders included some now-familiar names: the Nat Brandwynne Orchestra from Caesars Palace, the Tony Costa Orchestra from the MGM Grand Ziegfeld Room, the Jack Eglash Orchestra at the Sahara, the Joe Guercio Orchestra from the Las Vegas Hilton, the Johnny Haig Relief Orchestra, and the Dick Palombi Orchestra from the Riviera. The winner in 1976 was the Johnny Haig Relief Orchestra. Another award, established for show orchestras of "nine men or under," was contested in the same year by the Ron Andrews Orchestra for "Spice on Ice," the Mickey Finn Orchestra for the "Mickey Finn Show," the Mike Montano Orchestra for "Playgirls on Ice," Otto Ortwein's Orchestra from "Bottoms Up '77," Jimmy Packard's Orchestra from "Bare Touch of Vegas," and Brent Price's Orchestra from "The Orphan's Revenge." The winner that year was Jimmy Packard's group.[1]

Many headliners still preferred to work in Las Vegas because of the talented musicians that made up the hotel bands. Some noticed that when they toured they could not find musicians of the same high quality in many other cities. Comedian Pete Barbutti complained about the difficulty of finding good musicians, and about having to "dumb down" his charts. "You'd be surprised," he said. "It could happen in Miami, it happened to me in New York City. It can happen anywhere. . . . They may be the hottest players in Miami, Cleveland, or Philly, but they still aren't very good. So you're trapped. You can't put in the contract 'must be good.'"[2]

A number of musicians who still work in Las Vegas today arrived during the 1970s. Violinist and contractor Rebecca Ramsey came to Las Vegas in 1974 when a friend in one of the relief bands suggested that she spend the summer working on the Strip to earn money for school. Upon arrival, she joined the union and, after the waiting period, started searching for gigs. She auditioned for the Wayne Newton show at the Sands by playing the first page of the Mendelssohn *Violin Concerto* and was hired on the spot. Her first job was for three weeks, a fairly typical engagement in those days. She was delighted with the money she earned: "It was a fortune for me at the time. I had no money at all. I didn't even have a car, I didn't own my own violin."

When she finished her first engagement, she thought that she would continue with the same orchestra, but soon found out that she was not to be used for the next act. Ramsey said, "It's pretty much the same as it is now. You have your pecking order. . . . I'm not quite sure what the underlying rules are for the band side, but for the strings, everyone knows what their chair is and where they are in the pecking order . . . who the first two are, who the first four are, and then the added people. I was an added person." Fortunately, a friend helped her land her next three-week gig at the Thunderbird Hotel.

Al Ramsey (later Rebecca's husband), the contractor for the Thunderbird Hotel gig, was never there but he heard good things about Rebecca. Sometimes, that was enough. Rebecca noted, "That's another thing. It doesn't really matter how you play too much, it's just what people say about you. If your reputation is good, you are going to get hired. It takes a long time to mess that up! So, I was on a roll now." With six weeks of work under her belt, her friend suggested that she write a letter to Al Ramsey to let him know that she would be available for the summer, but told her, "Don't send him a résumé. He hates that!" Rebecca took this advice and Al hired her to play at Caesars Palace for Harry Belafonte. Almost all the other string players in the Caesars Palace orchestra were much older than she was. Rebecca was only twenty years old at the time and said she did not feel particularly welcome. "But I sat in the back and did the best that I could." Al said, "We like you and we want some younger players in the orchestra," and then hired her to work full-time in the Caesars Palace showroom, one of the best jobs on the Strip at the time.

Frank Sinatra was now a regular performer at Caesars Palace and Rebecca had several memorable personal encounters with him. The first was in her early days in Las Vegas when she was a twenty-two-year old section string player. The orchestra was rehearsing a new song that featured a string melody with a lift (lifting the bow off the string in a particular manner). During rehearsal, the lift had not gone well for the section; to ensure that she got it right Rebecca spent her ten-minute break practicing it. "All of a sudden, I felt this presence behind me. 'If they all played like that, honey, it would sound perfect.' It was Frank Sinatra!"

Her second encounter with the legendary singer ultimately resulted in a job with Sinatra's touring orchestra. Rebecca came to the showroom for Sinatra's Las Vegas show expecting to see all of the usual arrangements and was instead given a folder with music that she had never seen before. "Every single piece had a huge violin solo [for her]. We started rehearsing and he [Sinatra] was standing right next to me. . . . We went through four or five songs." Clearly, Sinatra liked what he heard because his touring drummer invited her to do some roadwork with them immediately after this rehearsal "audition." Rebecca was prepared for the unexpected. "You never know what music is going to come through. It could be very easy or it could have lots of solos."

Trumpeter Tom Snelson was touring with Frank Sinatra Jr. when the bandleader at the Frontier Hotel said, "Why don't you quit and stay in town? See that guy right down there? I'm gonna fire him!" Snelson replied, "I don't want a job that way!" The bandleader assured Snelson that it would be easy for him to find steady work in Las Vegas. Snelson remembered, "My first job in this town . . . officially . . . was [with] Al Hirt and Pete Fountain. It was interesting because the bandleader . . . got very angry about the marquee because his name was too small. So after the rehearsal he drove back to the airport and went back to New Orleans. He wouldn't even do the show! That was my introduction to show business here in Las Vegas."

By 1976 it was more difficult to get started as a newcomer. "You had to wait your turn," said cellist Barbara Gurley. She remembered waiting three months to get her union card and six months to get steady work. While she waited, she had to sign in at the union office once a week. Eventually, Lew Elias began to call her for his relief band if someone was sick or out of town.

Violist Sharon Street-Caldwell said, "It was tough when I first came to town." The biggest hurdle was the wait to get her union card, but once she did, she began to get work. Street-Caldwell had been teaching school in Iowa and playing with the Omaha Symphony. "Everybody that I told I was leaving thought I would be a stripper! . . . I'll never forget my very first job. I had no idea where I was going. It was at Caesars Palace, and it was going to be Andy Williams. I grew up watching Andy Williams, and I'm thinking, 'Oh, my word!'" She was so excited that as she drove to a rehearsal she rear-ended a car full of people near the valet parking area. "I was just hysterical, [saying] 'It's my first job!'" Fortunately no one was hurt and the valet parking attendant found the contractor and explained that Street-Caldwell would be late.

Street-Caldwell recalled that in this show each musician had his or her own riser encased in Plexiglas, with smoke effects surrounding them. After the rehearsal, she said: "I called my Mom, 'I'M PLAYING IN VEGAS WITH ANDY WILLIAMS!' I never knew string players could do stuff like this. . . . I grew up in Wyoming. I didn't even know you could do anything but classical music. The idea of playing jazz, or gigging in hotels . . . was absolutely alien to me. I really didn't think there was going to be any work at all. But it worked out okay!"

Trumpeter Tom Wright first began getting work on the Strip while working on his master's degree at UNLV. His trumpet teacher, Ralph Kimball, was also a member of the Lew Elias Relief Band and knew how Las Vegas worked. Wright told himself that if he was not working steadily by the time he finished the degree that he would move back to California, but it never came to that. His first work was on a new production show at the Desert Inn. Eventually he landed a spot in the "Folies Bergere" orchestra at the Tropicana.

Wright remembered the tremendously talented trumpet players in town when he was auditioning for jobs. According to Wright, contractor Jim Trimble had invited Wright to audition for a show at the Dunes Hotel and had him come in to observe the production. Wright looked at the book (containing all the sheet music, or charts) before the show and said it seemed okay to him. Then he watched the current trumpet player Brad Allison play the show. "He starts playing stuff up an octave, up a 6th." When it came time for Wright to audition, he asked Trimble, "Do you want what's on the page or what Brad has been playing?" Trimble replied, "Well, what's on the page, what he's been playing." And Wright said, "I can play what's on the page. I can't play what Brad's been playing!" Allison was not the only musician to improvise off the charts. Musicians recalled that some of the most difficult shows, such as "Siegfried and Roy," had changed so much over time that only about 20 percent of the show was written down. If you played the actual chart, it was wrong.

Violinist and contractor Lisa Viscuglia arrived in 1979, interested in having a good time and making money. Viscuglia said she would "probably flirt with whoever the band was for the act that was I playing. . . . I was in my twenties and wore the tightest dresses and had the biggest hair. So, I was 'that' girl during the period, the one everyone liked to talk about, but now I'm not anymore, so they forget about it! I was young, single." Once, in the Caesars showroom, Viscuglia remembered Mary Trimble yelling from the viola section that she "couldn't see over my hair!"

A specific type of work done by the string players in Las Vegas was called "strolling." This type of performing was classic, old-style strolling with five musicians coming up to a table and then playing for the customers. Viscuglia was a member of Sasha Semenoff and His Romantic Strings, which had played at the MGM Grand since it had opened in 1973. When Viscuglia arrived, the group consisted of Sasha Semenoff and Viscuglia on violins, violist Susan Shoemaker, accordion player John Linger, and Semnoff's son Paul on the bass. Viscuglia remembered strolling for seven years, six nights a week. A typical evening might find her group playing for fifteen minutes in the lounge, fifteen minutes in the French gourmet room, then fifteen minutes in the Italian restaurant. [3]

"We annoyed a lot of people," Viscuglia said with a laugh. She added, "We played for billionaires, literally." One wealthy client, an international arms dealer, was especially memorable. Because he was known as a great tipper, the restaurant was held open late just for him. "Everyone was all a-twitter because we knew we were going to makes tons of money." Apparently, he had a routine with which everyone was familiar: He was always accompanied by a beautiful woman, a different woman each time. During the afternoon, his bodyguard would go downstairs to the hotel shops and buy her a "bauble" and a new outfit. When the couple arrived, Sasha would bring his group over to the table and the wealthy dealer would say, "Sasha and I wrote a song for you this afternoon." In fact, the song was Sasha's own composition written for his wife, "The Song I Wrote for You," but the woman would inevitably believe that her date had written it just for her. Viscuglia said, "We would play the song, the girl would swoon."

Another man's attempt to impress a woman using the strolling strings did not go nearly as well. He had arranged to have a group of the twelve hired violinists each arrive at the table one by one, with a rose to put at his girlfriend's feet before they began to play. When all twelve strings were serenading her, the man proposed. Much to his shock, she said no and a heated argument immediately ensued. Viscuglia remarked, "We backed out of there as fast as we could!"

Viscuglia remembered the group being asked to play for a very strange private party where everyone was asked to wear yellow. When the musicians arrived, they saw that the fireplace was made up like an altar. The musicians were then asked to play facing the altar, with their backs to the guests. When cake was served, the first piece was served to a mummified chicken in the corner. Later, Viscuglia noticed that the cake and chicken were covered with ants.

As one of only two females in Sasha's group, Viscuglia spent a lot of money on matching gowns with the other woman. "By the time I was twenty-three, God help me, I had a mink and a Mercedes. A used mink and a used Mercedes, but it doesn't matter! I was twenty-three and living large, not saving a penny. . . . [I] had a great time. If I only knew then what I know now!"

The work was challenging and different from work in other cities. There were still instances where individual musicians or entire musical groups would perform more than one gig in an evening. Johnny Haig spent many years working in the Las Vegas music business, but he never forgot one especially eventful night on the job. His band, which had a regular showroom job at the Sahara Hotel starting at 7:00 P.M., was also playing the Ford convention show at the Sands Convention Center and was running very late. The group should have already ended the Ford show with just enough time for the musicians to pack up their instruments, drive a few blocks to the Sahara Hotel, and set up again to start their regular show. As the Ford show got more and more behind schedule, Haig realized he was in trouble.

Acting quickly, he called a limousine service and arranged to have three stretch limousines waiting outside the back door of the convention center. When the band finally finished at 6:45, Haig told them to run for it. Leaving behind their cars and extra belongings and not bothering to pack their instruments in cases, the musicians raced to the limos. The players quickly stuffed themselves inside the three waiting cars: the woodwind doublers with assorted saxophones, flutes, and clarinets; the trumpeters and trombonists; and the rhythm section players. After a chaotic ride to the Sahara Hotel, the band members scrambled out of the cars and dashed for the bandstand.

Leaping over the rails, they hit their seats just as the curtain was going up. Haig gave the downbeat to start the music and the band began to play, as usual, and the audience never knew just how close they came to having no band. The backstage hotel staff must have been amused, though the hard-working hotel employees in Las Vegas undoubtedly have seen many strange and unusual things. Years later Johnny Haig remembered that night with amusement. His ability to think on his feet was just one of many reasons he was so highly respected during his years as a great contractor and con-ductor on the Las Vegas music scene. No doubt his usually calm disposi-tion was another.

When the relief band jobs disappeared after the 1989 musicians strike, in part because the corporate owners did not care if the showroom was dark for a night, Haig had already transitioned into a new phase of his career as the music director for Caesar's Palace. He remained in that position until the casino closed its original showroom in 2000. He continued to put together bands for events until his final show in June of 2006.[4] Haig died a year later, and is remembered with respect by the musicians who worked for him. "He's the best. He's the best I ever worked for," said Ronnie Simone. Band member Thom Pastor said that Haig was "the crème de la crème."

In the 1970s and 1980s "Vegas Spectacular" productions became more prolific than ever. These shows mainly featured variety acts and musical numbers, often with very difficult music. They were fast-paced and demand-ing in a number of ways, much more difficult than the shows that musicians played for the boys. In spite of the difficulties involved, these types of shows often became boring for the musicians over time because the music was the same night after night, making it difficult to stay focused. "The work back then was just way too hard," Wright said. "I was kind of fortunate because I never did any star rooms . . . but a lot the guys . . . you got guys that had done Tony Bennett, Frank Sinatra, Sammy Davis, playing good music with good orchestras, and not that taxing. And now they're going into twelve shows a week of this non-stop blasting. . . . You were too close. The lead trumpet, when he cracked a note, it was pretty much four thousand watts of power going. . . . Even the sound man would look up!"

Sometimes, a player experienced a mental crisis brought on by fac-ing the same difficulties every night. Once having played something well a few times, the pressure to never miss anything became an almost-insur-mountable obstacle. Perfectionism and overthinking could lead to mis-takes, which in turn could cause the performer to self-doubt, leading to more mistakes. Tom Wright explained, "The mental thing. . . . If you don't have the mind set that you're going to take over the world, and you're afraid you're going to miss something, then you start missing more, and it wears you out. Not that any of these guys that got let go or quit weren't capa-ble. . . . It's just a matter of time. If you play it perfect, all you can do is mess up. Trying to keep your mental alertness after you've played the same show for four years . . . it's hard."

Once again, the trumpeters seemed to have the most challenging obsta-cles. Don Hannah remembered a particularly frustrated trumpeter play-ing the same show night after night on the lead trumpet part, which called repeatedly for extremely high notes. He started to miss small things, to make mistakes. As his confidence decreased, the mistakes kept coming. The pro-verbial final straw was when, after missing one high note too many, the trumpet player stood up, pitched his horn across the pit, and walked out. Hannah reported that the trumpeter, somewhat calmer, later returned to finish the show with his dented instrument, probably after considering some less-appealing alternatives.

Tom Snelson recalled playing lead trumpet for the "Folies Bergere" show in the Tropicana Hotel showroom. "That was a very hard job for me, it was horribly hard. It was a lot of piccolo trumpet. . . . It was brutally hard work. We did twelve shows a week. You just had to spend a lot of time warming up the next day to get the [lip] swelling down." Tom Wright told of another lead trumpet player who was found lying on the hood of his car with congestive heart failure and was sent to the hospital in an ambulance. Then he was so worried about his job that he came back to work too early and eventually ended up quitting altogether.

All the musicians had to be excellent sight readers and to know lots of music from memory, though many considered this part of the work fun. Rebecca Ramsey performed with a group for champagne brunches, play-ing tunes for four hours at a time. "I learned so many songs from the Amer-ican Songbook . . . all in the original keys. . . . You name a song, I'll tell you what key its in! You've got to know what key you're in. . . . You don't rehearse, ever. You walk in, they name the song, and you've got to know the key." This type of challenging work is rarely found on the Strip anymore.

The pressure was intense. Tom McDermott recalled "a wonderful saxophone player . . . saying 'Just remember guys—you're only as good as your last solo!'" Dave Hawley said, "One of the things you learn when you are in a business like we were in . . . is that there is always a better player. . . . There is always somebody better." There was no real job security and, because of this, some people were even afraid to take vacations. If the contractor liked the substitute better, they might just fire the original musician and hire the substitute to take his or her place. One musician remembered, "Musicians are so insecure about money, that [they] would often want to work on their night off. . . . Many musicians would work a whole year without a night off."

One contractor fired so many people that the hotel owner he worked for eventually told him he could not fire anyone else. "It's not good for a band, not good for morale, makes people uneasy," said one musician about those abuses of power. Ed Boyer said that he was once put on notice for not smiling enough. "All they [the contractors] had to say was that you weren't acceptable," said Sharon Street-Caldwell. "In the end, you didn't tell people no." One assistant conductor recalled having to fire people for his boss. "I would see the look in these people's eyes when I would walk up to them. . . . I did not want to be there."

Another contractor was known for always having a "whipping boy." Trombonist Ken Hanlon, who recounted this story, remembered that a trumpet player in his band "could not breathe hard" without attracting the ire of the contractor. When Hanlon once reacted by making a face, he found himself as the new whipping boy. Soon, the contractor was yelling at him: "All I can hear is you. I can't hear anybody else in the band but you!" Hanlon left the job and moved on to another before the bandleader could fire him. Still, everybody told him, "You're not a pro until you've been fired." Other contractors, like Johnny Haig, were more tolerant. "I just don't want to get into any negatives. . . . Some of the people in this town were negative. There was a lot of stuff I had to overlook where people weren't up to where they ought to be," he said.

Female musicians were rare before the 1970s. "There were not as many as there are now," according to Rebecca Ramsey. "When I started at

Caesars, it was mostly men. Now, it is almost all women in the string section. I didn't realize it was happening at the time but I had to work a little
bit harder to gain respect as the concert master." She never noticed gender
being a real problem, but she knew there was some resentment. "If anything
like that was going on, I would just laugh it off." Sharon Street-Caldwell
said she missed the worst of the discrimination, though she pointed out that
reverse discrimination was also possible. She remembered that Paul Anka
requested an all-girl string section.

Cellist Barbara Gurley said that she refused to flirt when contractors
would start coming on to her because she wanted to be accepted on merit.
Another female musician mentioned a particular contractor with a reputation as a casting couch contractor. She brought her boyfriend with her
for the solo audition. Some of the female musicians did not like to spend
too much time in the casinos because they were occasionally mistaken for
hookers. Pat Harrell said that the single women sometimes had a rough
time with the stars.

Both racial and gender discrimination were definitely a factor. And
even after desegregation finally took hold, old ways died hard. Many minor-
ities and women found it easier to get work in the showrooms off the Strip.
And some entertainers, such as Sammy Davis Jr., would ask specifically
to have some black musicians in his orchestra if possible; these musicians
tended to be wind or percussion players as there were few black string players in Las Vegas at the time.

As late as 1971 women were still barred from dealing in most casinos
even though casinos later learned that gamblers often preferred them.
Women casino workers were often relegated to the "girl's ghetto" of Keno
running and cocktail serving.[5] Or women were hired as a sexy novelty, such
as the two female blackjack dealers hired in 1966. They were the only dealers in the casino required to wear see-through tops and pasties.[6]

By the early 1970s, more casinos such as the Silver Slipper and some
other downtown properties were willing to use female dealers. Still, the
women hired had to be young and good looking. Frank Rosenthal agreed
to hire twelve female dealers for the Stardust, but stipulated that he wanted
only "the most qualified and attractive." There was also a glass ceiling for
the women who worked in the casinos and few thought that these women

could do more than look decorative while working low-paying jobs such as dealing, Keno running, or serving food or cocktails. Even as more female dealers were hired, it was rare that a woman moved up in the organization. One woman who eventually became a director of operations for a casino started her career as a dealer. She remembered, "There were plenty of women dealers. We were the eye candy behind the table. But I don't know if it ever occurred to the guys [in charge] that we might one day want to do more than deal."[7]

One unfair practice was to hire women for what was called a probationary period for about ninety days. When the ninety days were up, the management would replace her with a different woman. Casinos did not allow women to work for more than eight hours a day or for more than forty hours a week. In 1975 Nevada legislator Jean Ford succeeded in pushing through a bill that required employers to give "equal pay, hours, and working conditions regardless of gender."[8]

Regardless, musicians and other entertainers were usually hired on a purely subjective basis. Even now, most hiring for musicians is subjective, with contractors holding a great deal of power. This is true of the music business in general, and is unlikely to change.

Musician D. Gause arrived during the 1970s and soon found out the hard way that gender discrimination was alive and well in Las Vegas. "When I came here, I had to make some decisions. I was a clarinet player and a keyboard player. . . . Doing one thing was difficult enough, being female." At that time in the Strip bands, the string sections were almost all women, while the wind and rhythm sections were almost all men. Gause recalled, "The first year I was here, I didn't gig at all. There were many openings in the show bands, but I was not allowed to audition for any of them because I was female. The worst thing was just not being allowed to do what it is that I do. . . . That first year was painful. It was a lesson, that if we are not mindful of where we are today that we can always backslide. . . . [We need to remain] mindful of women's rights, of human rights, of civil rights." Still, she persevered. "It was choosing my battles and winning my wars. I was working in a hostile environment. It was a long hard road."

The first gig that Gause played was in a jazz club owned by a prominent black businessman in the black section of town. She recalled that the mostly black ensemble played until 3:00 in the morning. Soon she began to make connections, friends, and a name for herself. In 1979 she became the first female conductor on the Strip. "I never really thought about wanting to do it or not wanting to do it. . . . I was given the opportunity and I said sure." The small-scale production was housed at the Silver Slipper. "It was literally little. . . . The tallest girl was 5'6"!" There were four girl dancers, two stunt people, and a comic. "I would hang out with dancers and they couldn't eat before they went to work because of the weigh-ins. . . . That's where I got my habit of eating after the shows."

After the Silver Slipper production ended, Gause continued to work on the Strip in various capacities, though not without problems. She recalled that the upper management of the show "Legends in Concert" did not want a woman in the band and told the contractor to fire her. The contractor refused. "You fire her, you're firing me as well."

Certain headliners were known for firing musicians on the spot. One in particular watched the musicians constantly out of the corner of his eye while he was performing, looking for any mistakes. For those who were writing or arranging, projects would last only ten days or so. No matter how well one did, the project would end and the writer would be looking for the next job.

Unfortunately, there were those musicians who turned to alcohol and drugs to help them cope. This, in turn, exacerbated the stress of working in close quarters every night. Drunks would argue and get into fights over all the things that people argue about when working together for a long time in a confined space. Johnny Haig thought that alcohol was not a good factor to add into this equation. "With alcohol, words would come out. Great musicians would hold everything in during the job. Once they started drinking, it would come out. Then, it seemed like two guys would always end up having a fight." Drinking was a common pastime for many of the Strip musicians, though. One production show featured an eleven-minute video that allowed the band members to race to the bar where the bartender had already set out their drinks. "We would just book out, we'd go straight to the bar, the bartender would see us coming and set up the drinks. . . . We would just slam them back and take one for the road."

On May 21, 1972, the Musicians Union built an office with a rehearsal

hall and a bar just off the Strip, located at 155 East Tropicana.⁹ The previous office/rehearsal space was 1611 E. Fremont Street; the new location was
more central to the Strip action. Musicians went there after work, still keyed
up after their last shows. Many would go to the union to see their friends,
drink, or find out the gossip for the night. At the union rehearsal hall, musicians could try out working with a new or different player. Tom Wright said,
"You don't want somebody you hate sitting next to you."

As always, the musicians who arrived in Las Vegas during the 1970s
have a number of backstage stories to tell, sometimes repeated so often and
by so many that the origins become murky. One particular story stands out,
recounted by numerous musicians in slightly different ways. The gist of
the story seems to gel into the following account. Two cellists who shared
a music stand on the Liberace Show disliked each other with an unusual
intensity. Sharing the same music stand meant that they were forced to
work in close proximity reading from the same music night after night. Perhaps this was what caused them to dislike each other in the first place! In
any case, the Liberace Show had a number that was called the "Dancing
Waters," featuring fountains that were placed in front of the orchestra with
waters that would rise and fall in time with the music. On the final night
of this show, one of the two cellists finally reached the limits of his endur-
ance. Using his cello bow, he snatched the toupee off the head of his hapless
colleague and sent it flying into the fountains. As the dancing waters were
active at the time, the toupee became part of the show, rising and falling
with the fountain waters that were choreographed to the music, although
very little music was happening once the other musicians spotted the soggy
hairpiece bobbing up and down.

Some musicians did not enjoy the Liberace Show—but not because of
the entertainer himself. "He's a very nice man, the show was pleasing to a
lot of people," one musician recalled. "[But] the dancing waters absolutely
stank! That was a nasty smell and we were sitting right next to that foul water
after 6 weeks." Barbara Gurley remembered hearing about a Liberace Show
cellist who had played the act so often that he had memorized it. She went
to see for herself and found out that it was true; the player never opened the
music all night.

Bill Trujillo remembered another special effect from the Liberace

Show while playing with one of Johnny Haig's bands at the Hilton. At the end of the show, Liberace, pulled by ceiling cables, flew over the audience's heads as he yelled, "Whee, whee!" One night the famous entertainer was lifted to the ceiling and was stuck in the rafters for more than ten minutes while the stagehands tried to get him back down.

Trumpeter Tom Snelson recalled something similar that happened to Bob Newhart during one of his comedy shows. Newhart ended his performances sitting in the "O" of a large neon sign that spelled "BOB." As the audience applauded, the "BOB" sign, with Newhart still in it, was raised offstage and the curtains closed. One night the stagehands forgot about Newhart, and left him stuck near the ceiling in his "O," until they heard his unmistakable voice coming over their heads, "Guys? Guys? Hey, guys!"

Trombonist Ken Hanlon remembered another opening night foul-up on a new production. There was a sequence done on a movie screen of a beautiful woman being chased by a man. The action took place on a ski slope and was planned to come to a dramatic finish: as the actress in the movie skied rapidly down a slope toward the audience, a live showgirl was supposed to burst through the screen and fly over the heads of the audience. The unfortunate showgirl got stuck about halfway across the theater and the production was halted until she could be freed.

Some stage mishaps had unfortunate consequences for the performers. Tom Wright recalled a particular production show that had been brought to the Desert Inn from Paris. The cast was so used to rehearsing with tapes that they had trouble performing the show with the live band. In addition, the star that was supposed to drop from the ceiling on a rope to sing the opening number took a serious fall when the rope broke, and someone else had to fill in on opening night.

Several of the musicians recalled another toupee incident that occurred one night at the Riviera Hotel and Casino. As the conductor was exuberantly leading a Broadway-type show, he flailed his arms a bit too much and caught his toupee with his baton. Unfortunately for him, the toupee did not stay on his baton but flew off into the far reaches of the audience. The audience members thoughtfully passed it back to him slowly overhead. Presumably, this particular conductor restrained his more vigorous motions after that.

Musicians, especially when bored in the production shows, were not above playing practical jokes on their colleagues to keep things interesting. "At the Frontier, there were things happening every minute," recalled trombonist Ralph Pressler. There were spitballs, people throwing things and aiming for the lights. "Band members would play pranks on each other every night." Howard Agster noted, "Nothing is harder than playing the same show for years." He added, "We had a trumpet player who would come in between shows and move everybody's [tuning] slide!"

Agster, a percussionist, remembered another incident at the Tropicana on the "Folies Bergere" show when he missed hitting the cymbal three or four times. He was disturbed because "I had never done that before." Soon enough, he discovered the reason. The pianist was gradually pulling his cymbal away from him on a rope whenever Agster was looking the other way. Agster got his revenge by piling all the guest chairs around the pianist's bench. Sometimes, the pranks could get out of hand. Pianist Ronnie Simone remembered a saxophone player who squirted a water pistol in the conductor's face because he was angry. The frightened conductor believed it was a real gun and crawled under the bandstand.

Guitarist Joe Lano spent eight and a half years working at the Dunes with a conductor that he described as being "uptight, no sense of humor." When this conductor took a vacation, the relief conductor took over and was not nearly as tough. The band members immediately took advantage of the situation, making the most of the opportunity to relieve their boredom with the long-running "Casino de Paris" show. For the entire time that the relief conductor was in front of the group, the saxophone section and the percussion section did battle with spitballs.

Another incident from the same show was almost a disaster. With twenty-two band members in the balcony, it was a very tight fit. One percussionist required so much equipment that there was no room left in the balcony for his huge gong. Stagehands welded a rod onto the balcony and hung the gong over the edge. One night the percussionist hit the gong as usual but was startled to watch it fall into the audience, barely missing two people seated at a table below the band. "They could have been killed!" said Lano.

More than one musician got confused about where they were supposed to play, particularly those who worked with the relief bands. Howard Agster

Violinist and banjo player in the Arizona Club. The Helen J. Stewart Collection, 0104–0089, Special Collections, UNLV Libraries, University of Nevada, Las Vegas.

Musicians standing in front of the Las Vegas Courthouse, 1930. Sherwin "Scoop" Garside collection, 0067 0119, Special Collections, UNLV Libraries, University of Nevada, Las Vegas.

Veterans of Foreign Wars (VFW) Post band seated on steps of Las Vegas Courthouse (Vegas Studio, Las Vegas), 1930. Sherwin "Scoop" Garside collection, 0067 0059, Special Collections, UNLV Libraries, University of Nevada, Las Vegas.

Interior of the Ramona Room at the Last Frontier Hotel and Casino, 1945. Manis collection, 0100 0110, Special Collections, UNLV Libraries, University of Nevada, Las Vegas.

Girls dance on top of the bar in the Gay 90's room at the Last Frontier Hotel and Casino, 1945. Manis collection, 0100 0114, Special Collections, UNLV Libraries, University of Nevada, Las Vegas.

Harold Stern Strolling Orchestra at the Flamingo, 1955. J. Florian Mitchell collection, VR-373-H, June 6, 1955, Photo collections at Nevada State Museum, Las Vegas, J. Florian Mitchell, photographer.

Royal Nevada Stage Show, 1955. J. Florian Mitchell collection,
VR-384-B, 06-14-1955, Photo collections at Nevada State Museum,
Las Vegas, J. Florian Mitchell, photographer.

Antonio Morelli with the Sands Orchestra, 1960s. Antonio Morelli collection, 0365
0009, Donated by the Junior League of Las Vegas, Inc. Endowment Fund, Special
Collections, UNLV Libraries, University of Nevada, Las Vegas (Las Vegas News Bureau:
Don English, Jerry Abbott, Joe Buck, Milt Palmer, John Cook).

said, "At times I would have to drive up to the hotel marquis to see who was playing. . . . You could forget." He felt fortunate that after twenty-five years in the Lew Elias Relief Band he went to the wrong hotel only once. On that occasion, Agster recalled thinking, "Gee, look at the substitutes we have. . . . A lot of guys must be taking vacations." Luckily, he realized his mistake in time to make it across the street to where he was really supposed to be. He remembered another relief band musician who showed up at the Dunes on the regular band night. That musician told his counterpart, "As long as I'm here and I'm dressed up in a tuxedo, you can go home and I'll play the show."

The live animals used in many shows presented the most frequent issues. No one ever knew what they would do. Several musicians remembered the cheetah that arrived in the orchestra pit with the apparent intent of silencing the cymbals. The drummer for the show was right in front of the cat stool, and the cat was very disturbed by the cymbal sound. Dave Hawley said that some musicians kept on playing but that "we didn't want the drummer to keep playing!" He does not remember how the cat eventually got out of the pit. "I felt safe because I knew he would have to go through other people before he got to me!"

At the Desert Inn, bassist Tom McDermott remembered the birds that took part in the finale. All the showgirls had birdseed hidden in their headdresses and the birds would fly to them from the back of the audience. Often the birds would let loose, and "we'd look out to see who 'got mail'!" He also remembered his bandleader trying to conduct the band with some misguided doves perched on his arms. Pianist Ronnie Simone once had to finish the Lance Burton Show with a pigeon sitting on his head. Since he had to keep both hands on the piano, stagehands came to take the pigeon off stage.

Bass trombonist Ralph Pressler recalled an incident involving stagehands and a tiger named Magic used in the Siegfried and Roy Show. "One of the nights Magic decided to go right instead of left, so everybody said 'Scatter!' It was not familiar territory for him [Magic]. He just wanted to find a safe place to go, so he headed for the corner." Some of the stagehands were unfortunately already in the corner where Magic was determined to go. Most of them got out of the way quickly, but one rather large stagehand was not fast enough and decided to climb the ladder attached to the corner wall instead. Because the ladder had safety rungs wrapped around it in a tunnel shape, the stagehand was too big to get far and got stuck partially up the ladder. Unfortunately for him, Magic decided to curl up under the ladder for the duration of the show. Years later, in 2003, another tiger would nearly kill Roy Horn and cause the Siegfried and Roy Show to permanently close.

The "Casino de Paris" production at the Dunes featured an act within the show called the "Rupert Bears," featuring brown bears from Germany. The finale of their act was on a seesaw-type rig. On one end, a bear dressed in a hat and goggles sat on a motorcycle, while another bear perched on the opposite end. Each time the motorcycle wheels hit the ground, the seesawing motion of the rig got faster and faster. Joe Lano remembered one memorable occasion when a bear pooped while the rig was at top speed, sending bear poop flying all over the audience as they ducked for cover.

The stagehands were often involved with the animals used in the show, and with the removal of whatever an animal might have left behind. Simone said that the stagehands in one of his shows had a lottery to predict when the horse would "do a number onstage." According to percussionist Tommy Check, Debbie Reynolds once cleaned her own stage following the elephant act. The elephant had done a big number onstage just as the announcer said, "And now, ladies and gentleman, the star of our show, Debbie Reynolds!" So Reynolds "came out with bucket and shovel, cleans it up and then gives to the stagehand. 'Can we start now?'" Trumpeter Tom Wright remembered hearing about a Royal Lipizzaner stallion that slipped and fell into the audience, and monkeys at the Dunes who pooped onstage and started throwing it at the audience. "Live animals are hard," he mused.

Audience members sometimes provided extra entertainment by heckling the performers or getting into fights among themselves. One musician recalled an incident at the Desert Inn at the end of the show after the curtain came down. Hearing a commotion in the audience, the musicians looked out to see two men fighting, but it did not last for long. The mob owners prided themselves on keeping Las Vegas clean. Norman Kaye remembered, "Drunks and hecklers were made short work of in those days by bouncers. Anybody that got out of line was fast removed . . . somebody would just pass an eye to somebody and the person who was the offending party was really put out very fast."[10]

Woodwind doubler Sam Pisciotta remembered a fight that took place between a trombonist and a drummer on a revolving stage at the Stardust Hotel. One group would perform while the other would set up on the stage facing away from the audience. The fight began when his group was backstage and was revolving to the audience side. Pisciotta remembered the musicians yelling, "Keep the stage turning!"

Another musician recalled being part of a notorious fight. Normally a member of the relief band, he had been called to fill in on a production show. "I knew the show cold from being in the relief band," recalls one musician. One of the other musicians became enraged because the relief musician was reading *Time* magazine on his stand during the show. Another musician complained, "You are bringing heat on the sax section!" This small incident escalated until the two became involved in a scuffle and both were fired. Dick McGee, who was not involved but remembered hearing about the fight, was not too surprised. "We all heard about that. . . . I wasn't there, but I heard!"

Musicians in Las Vegas had to get used to thinking of themselves as part of show business, much more than their counterparts in other cities. Onstage and featured, many took to wearing more-glamorous clothing or even costumes. One musician recalled that a musician quit the house band because Bobbie Gentry wanted them to wear special hats. "It's funny how some musicians resist. It was no big deal to me."

Between the shows, the players would go home, visit others in the coffee shops, or involve themselves with hobbies. Tom Snelson told the story of an infamous long-running card game among the band members at the Tropicana between shows. Apparently two of the players had devised a way of cheating through hand signals. One night, the other players finally caught on. "This one trumpet player got so mad he called the bandleader up! And he [the bandleader] was out for dinner with Phyllis McGuire. . . . So the bandleader says 'Guys I'm at dinner.' 'Well, we don't care, these guys are cheating. What are you going to do about it?' He hangs up and tells Phyllis about it and she says, 'You go back there and give those cheaters a raise!'"

While going home between the shows was clearly beneficial for some, not all of the musicians were able to stay focused if they left the workplace. The musician who went home was always taking a chance: he or she might get too comfortable and lose track of time. Percussionist Tommy Check said that he stopped going home between shows after falling asleep on his couch in his underwear. He arrived ten minutes late to his 12:00 A.M. show and he remembered that his bandleader was "hysterical." Violist Sharon Street-Caldwell said, "I made the mistake one time of going home. . . . I fell asleep! I only did that once. After that, I never went home again. . . . The hardest thing physically was eating so late . . . [and] having no normal life with people." Their unusual schedules meant that Strip musicians started work when most families were putting their children to bed.

Cellist Barbara Gurley liked to go home between shows. Because she liked to play chamber music during the day, she was not really interested in staying out after work, either. She was, in her words, an "early-to-bed person." Violinist Rebecca Ramsey said, "What I was doing all these years was practicing. . . . I would go home after the show, go to bed, get up and practice 4 or 5 hours. I was always studying. For me, it was very important to get better on the violin."

Brass players generally were not able to practice or play chamber music during show days. Trumpeter Tom Wright said that he always tried to do something else. "You had to get your muscles [to relax], let your face rebuild itself." Wright liked to work on his own cars and those of his friends. He also liked to visit the new car lots after work. "Dick [McGee] and I always found each other browsing in car lots at three in the morning."

Working with the stars was exciting for many people, and most of the big-name entertainers were very good to the hotel musicians. D. Gause remarked, "Almost all the stars I worked for were wonderful." Sharon Street-Caldwell agreed. "The entertainers we really fell in love with . . . you really wanted to do well for them." Musician Don Hannah also noted, "People with big salaries and big reputations were usually very nice."

Jerry Lewis was a favorite of Lisa Viscuglia. She recalled that when she was pregnant and playing his show that Lewis would yell into her stomach each night, "Nice LA-dy, nice BA-by!" After her son Jack was born, she sent Lewis's manager a picture of him. Lewis gave her son a Tiffany rattle, engraved "To Jack, Love, Jerry." When she next saw Lewis, Viscuglia was touched to see that he had baby Jack's picture in his wallet. "He was so wonderful."

Another favorite comedian was Dom DeLuise. He was "hysterically funny," according to trumpet player Tom Snelson. And, said Snelson, he was a good sport too. The band once played a trick on him during his performance of the song "O Sole Mio," changing the key of the music by going up one-half step in pitch without telling him. Each night, the band raised the pitch another half step, making it more and more difficult for DeLuise to reach his high notes. DeLuise kept wondering what had happened to his voice. When he finally figured it out, he got a big kick out of it.

Percussionist Howard Agster liked Debbie Reynolds. "She treated us well and she was fun to watch because people really liked her . . . very professional. She would throw parties in the gourmet room and let you bring your wife, would have a jazz trio playing." He also mentioned Jimmy Durante, who would do extra performances between shows in other venues to help the musicians raise money for various causes. D. Gause enjoyed jazz singer Shirley Bassey. "She was such a class act . . . [and] such a magical woman. What a performer."

Many times the public perception of stars would be quite different from how they were in person. Ronnie Simone remembered that Jayne Mansfield "was entirely different from her public image. Delightful. Didn't complain at all, very nice." Don Hannah really liked Barbra Streisand. "All she wanted was 'Do the job right.' I enjoyed working with her. She was really very nice." Percussionist Tommy Check admired Streisand because of her incredible work ethic. She would work shooting a movie on location all day and then come to Las Vegas and do a live, recorded show.

Some of the most fun was working with entertainers who had good musical arrangements for the orchestra to play, such as Burt Bacharach. "Burt. Magnificent arrangements," said Lisa Viscuglia, who also liked playing the classic repertoire of Johnny Mathis. Trombone player Ralph Pressler mentioned the arrangements and big band charts of Natalie Cole and Bobby Darin. Sharon Street-Caldwell added, "The charts back then used to be absolutely wonderful." Because the music was also quite difficult, Street-Caldwell said that the headliners really liked working with the Las Vegas musicians. "When they toured, they couldn't find orchestras that could play the books (perform the music) . . . they could [only] cover them in New York, LA, and Vegas [because the musicians were used to the style]."

Lisa Viscuglia remembered performing with Bacharach during the World Series. The show had a solo violin and solo saxophone feature. Normally, Rebecca Ramsey performed the solo, but she had cut her finger and could not do it on this occasion. "Becky is brilliant at leading the section; she taught me a lot," Viscuglia noted. She was told to go up to Bacharach's suite to play for him and the music director. When she called up, he told her, "The World Series is on. I have to go!" So, she played the solo with no audition and everything went well. The start of the show was delayed, though, because the baseball game went on for twelve innings that day.

Tom Snelson said, "Musically, I always looked forward to Shirley MacLaine's show. It was very difficult and she had a great conductor who was wonderful to work for, demanding. One Thanksgiving, she felt really bad because we had to rehearse and do two shows that night. She flew in her chef who fixed a wonderful soul food meal for everyone." Pianist Ronnie Simone also has a lot of respect for Shirley MacLaine. "She was a tough taskmaster but the thing about Shirley . . . [was that] she drove herself that hard. . . . She wasn't going to demand it from you unless she demanded it from herself. She went on with legs that hurt. . . . She'd have to have reflexology after every show." Joe Lano, who traveled with Lena Horne for five years, appreciated the way that the singer varied her show. "She never sang the tunes the same way twice. That was the most fun. . . . We never knew what to expect."

The comedians often developed a rapport with band members and would sometimes joke with them onstage. Sharon Street-Caldwell remembered Rip Taylor: "One time this audience was staring at him like he was an absolute freak. He turned his whole set around and did his whole show to the band." Working with comedians meant hearing their material delivered, sometimes in exactly the same way, for many nights in a row. Flip Wilson did not want to subject the musicians to this, remembered trombonist Ken Hanlon. During rehearsal, Wilson said, "Guys, here's the deal. You play me on. They're going to close the curtain. When you hear this joke, go get lost. . . . When you hear this story, get back on and play me off. The last thing I want is you guys sitting back there with those dead faces because you've been hearing my stories every night!"

Other comedians dealt with this problem in a different way. Milton Berle kept the band members onstage and had them shake their shoulders up and down as though they were laughing at his jokes. "He was not a happy person," said a musician. Another player thought that Berle was intimidating, and said that he got very upset if you did not laugh at his jokes. According to showgirl Kathy Saxe, Berle had all the dancers at the Flamingo fired because "he didn't want to work with anyone taller than him onstage!"[11]

Berle was one of the few unpopular headliners; most are remembered fondly. When asked if there were those he didn't like, Johnny Haig said, "I can't think of anybody. . . . I've had about 400 names." There were some names that came up repeatedly from most of the other musicians, however. These types of stars were abusive or unhappy. Joe Lano was one of the rare musicians who did not care for Frank Sinatra. He said that Sinatra once shorted him $1,000 on a check, while Sinatra and Caesars argued over who should pay it.

There is one entertainer whose personality was truly divisive: Wayne Newton. In the interviews, musicians either loved or hated him. One musician recalled, "He was treacherous. He would watch you out of the corner of his eye. . . . You had to be careful. . . . You had to look interested in his show. . . . You certainly didn't talk to any one else. He just might glance back while you are doing that. He'd have a person fired." Another player made the mistake of being seen looking at his watch during a meeting. "Have to take a pill?" snapped Newton. Another musicians recalled, "The one show I found I had to drink to get through was Wayne Newton. . . . To get through his show, you can't do it sober. There's no way. I used to start getting my headache; I called it my 'Wayne Newton headache,' about three in the afternoon when I knew I had to work [with] him. It's like giving a pint of blood."

Part of the problem was that the showroom allowed Newton unlimited overtime. "If you didn't go to the bathroom before you went on to do that show, you were dead," said one player. Newton would often stay until the crowd was going crazy, going on long after the musicians should have been finished. He also was allowed nine-week engagements, something no other entertainer had at the time.

One musician remembered him as "so arrogant, so condescending. Patronizing. In public, you would think he was our best friend. He would keep you waiting in the hall [after a show] for an hour . . . [and] would berate one person in front of the entire band. People lost their minds on his jobs because of the mental games he would play." Newton always had a regular entourage of players that met after every show. "Soup's on," his manager would say, and the entourage members would gather first to hear Newton's comments. Then, the players would often be yelled at and humiliated in front of the others for small mistakes.

One of Newton's band members who had worked and toured with Newton for several years got married and then became pregnant with her first baby. While she was still in the hospital, one of his representatives called and asked if she was going out on the road with them and said that they were leaving almost immediately. When she told them no, she was informed, "If you are not going on the road, then we can't have you." Finding herself suddenly out of work and disoriented as a new mom was a painful experience, but fortunately she was quickly absorbed into regular Las Vegas work.

Another musician, working the lounge of the hotel, was asked to fill in on Newton's act in the main showroom. He worked for three weeks and Newton told him, "You did a nice job. You can do all my shows," but Newton never called him again. Some musicians were blackballed by Newton for years, suffering some of the worst abuses. Even now, years after they worked with him, they are unwilling to make their stories public for fear of reprisal from Newton.

Still, there are quite a few musicians who love Wayne Newton. One musician said, "To me, he was great." In particular, this person thought that Newton was at his best on a one-to-one level. "I came out of each meeting unscathed, but others were not so lucky." He also has a loyal group of long-time players who are happy to continue working with him in spite of the fact that he is currently on the American Federation of Musicians' International Unfair List. Newton was placed on the list during labor disputes in 2006. At this time, no Musicians Union members are allowed to render services for his performances anywhere in the world. So the players who continue to work with him quit the union in order to do so. That kind of loyalty to a performer is truly rare.

As the corporations moved in during the 1970s and 1980s, they continued to have combative relationships with the various Las Vegas unions connected to the hotels. Negotiations were no longer easy, friendly, or painless, and gradually led to serious rifts between the union members and the corporate management, and in 1976 workers walked out of the casinos for a strike that lasted fifteen months to protest low pay and poor working conditions. Showgirl Tracy Heberling thought that Howard Hughes played a big role influencing the attitude of management toward the union. "He never made any secret that he was anti-union. And he said very plainly that he was going to bust the union while he was here. . . . There had never been any problems with stagehands or culinary unions before, but those problems started to arise. And the town changed in atmosphere. . . . He brought in that corporate mentality, the bottom line mentality, and very much changed the atmosphere of the town. He bought up large portions of Nevada. There was a lot of resentment towards him."[12]

Mark Tan first reported the trouble on March 8, 1976, in the *Hollywood Reporter*: "March 10 is looming to be the day to watch, and could conceivably be one of the Strip's darkest. That's the date the three biggest unions— Culinary, Musicians, and Stagehands—will decide whether to sign new contracts with the hotels or walk. . . . Both the musicians and stagehands are [and have been] on the job without new contracts, agreeing to wait until the March 10 deadline."[13]

There was indeed a walkout that immediately impacted the Strip. On March 15, Mark Tan wrote,

> While the hotel members of the Nevada Resort Association and three separate unions conducted chaotic contract talks, it was the Strip performers who were hit first with last week's walkout by Musicians Union (Local 369), Stage Hands (Local 720), Culinary Union (Local 226) and Bartenders Union (Local 165). With the exception of the NRA's non-member hotels—the Riviera, Stardust, Hacienda, Aladdin, Marina, and Fremont—all major showrooms were dark with all performers out of work and out of pay without protective "pay or play" contracts. Performers in shows

like *Hallelujah Hollywood!*, *Casino des Paris*, *Folies Bergere* are on "forced vacations" without pay since their contracts are with individual producers and hotels. Again, the nonmember hotels are unaffected and have already signed a separate contract with the Culinary Union, and will remain in full operation. At press time, reports were that the Nevada Resort Association hotels were ready to close down for a month or longer.[14]

There were competing stories from both sides, but in this case the union ultimately prevailed. Nevertheless, this was a difficult and stressful time for the hotel musicians, some of whom did not really understand the issues in the first place and resented the loss of income. It is worth noting that the Musicians Union strongly supported what appeared to be primarily a Culinary Union issue in 1989, but when it was the musicians who were under fire, they got no such help from that union.

Mark Tan wrote with strong disapproval in the aftermath of the strike, noting that "the tourist industry is Las Vegas' ONLY industry" and that it was shortsighted of both sides to cause tourism to be impacted so negatively. He wrote, "The agonizing statistics of the recently ended five union strike should prove sobering. The estimated loss in revenue to the Strip is in excess of $150 million and more than 250,000 visitors. . . . Neither side is totally wrong or totally right, but where oh where were the cool heads that should have prevailed? As individuals, neither hotel management executives or union bosses suffered, only the employees, the showfolk, and thousands of others who live, work, and depend on the liveliness of the lone industry for livelihood."[15]

Unfortunately, these strikes would be repeated again in the 1980s, most disastrously for the hotel musicians in 1989.

NOTES

1. 1976 Program with notations by Bill Willard, Bill Willard Collection, Box 10, Folder 2, MS 2001-17.

2. Interview with Pete Barbutti by Bill Willard, Bill Willard Collection, MS 2001-17.

3. Box 20, Folder 11, Dunes Hotel Collection, MS 93-08.

4. Weatherford, "Bandleader Johnny Haig Dies of Cancer."

5. Moehring and Green, *Las Vegas*, 201.

6. Niemann, *Las Vegas Legends*, 116.

7. Ibid., 116 ("the most qualified"), 117 ("There were plenty").

8. Hopkins and Evans, *The First 100*, 338.

9. Musicians' Wives Club Collection, Box 1, MS 2004–13.

10. Interview with Norman Kaye by Mark Tan, November 20, 1976, Box 1, Folder 38, Mark Tan Collection, MS 089.

11. Interview with Kathy Saxe, KNPR *Vegas I Remember* transcripts, Box 1, Folder 23, MS 063.

12. Interview with Heberling, KNPR *Vegas I Remember* transcripts, Box 1, Folder 11, MS 063.

13. Mark Tan, *Hollywood Reporter*, March 8, 1976, Box 2, Folder 26, Mark Tan Collection, MS 089.

14. Mark Tan, *Hollywood Reporter*, March 15, 1976, Box 2, Folder 26, Mark Tan Collection, MS 089.

15. Mark Tan, *Hollywood Reporter*, April 12, 1976, Box 2, Folder 26, Mark Tan Collection, MS 089.

CHAPTER SIX

1980–1989:
The Dog Days

Times have changed.

BURTON COHEN, Casino Executive

It's all over, you missed it, it's done.

GARY QUEEN, Musician

*L*AS VEGAS ENTERTAINMENT had reached a new low point by the 1980s. Cut-rate shows and has-been performers made up the bulk of the showroom offerings. "Las Vegas reached its peak as an entertainment force in 1965 and has been going downhill erratically since the mid-60s," remarked Bill Willard in a 1976 interview. "Yet the myth still persists that Las Vegas is the 'Entertainment Capital of the World.'"[1] *Las Vegas Review Journal* entertainment writer Mike Weatherford thought,

Gradually, between 1968 and 1975, Vegas found itself pushed across the generational line that divides cool from laughable. . . . A random look at the showroom lineup in May 1982, the dawn of the MTV era, reveals the dog days of entertainment inertia. A couple of celebrated veterans, Sammy Davis Jr. and Shecky Green. A quartet of younger but out-of-phase traditionalists—Robert Goulet, Crystal Gayle, Neal Sedaka, and Paul Anka. Two journeymen making valiant attempts to become homegrown 'stars' in the Wayne Newton mode: singer Lovelace Watkins and female impersonator Jim Bailey. . . . The rest of it was dinner theater comedies or showgirl revues, ranging from famous extravaganzas ["Lido de Paris"] to low-budget burlesque.[2]

A particularly reviled show of 1980, "Alcazar de Paris" at the Desert Inn, was skewered by Mark Tan in the *Hollywood Reporter*: "There has NEVER been a Las Vegas mainroom show as sloppy, boring, or as insulting as 'Alcazar de Paris,' now supposedly making its 'breakthrough' at the Desert Inn. . . . Barbra Streisand, Barry Manilow, the late Josephine Baker, Liza Minelli, and the original casts of shows including 'Gypsy,' 'Side by Side,' 'A Chorus Line,' etc., are the unwitting (and certainly unwilling) accomplices in 'Alcazar,' wherein their genuine talents via lip-synced recordings are at least 80% of the show's 'musical' content."[3]

"Alcazar" was a harbinger of things to come: the use of recordings rather than live music. The corporate hotel owners were no longer willing to pay big salaries for stars or productions, and were seeking other options. The entertainment writers complained vociferously about the results. The recorded music in "Alcazar" was just one of its issues. Tan thought almost everything in the show looked cheap and that the production appeared to be thrown together. He complained, "The lack of originality is particularly offensive in Las Vegas, where most of the major spectaculars have a history of being class 'A' (meaning Arden, Apcar, and Ashton.)"[4]

In a 1982 interview with Bill Willard, Desert Inn casino executive Burton Cohen blamed changing tastes for the budget cuts. "Let's make one thing clear: Every entertainer that we've had appearing in a major showroom in Las Vegas is a superb performer. . . . What has happened is that the taste of the consumer has changed. It's the inability of that consummate performer that you and I both like and love to fill the showroom. So, times have changed."[5] Cohen also argued that the "Alcazar" show was misunderstood. He championed it as a cabaret and said that people made unfair comparisons to the full production shows.

Cohen was clearly planning to continue taking the Desert Inn in a new direction. To illustrate his thinking, Cohen told Willard the following story: "Last New Year, we had the Jimmy Dorsey Orchestra here for a private party, big band, the old standards. When the Jimmy Dorsey Orchestra performed it was me, my girl friend, and one other couple up dancing. In between, at intermissions, we had a disco. You couldn't get on the dance floor. These were all my prime customers. I lit up my cigar and I said 'ooooo, times have changed.'"[6] Other executives and entertainment directors were also seeking showroom productions that were more afford-able and geared toward younger audiences.

Some of the hotels still maintained the old standards, most notably Caesars Palace. Caesars Palace was still maintaining a star room policy, and the musical director there was Al Ramsey. In 1981 there was still enough interest in the hotel orchestras for the *Las Vegas Sun Magazine* to serialize a feature about the main bandleaders in town, and Ramsey was featured. Ramsey got his Las Vegas start in the late 1950s as part of the Nat Brand-wynne Orchestra and came to Caesars when it opened. He booked the lounge and contracted the orchestra, and "as Caesars grew, so did my job," he said. Ramsey said he was one of the only directors left with a large bud-get—over $2.5 million for the three Caesars properties—and he was very proud of his orchestra. "I know that everyone else [the other orchestra lead-ers] feels the same way, but our group thinks alike, talks alike and, as for our string section, it really is second to none," he said.[7] The quality of enter-tainment at Caesars had always been high, but now Caesars was more the exception than the norm.

The continued downward spiral of casino entertainment worried many of the long-time participants in the industry. What should be done? In an interview in 1984 producer Matt Gregory reminded readers that entertain-ment was the main attraction in Las Vegas. "If the attraction was gaming, the guy who has the little casino at the Nevada-California border would be get-ting all the business," he said. He worried hotel executives who knew noth-ing about the business were playing too large a role in the hiring decisions. In a remark that seemed to be directed to executives like Burton Cohen, he said, "A hotel owner who suddenly becomes a talent buyer isn't doing the establishment any good. He's satisfying his own ego." Worst of all, Gregory stated, was that Las Vegas had lost its pride. He remarked, "From the man-agement to the lowest worker, pride has been beaten out of them. . . . Peo-ple look down on our city, but we've done nothing to correct it. We respond to stupid comments regarding Las Vegas, but we do nothing to get the piz-zazz back. We've always said Las Vegas is the Entertainment Capital of the World, but we haven't paid any attention to it."[8]

The staleness was not confined to the area of entertainment: everything on the Strip seemed to be stagnant. There were no new casinos being built, no new ideas, and very little forward momentum. Historian Eugene Moehring said that most people want to forget the Las Vegas of the 1980s, the early 1980s in particular. "Las Vegas was in an unusual transition," he said. "The town was dying and needed something new."[9]

Casino workers in general began to report less job satisfaction after the corporations took over management of the hotels. Barney Vinson, an author and a casino executive of the Dunes Hotel, cited a survey taken during the 1980s that showed 80 percent of all dealers in Las Vegas would rather be working at something else. The main problem was the poor treatment they received. One dealer complained, "[The casino will] leave you on a table without even telling you you're working overtime. Like your life is nothing, and it doesn't matter if your husband is out in the parking lot waiting for you at 4:00 in the morning." Vinson noted, "On the average, a dealer makes $27 a day plus tips. He's at the tables eight hours a day, seeing people lose their money, their temper, and drink themselves into oblivion. It's enough to send anyone to the monkey house." While conceding that the corporations were increasing profits exponentially, Vinson was still troubled. "Certainly, Las Vegas is on the move," Vinson admitted. "The biggest, most glamorous hotels in the world are here. But I think the casinos are going to have to change their attitude towards their employees *and* their customers in order to keep the people coming in."[10]

The 1980s started badly. One of the greatest disasters in Las Vegas history occurred when the MGM Hotel caught fire on November 21, 1980, killing eighty-five tourists and hotel employees and injuring another seven hundred.[11] This shocking event raised numerous questions in the public mind about hotel safety. It took months to discover what had caused the fire and what had made it spread so quickly. The investigation of the disaster eventually focused on "the hotel's greed in constructing the resort and on a series of installation and building design flaws," according to *Las Vegas Review Journal* reporter Glenn Puit.[12] Ignoring the recommendations of the fire marshal, the hotel builders had refused to install a $192,000 sprinkler system during construction, and a Clark County building official had sided with the resort. "All they wanted to know is what the code stated," said Clark County fire marshal Carl Lowe. "A fireman can see a lot more than the average citizen. But with builders, all they see is dollar signs. The building code was a little outdated for that time in Las Vegas." Authorities later said the sprinkler system could have prevented the disaster.[13]

The MGM was not the only hotel without a sprinkler system in 1980: the Las Vegas Hilton, the Flamingo Hilton, the Desert Inn, and the Riviera did not have sprinkler systems either. After the catastrophic MGM fire, some hotel owners chose to retrofit sprinkler systems and some did not. Then, on February 10, 1981, the Las Vegas Hilton caught fire with 79 percent of its 2,700 rooms booked, in the prime time of the casino occupancy. Juliet Prowse had just performed her opening number when Hilton Entertainment Director Dick Lane quietly interrupted to ask the audience to evacuate in an orderly fashion.[14]

Eight people died and 252 were injured in the fire, later determined to have been set by an arsonist. After this new disaster, a bill that required all hotels, motels, office buildings, and apartments higher than fifty-five feet to have sprinkler systems was passed by a large majority in the Nevada legislature. This new law also required sprinkler systems in the showrooms and other gathering places of more than five thousand square feet.[15]

The first fire at the MGM Grand had other consequences—less deadly but still serious. The MGM Grand was home to "Jubilee!," a Donn Arden spectacular with a cast of 124 and 1,100 costumes designed by Bob Mackie, Ray Aghayan, and Pete Menefee. The show, which was in rehearsals at the time of the fire, was a typical Arden over-the-top epic that included a forty-foot replica of the Titanic. Arden and his choreographers were all staying at the hotel in rooms on the seventh floor. Though all of them were able to escape, the fire destroyed the "Jubilee!" sets and costumes and caused a nine-month delay opening the show. Additionally, almost four thousand people were put out of work with no warning.[16]

Lisa Viscuglia was working with Sasha Semenoff's strolling string group for the MGM Grand Hotel at that time. Fortunately, she was not in the hotel when the fire broke out, though she heard later that it had been smoldering behind the wall during their set. In the early morning, she received a phone call from her mother telling her that the MGM was burning. Viscuglia described the eeriness of walking through the completely blackened halls of the hotel with security on the day after the fire. Even though the musicians' dressing room had not caught fire, the smoke and water damage were so severe that all the costumes were ruined, and one violinist had water damage to his violin. Still, she felt very lucky: many people had lost their lives in the disaster, most from smoke inhalation.

The fires were the first problems in a long decade of depression. Financially, the corporations were showing profits but Las Vegas was no longer a glamorous place, and the changes saddened many. By now, few hotels still maintained connections to organized crime and corporations owned many casinos. One of the final Mafia holdovers, Frank "Lefty" Rosenthal of the Stardust, narrowly survived a car bombing on October 4, 1982. After that, he left Las Vegas and lived in Miami until his death at age seventy-nine. His colleague, the notorious Tony "the Ant" Spilotro, was killed by the mob in 1986. These violent events signaled the end of an era.

The corporations had made the gaming industry more respectable, with regulations that stopped the profit skimming and kept organized crime away. Now the executives were looking for different kinds of tourists. For a brief period, Las Vegas was even advertised as a family destination. In 1985 the National Finals Rodeo was held in Las Vegas for the first time. Revenues from the former loss leaders like food and beverage services and entertainment were greater than those from gaming.[17] Arguably, the corporations managed this on the backs of the workers, as they struck for better pay, better working conditions, better benefits, and job security through the 1980s and 1990s.

All the while, musicians continued to move to Las Vegas, unaware that the business had changed. The music industry was saturated and the competition was tough. Local musicians sometimes resented the newcomers, particularly if they perceived the recent arrivals as a threat. The union took steps to protect the local jobs, requiring longer residencies before a musician could accept work. By the time trombone player and conductor Dick McGee moved to Las Vegas in the 1980s, the union rule was that a person had to live in Las Vegas for at least thirteen weeks before being hired for full-time work. While waiting out his time, McGee worked as a substitute teacher. McGee remembered,

> I knew that what I needed to do was to get my name around, and so the best way to do that in those days was to hang out at the union building. They had a bar, a nightclub in there; and they had

kicks bands, rehearsal bands, that would play every night. And so for the first few nights I went to the Musicians Union and just sat there listening to the bands. It wasn't very long, just a few nights, before somebody needed a trombone player. . . . The guy I was sitting next to was a great trombonist here in town. . . . He kept throwing me lead trombone parts. And I knew what he was doing; he was trying to see what kind of player I was. And so I did okay.

It turned out that the trombonist was the contractor for the Dunes Hotel, and because he liked what he heard, he said he would try to hire McGee as soon as there was an opening. McGee was elated, but three weeks after making his connection, the contractor was fired from his Dunes job. McGee said, "My whole world came crashing down."

In the meantime, McGee was getting calls for the kicks bands. He said, "Within just a few weeks, I was playing in nine bands . . . for nothing! But, it was great! You started getting to know the people. . . . A lot of working people would play in the late bands for fun, and they would drink, and they'd party and go home at sunrise. The downside of that lifestyle was that I would get home at 5:30 in the morning, then at 5:45, the phone would ring and it's the substitute office at the school district." For a few months, McGee continued to substitute teach for money during the day and network with musicians at night. Eventually, he landed full-time work and was on his way.

Two musicians from out of town who were resented by the local players were horn player Beth Lano and harpist Kimberly Glennie. They came to Las Vegas together from Indiana in 1982 at the request of Wayne Newton and were almost tricked into leaving town. Lano recalled, "We were to start at Caesars Palace. We were [staying] in the Tropicana Travelodge and we were told we would have rooms when we got there. I'd been little Mary Sunshine, jamming in the car . . . hanging the horn out the window sometimes. Just having a great time! She [Glennie] was the one that was a little bit concerned that this might not be a good idea. I had borrowed $200 from my Mom's boss and that was all the money that I had."

When they arrived, there were no rooms reserved for them. The Travelodge had one room left, with one bed, so they shared. In the morning they discovered that the windshield of their car had been deliberately cracked. The two women stayed at the motel and waited for a phone call from

Newton's organization. And they did get a call, just not the one they were expecting: "We don't need you. Go back. We hired two guys from Detroit."

"I was pissed," said Lano. "Now, it was Kim's turn to be little Mary Sunshine: 'No, we are going to get dressed up and go to Caesar's Palace and tell them that they can't do that to us!'" Glennie added, "I became livid." Glennie was suspicious of the caller because she did not recognize the person's name, so she called the Newton organization directly. It had all been a hoax from someone who clearly wanted them to leave town.

Though gender discrimination was still a reality, Glennie said that she never believed that this was the cause of their troubles. More likely, it was a local musician who resented outsiders coming to town to take work away. Glennie said, "It would be . . . [someone who] would hate the thought of bringing somebody in to do a job that somebody here could do. . . . It was totally ridiculous because they're bringing in, I mean, a harpist and a horn player? What kind of multi-level threat are we? I still have experiences out here where people are so territorial."

Violinist Patricia Saarinen (later Harrell) first came to Las Vegas for the wedding of a friend who was marrying Liberace's orchestra conductor. She saw many of her college friends from Indiana University who all wanted her to come back to town for the summer and work, so she did. Marty Harrell, her boyfriend at the time, was a bass trombone player for Caesars Palace. The Caesars's contractor Al Ramsey hired her to substitute for another violinist, one who was going on maternity leave. Soon Harrell was working at Caesars Palace full time playing for stars like Frank Sinatra, Ann Margaret, Tom Jones, Sammy Davis Jr., and Dean Martin.

Almost immediately Harrell was asked to become a member of a new string ensemble called the Palace Pops, for which she did some writing. She also strolled a lot at the old MGM with other string players, walking around the restaurants playing popular songs and taking some requests. Harrell strolled from 6:00 P.M. to 12:00 A.M., changing costumes three times. She performed in evening gowns, and wore the highest stiletto heels.

Because she also had her teaching credentials and a master's degree in music education, Harrell spent her days teaching in the new string program for the schools. Harrell also played the usual gigs and weddings. One gig in particular stood out in her memory: "I played for the wedding of two

Labrador retrievers! We played things like 'How Much Is That Doggie in the Window?'" She remembered that she got the job through Liberace. "The wedding cake was in the shape of a fire hydrant. . . . It was a double collar ceremony. The owner of the female came out with a shotgun!"

Guitarist Gary Queen first came to Las Vegas with a touring production of "Chorus Line" that performed at the Desert Inn in the early 1980s.[18] Las Vegas had much more desert when he first arrived. "The landscape was like being on the moon!" The cost of living at the time was very low. "It was really nice living. An incredibly easy place to live, the 24-hour aspect, the town was small then." Queen decided to buy a house in Vegas to use as home base. "However, in 1983 when I told some of the musicians that I was thinking of moving here, most of them said to me, 'It's all over, you missed it, it's done.'" And it did seem that things were slowing down. Still, he was able to work, although, he said, "I certainly wasn't working steady." For the first year, he earned only about $11,000, playing sporadically. Still, he thought, "I think I got extremely lucky right away, because I had only been here a few months."

When he was not performing, Queen worked the phones, talking to all the guitar players who were in the showrooms about subbing for them. Between 1983 and 1987 he worked many small gigs. "I was working the phone, sending out résumés." Queen also did the kicks bands. "I didn't sit and wait for the phone to ring. Also, at the same time, I was cultivating . . . more classical guitar, doing solo gigs." He was able to substitute for the harpists who worked in the gourmet room, playing classical guitar. "I feel very lucky that I play the instrument that I do."

Finally, he became a part of the Hilton house band in 1987. "That was a lucky break." Still, it was not the gig he hoped it would be. "My job at the Hilton would be to come sign in on a list, make sure his [the star's] guitar player was there, and leave! And that was my job. And it was 80 percent pay at the time. I would leave the house, sign in, and be back in my house within an hour's time." Queen, who really wanted to work, found it frustrating. Still, there were times when he could live the Las Vegas musician life that he had heard so much about. "There were a few weeks where I would do the opening act in one hotel, run down the street and do the star in the other hotel."

In spite of the difficulties, the hotel musicians were still having some fun, still playing pranks on each other, and still enjoying most of the stars. Kim Glennie recalled the freewheeling atmosphere that usually prevailed on the Wayne Newton shows. "I had no harp parts . . . so I could play anything I wanted whenever I thought I should be playing and pretty much Wayne wanted that from anybody. If you had something that you thought you should inject, inject it! . . . We had this one drummer. . . . Les was famous for being able to play everybody's part from his drum kit." Beth Lano agreed. "I think Wayne sensed that we would get bored. . . . We had surprises which did keep it somewhat interesting." She noted that Newton would give out bottles of liquor at each show: one for the strings, one for the winds and brass, and one for the rhythm section. Howard Agster recalled a trumpet player who came out onstage during Newton's last number, dancing and covered with balloons. As he danced, he would stick pins in the balloons, bursting them, until he was finally dancing in only his jockey shorts.

When Newton sang "MacArthur Park" he used a rain curtain, a type of water feature that made it appear to be raining a wall of water at the front of the stage. One night, the band got particularly rowdy and many of them began taking off parts of their clothing and throwing them down on the stage, to the great amusement of Newton. Fortunately, the audience could see none of this. "Nobody got naked or anything!" Lano said. "It wasn't as if we completely disrobed. People were pulling off shoes and I think there might have been a pair of pants down there." As it got closer to the time for Newton to sing "MacArthur Park," he devilishly began edging some of the clothing into the gutter for the rain curtain where it would become soaked. "Instead of wondering what we were going to do, I climbed down off the scaffolding," continued Lano. "I crawled down . . . and Wayne was standing up in front with his guitar singing 'Walkin' My Baby Back Home.' I got on my hands and knees and came out of stage left. . . . I'm picking the stuff out of the rain." When she got up to Wayne she looked up and said "Don't mind me." She added, "I thought for sure I'd get yelled at. But I thought, well, if I get yelled at I'll get out of it somehow." In the end, the musicians got their clothes back and Lano got away without getting in trouble. But the band probably thought twice about tempting Newton like that again.

Glennie recalled the time a musician's bouffant hairdo caught fire from something in the lights during the Newton show. Another fire, this one at the "Solid Gold" show, was apparently caused by the musicians themselves. Trumpet player Tom Snelson recalled smelling smoke as firefighters came onstage and ended the show. Later, Snelson said, "I see the fire marshal, the stage manager and the bandleader, and this fire marshal is standing there with this smoldering paper airplane." Bored, some of the musicians had tossed paper airplanes that accidentally found their way into the hot stage lights.

Rebecca Ramsey recalled one incident that was remembered slightly differently by many, involving a fish and Bobby Scann's trombone bell. "This is the way I remember it: They'd been out on a fishing trip. We were playing the Cher show. These guys took a frozen fish and stuck it in Bobby's horn. . . . All of a sudden, he blew out a really loud note and blew out that fish. It landed right at Cher's foot!" D. Gause added, "He took a mighty breath, and blew mighty hard. [Cher] didn't miss a beat, not Cher. That's one bright woman." Patricia Harrell added that she was the one who actually put the fish in Scann's horn. Harrell said that Scann told her the story this way: He had just returned from a fishing trip in Utah without any fish. Some of the band guys went out and bought a frozen fish before the show. During the opening act of Cher, the male band members took off their ties and jackets and left them hanging on the backs of the chairs. Just before Cher came on, Scann got on the bandstand, reached into his pocket, and found a fish tail and scales. He just laughed it off, but wondered why his trombone still had a fishy odor to it. The guys had also put a frozen fish in his trombone bell and the cold temperature on the stage caused it to stick to the inside bell of his trombone until his horn warmed up and the fish came flying out of the bell. He thought that Cher never saw it.

Las Vegas shows were still very dressy affairs at that time, and some entertainers had specific costume requests. Harrell said, "We dressed! We dressed like crazy." Beth Lano enjoyed the glamour of dressing up for a show with one exception: a show that called for white dinner jackets for the men, all-white "something" for the women. "If you've got an ass at all, and you're wearing white, you might as well be a Queen size bed. Freshly laundered. That was pretty disgusting. The white outfits and the big hair!" While most musicians are used to dressing up for concerts, Lano pointed

out, "Strip black is way different than concert black. It was almost a contest sometimes to see who could wear the 'strippiest' dress. Even if it wasn't
sequins it had to be kind of a hot dress." Sometimes, she continued, there
were expectations concerning dress aside from the concerts. "Working for
Wayne, especially if you were a woman, you didn't go to McCarran airport
if you weren't dressed up. There was an image there."

Harrell enjoyed the glamour: "'Vegasy' dressing was all our idea. Basically because we wanted to glam it up, because we could!" She recalled
wearing white dresses for Wayne Newton and blonde wigs for Bobby
Vinton. Unlike most classical musicians, "We could get away with a lot
more. . . . We could do what we wanted."

After the MGM fire disaster, Lisa Viscuglia found work at the Excalibur
as part of a variety show that went on all day featuring fifteen-minute spe-
cialty acts: jugglers, magicians, contortionists, and so on. With a friend, she
formed the act "Lisa and Laszlo," with "cheesy Hungarian accents and comedy," playing gypsy music and wearing gypsy costumes. Viscuglia adapted
to the changing industry successfully, more so than many others, because
of her flexible personality.

With so many of the traditional stars failing to attract enough tourists to
the hotel, many entertainment directors tried switching to a country music
focus, hiring famous singers like Dolly Parton for big salaries and featuring
large country music production shows. Viscuglia was part of one such spectacular called "Country Fever" at the Golden Nugget Hotel that featured
dancers, singers, and a full band. The musicians had some choreography
of their own, including a "step out" number for Viscuglia where she went
into the audience to perform, rather than staying with the band onstage.
The violin number, the *Smoking Fiddle,* ended when Viscuglia flicked a
switch with her chin and smoke came out of the special violin she used just
for that song.

The most memorable moments usually involved their interactions with
the famous headliners. Gary Queen played guitar for Bill Cosby's opening act and said that Cosby would wander onstage in his bathrobe and slip-
pers. One night, Cosby sat down next to him and started yelling out chord
changes.

Another night, woodwind doubler Thom Pastor was listening to the conductor of his group scolding the members for dress code infractions. George Burns, then in his nineties, walked out and tapped Pastor on the shoulder. "Relax. Don't you know none of this means shit?"

Bassist Ed Boyer remembered seeing Johnny Carson sitting backstage by himself before each show where anyone could easily approach him; most of the other entertainers tended to stay in their dressing rooms until it was time for them to perform.

McGee mentioned a lot of performers that he enjoyed and said that his favorites were all "nice people. Johnny Mathis. . . . If you had ever held a golf club, Mathis wanted to talk to you. Steve Lawrence, he's still got it. . . . Amazing. . . . A really nice guy. Musically they were always right on the money, very consistent." Beth Lano also considered Mathis a favorite: "Johnny has such a dedication to his own craft and to the musicians." Cellist Barbara Gurley added that Mathis was always careful to maintain his voice and was a gentleman. "It felt like family," she said. After the show there would often be parties and gifts.

Pat Harrell said that Smokey Robinson would bring a dozen roses for the women, bottles of wine for the men. "He would deliver them himself!" She added that Ann Margaret remembered everybody's name and that Diana Ross remembered "things you were doing." Some of the stars would hang out with the hotel musicians after the shows or during breaks. Harrell said that Johnny Mathis liked to get a softball game going with the orchestra during their time off. "We played 'Trivial Pursuit' with Natalie Cole," she recalled. "Doc Severinsen, fabulous player, would hang out with band. . . . [He] was one of us," said Dick McGee. Dean Martin was "a real gentleman . . . [and] so musical. Never got over his son's death. He just couldn't get over it. . . . I felt so sorry for him." Dean Martin's son was killed in an Air National Guard crash in 1987 and many of the Las Vegas musicians said that Martin was never the same after that. Tommy Check said that the usually social Martin became more reclusive.

Suzanne Somers, while she was still on the television show "Three's Company," also had a big Las Vegas show with multiple costume changes. She kept the show exciting by continuing to talk to the audience as she moved behind a screen, where two dressers would quickly change her from one costume to another. Dick McGee recalled one night when the costume changes did not go quite as planned. During the first show, Somers had emerged from the screen wearing a sexy, high-cut, slinky dress, with shorts underneath. "Second show, she goes out in the slinky dress. . . . I look up. . . . The girl [dresser] had forgotten to put them [the shorts] on. I started missing notes. . . . All of a sudden you started hearing everybody else in the band missing notes! She realized what was going on at some point, but she was a trouper! She finished the song." Later, McGee recalled, Somers told the band, "I knew there was something wrong when I felt this breeze."

As with any job, working with the same people every night could also take its toll. "It is not like you don't like everybody, but it's a lot of tension," said Kim Glennie. Tom Wright agreed, "I kept a lot of stuff in. It was like a family. You loved them and you hated them. I saw them more than I saw my wife." Sharon Street-Caldwell added that she started smoking just to have an excuse to leave the stage.

It was critical to have the right mental attitude. "I made it my business to get along with everyone. There were some difficult people for sure," said Beth Lano. One musician remembered a conductor that would turn his back while conducting if he was angry. Another remembered the concert-master who was so busy picking on people that he accidentally sat down on his own violin, smashing it. "I've never heard the string section be so quiet!"

Fights were not uncommon. D. Gause recalled that some couples who worked together fought viciously backstage, but who, once in front of an audience, behaved perfectly. Lisa Viscuglia once did three months of rehearsals, twelve hours a day, for a show that never opened. The hotel that cancelled it, owned by Steve Wynn, was loyal to the musicians and employed them as a show band called the Naked Martinis in the lounge. Sadly, Viscuglia recalled, that job "disintegrated into a pile of dust when the guitar player beat up the music director!" Viscuglia, who was on pregnancy leave, heard that there was some type of explosion between sets. The music director sued, the case was taken to court, and the music director still has hearing loss in one ear to this day. What were they fighting about? She answered, "Who knows! Personality difference is what we'll call it."

At the Tropicana, a corporate casino, there were fights, and the band room was filthy. Dick and Joan McGee came in once on a day off and cleaned. "It was an experience," Dick said wryly. They found trash and dead rats, as well as things that had rolled under the bandstand throughout the years. Tom Wright said, "It was not a healthy place."

It was especially difficult when production shows went on for years: "You take a bunch of people who are basically much higher in creativity than the average person and then make them work . . . in an assembly plant, so to speak," said Don Hannah. "I can remember how I felt when I found out that the show that we thought was going to change had been signed for another eighteen months. I was drinking probably three bottles of Maalox on the bandstand a week." Tom McDermott remarked, "That's tough . . . playing a production show over and over. Tougher on the horns, I'm sure. There were cliques, especially in production shows." When McDermott began doing production work, after having worked in the lounges, "it took its toll. I started to cook. . . . I wanted to do something creative."

The production show parts for brass players had become even more difficult and taxing than they were in the 1970s, and they played the same music over and over. "The problem with playing a production show like that two shows a night, six nights a week, is that you can do some serious damage to your chops," explained Beth Lano. "And I did, I did. I have some chop problems that I still feel the remnants of today. It's basically a flexibility problem that just doesn't seem to go away." She recalled that the mental and physical pressures could be devastating. "Nobody tells you when you take a job, 'What happened to the last guy?' 'Well, he hung himself.'" She realized that warming up carefully was the most important step for her. "I was one horn in a pretty loud brass section, so it was sink or swim." Tom Wright remarked, "These people who were true musicians, it just grated on them. . . . no matter how well you tried to play it . . . you go nuts." He would sometimes find that the nights ran together. "I've actually sat there, played like an hour, turned to the guy next to me, and said, 'Have I been playing?'"

Dick McGee, concerned about the lack of job security when working the star rooms, specifically sought production work to support his family. The trade-off was that the music was simultaneously more difficult and more dull. He said,

Production shows go on for almost two hours, and the band goes non-stop. A hundred twenty pages of music, twice a night. Really,

really hard work, like playing a circus. It was a whole different kind of thing than playing the star rooms, and in a lot of ways, not as fun. When you play the same music every night, I mean every night, twice a night . . . you get to know everybody's weaknesses in the band, and their strengths. You either learn to live with them, or you start saying things to people. . . . There were guys in the band who had not spoken to each other in months.

McGee played seven and a half years at the Tropicana in a production show six nights a week, twelve shows a week. He liked the steady work and the variety of musical styles in his particular show but thought everything else was a downside. Still, he said, "I prided myself on trying to keep a positive attitude. . . . I was very, very happy. . . . You could tell who the strong people were and who was going to survive." Production show jobs were great if you were looking for steady work, but "most people were not happy," said McGee. After the strike of 1989, he started teaching at the community college and found it very therapeutic. "I thought I had all this mental discipline, that it wasn't affecting me." McGee found that he loved working with the students. "It reminded me of why I got into music," he said.

The volume level in the showroom pits could be deafening. All of the musicians found themselves playing louder and louder to be heard. One musician called the Occupational Safety and Health Administration (OSHA) to complain. When the representative came with the decimal meter, the very first note of the opener pegged the meter at 135, well over the safety limit of 90 decibels. The OSHA agent refused to say the sound level was a health hazard, however, because the sound was too loud for him to take an accurate reading from the meter. More than one musician interviewed for this book has suffered extensive hearing loss.

Conditions were often cramped and uncomfortable, depending on where the band was placed. At the "Folies Bergere" show in the Tropicana showroom, Ronnie Simone said that the band was so packed into the pit that they called the union to complain. The bandleader said, "Alright guys, get into the pit and get out your instruments. I'll tell you what, those guys that feel uncomfortable . . . [,] why don't you get out and make more room?" No one was willing to take a chance, so no one got out. Simone continued, "The union guy said 'Any complaints?' Of course, no one said anything." One hotel built a hydraulic stage for the band and responded to one musician's fear of heights by giving him a seat belt. Ralph Pressler said that the air was so bad in his showroom that a white fan he kept on his stand turned black in just a few weeks of use.

As before, many musicians coped with the issues by drinking or doing drugs. It was hard on people and on their relationships. Kimberly Glennie remembered,

> It was a time when being a real character was . . . part of what was honored. . . . [It] was an asset. What they always said was, "Man, he's out. He's out there." The more "out" you were, the better. I don't know if anybody has mentioned how many of those people are dead. A higher number than average met an untimely end. If you didn't drink or do drugs, you were the exception. Drinking . . . on the road that would get so out of hand. Totally out of hand. I knew a gentlemen who is now dead who had to be cut out of his boots at night because he would have the DTs . . . and the band played on. I knew one of our players who visited . . . sex places, spent every free hour visiting all of that. He's dead of AIDS. . . . If you are somebody who is sucked into that, drugs and alcohol . . . that's a vortex. I don't care who you are. . . . You can't sustain a good marriage.

One musician did not want to remember the past. "I have nothing to say. Vegas destroyed everyone I loved."

An industry-wide strike in the early 1980s led to the demise of entertainment seven days a week. Now the hotel showrooms would have one or two dark nights with nothing going on. The Johnny Haig Relief Orchestra, formed in 1968 and working until 1983, was put out of work when the hotels no longer needed a seventh-night orchestra. Ever pragmatic, Haig concentrated on contracting for conventions, tirelessly promoting his musical groups and finding other types of performers for a wide variety of events. His business files contain many proposals and letters to various entities outlining the types of productions he was able to do for them.

Relentless self-promotion was becoming necessary for many musicians, and most had not had to do it in the past. Cellist Barbara Gurley wrote a promotional letter to Bill Willard, in his role as critic for the *Las Vegas Review Journal*:

> With the music situation being what it is . . . especially concerning string players . . . and the lack of work . . . I would like for more of Las Vegas to know TRIO SERENATA, simply because, as professional musicians . . . we make a living with music, and if Las Vegas turns into a ghost town for musicians . . . which it certainly seems to be doing . . . TRIO SERENATA will have to concertize elsewhere! I would hate to see Las Vegas lose all its best musicians, but without employment, and without support, the musicians will have no alternative but to pack up and go! So . . . while we are still alive, and very active . . . please find some time to join us on one of our next performances.[19]

Another observable trend was that the orchestra names were no longer mentioned in many of the show books; there was a gradual noticeable drop-off of mentions until none appeared. Though the individual musicians were seldom mentioned even in the golden age, the orchestras themselves, named for their leaders, appeared in the programs. This omission becomes more troubling when one realizes that every other person who had a role in the production, no matter how minute, appears to have been credited in print, down to the least-involved office worker. Many of the musicians already felt invisible, down in the pit or even in a separate basement, unseen by the audience. Their sounds were often manipulated by sound technicians, some who had no real right to that title and who knew very little about professional sound. Now they went without even the most basic recognition in the show program.

To be fair, these industry changes were taking place everywhere: often musicians receive little to no acknowledgement by name for their work. Most movie and television credits, scrolling down the screen long after the show is over, credit every individual person, even those distantly involved in the production, but almost never list the musicians by name, as though crediting these talented players is somehow excessive or would take too much effort. Omitting not just the individual names, but also any mention of an orchestra, was an unexpected development in the "Entertainment Capital of the World."

Many welcomed the innovations brought in by the millionaire owners and the corporations, and many were happy with the new legal Las Vegas. The growth of the city continued at a rapid pace and in 1985 a $315 million expansion project of the McCarran International Airport was finished.[20] Most of the citizens did not miss the mob owners, but some did miss the more personal business model.

Owner Jackie Gaughan tried to keep the spirit of old Las Vegas alive in his hotels. Gaughan owned a number of different properties in downtown Las Vegas, but he was usually associated with the El Cortez. Gaughan was a genuine and unique person. He routinely made the rounds of his hotel, speaking personally to his employees, most of whom he knew by name. He once kept his own son waiting while he chatted with a busboy, even though his son was holding a $300,000 check. In an interview given in 1989, Gaughan remarked, "They [the corporations] seem to operate them [the casinos] alright, doesn't seem to make that much difference. There's not the personal touch of the old days, but I'm still operating mine [his hotel] the same way. In the 50s and 60s, the hotels were owned by individuals and you knew them all. Now, they make a lot of quick changes."[21]

The most forward-thinking and influential individual in Las Vegas was, and probably still is, Steve Wynn. Wynn arrived in Las Vegas in 1967 and started out small downtown, eventually revamping the Golden Nugget gambling hall into a resort hotel and casino. A visionary, Wynn brought a new look and level of class to the Strip when he built the Mirage Resort Hotel and Casino, which opened on November 22, 1989. The Mirage was the first new Strip property in sixteen years, and it is impossible to overstate the impact that Wynn had on Las Vegas from then on. Historian Hal Rothman said, "Calling Steve Wynn a genius and a visionary is a cliché, but his conception and the boldness of his execution still inspire awe. . . . The corporations that owned the hotels were endowed with cash, but lacked imagination. . . . Wynn understood the public's desires: experience they could taste that gave them the illusion of culture. The gamblers understood only their wallets, and the corporate hotels their business needs."[22] Wynn brought back the specialness and glamour of early Las Vegas without the profit-skimming and corruption.

His ideas about showroom entertainment were also revolutionary. He

gave the magicians Siegfried and Roy their own showroom for a production
that thrived for years, he was responsible for bringing in the wildly successful Cirque du Soleil shows, and he supported homegrown talent like popular impressionist Danny Gans. Most of his shows used live music, though
some, like Siegfried and Roy, eventually used taped music. Wynn played
no real role in the 1989 strike, but was largely supportive of live music, with
a few exceptions.

For the hotel musicians the building boom that followed the opening
of the Mirage came too late. Liberace died in 1987, the same year Dean
Martin's son was killed, and other tried-and-true entertainers were no longer a draw. Corporate casino ownership was the norm and the glory days for
hotel musicians were about to come to a definitive end. When the corporate
owners decided to cut the hotel bands in favor of synthesizers and tapes, the
rank-and-file of the union musicians were left behind while the rest of Las
Vegas boomed. When you speak to Las Vegas musicians, especially those
who have been in town for a long time, you cannot avoid talking about "the
strike of '89." It was this strike that ended the golden age of live music in Las
Vegas and forever altered the lives and careers of all the working musicians
in town. The good times and good money were over.

NOTES

1. Interview with Bill Willard by Mark Tan, 1976, Box 1, Folder 84.

2. Weatherford, *Cult Vegas*, 6.

3. Mark Tan, "Las Vegas Review: Alcazar de Paris," *Hollywood Reporter*, April 22,
1980, Box 2, Folder 28, Mark Tan Collection, MS 089.

4. Ibid.

5. Interview with Burton Cohen by Bill Willard, November 26, 1982, Bill Willard
Collection, MS 2001-17.

6. Ibid.

7. Elliot S. Krane, "Orchestra Leaders of the Strip: 6. Al Ramsey of Caesars Palace,"
Las Vegas Sun Magazine, March 18, 1981 ("as Caesars grew," "I know that everyone").

8. Barbara Lawry, "Las Vegas May No Longer Play the Starring Role in modern 'Tale
of Two Gaming Cities,'" *Las Vegas Sun*, July 22, 1984 ("If the attraction," "A hotel owner
who," "From the management").

9. Ed Koch, "Another Stardust Tale," *Las Vegas Sun*, November 12, 2006.

10. "Working in Las Vegas Casinos Not So Glamorous, Says Author," *PR Newswire*,
March 1, 1988, Bill Willard Collection, MS 2001-17 (all quotes).

11. Timeline, *Las Vegas Sun*, http://www.clarkcountynv.gov/depts/fire/Pages/MGMHotelFire.aspx.

12. Glenn Puit, "MGM Grand Fire: The Deadliest Day," *Las Vegas Review Journal*, November 19, 2000.

13. Deidre Coakley, *The Day the MGM Grand Hotel Burned* (Seacaucus, NJ: Lyle Stuart, 1982), 161.

14. Ibid., 159, 181.

15. Ibid., 184.

16. Ibid., 17, 185.

17. Ainlay and Gabaldon, *Las Vegas*, 141.

18. "Desert Inn Las Vegas NV, A Chorus Line 12 pg prog. 1982," *Worth Point*, http://www.worthpoint.com/worthopedia/desert-inn-las-vegas-nv-a-chorus-line-12-pg-prog.

19. Letter from Barbara Gurley to Bill Willard, March 1, 1984, Bill Willard Collection, MS 2001-17.

20. Hall-Patton, Mark. "McCarren International Airport," *Online Nevada Encyclopedia*, *(ONE)*, September 27, 2010. http://www.onlinenevada.org/articles/mccarran-international-airport

21. Bill Moody, "Jackie Gaughan: Others Move, but He Keeps the Faith on Fremont Street," *Nevadan*, September 17, 1989.

22. Rothman, *Neon Metropolis*, 45, 46.

CHAPTER SEVEN

The Strike of 1989

*The hotels have taken a small union and beaten
it into the ground. I hope they're happy.*[1]

BILL CALLANAN, Musician

It was a losing cause.

HOWARD AGSTER, Musician

ON JUNE 3 OF 1989, when the Musicians Union went on strike against five major hotel-casinos in Las Vegas, the union took on technology and technology won. When the smoke cleared one year later, the union had lost pretty much everything, and the corporations that owned the casinos had won a major victory: the right to use taped music and synthesizers in place of live musicians. Many musicians lost their jobs and left town permanently. Those who stayed had to find new ways to make ends meet. And while they may not agree on the cause of the strike or the way the strike was handled, they feel sadness for a way of life and work that many believe will never come back.

A variety of events have been singled out as the first indication of trouble, or the beginning of the end. One of the earliest signs was when the pay scale for lounge musicians was separated from the pay scale for showroom musicians and then lowered in the mid-1970s. Lounge musician Ken Harkins, interviewed by Bill Willard in 1976, said, "They [the union] excluded us from the bargaining agreement." Both the local and national union leaders disputed this claim, but the complicated legal difficulties arising from contract negotiations were the cause of much bitterness.[2]

Ed Boyer was one of the musicians who worked in both the lounges and the showrooms. He attempted to be philosophical when the lounge pay was lowered. "The hotels are always trying to save money," he remarked, "and that's just a part of doing business from their standpoint. I can understand it. I don't like it, but I can understand it. They don't want to pay us any more than they can help, and we want to make as much as we can." Nevertheless, Boyer thought that this issue was the first sign that there might be trouble in the future. Ralph Pressler agreed: "They put a pretty good wedge in the union when they separated the lounges from the showrooms."

Another factor that led up to the 1989 strike was that the cost of bringing stars to Las Vegas continued to increase exponentially. With certain popular stars, the hotels got into bidding wars for entertainers. Sharon Street-Caldwell, along with several other musicians, thought that this signaled "the beginning of the end." The bidding wars were one constant between the mob casino owners and the corporate owners; another was copying successful ideas to death.

The scrutiny of costs and the resulting budget cuts played a major role in setting up the strike. The corporation rule was that every department had to pay its own way, meaning the entertainment division had to support itself on ticket sales. President Frank Leone mentioned some of the earliest cuts in the 1970s such as the elimination of the dinner show and the end of seating captains and food servers. Soon the corporate analysts were questioning the numbers of musicians being used and the kinds of instrumentation. Ed Boyer said, "They brought in the bean counters."

The early casino owners were willing for entertainment and food to take a loss as long as they made money in the casinos, and they wanted only the best musicians and headliners to make their clients happy. "In my opinion, it was a lot better for us then," said Boyer. Composer, arranger, and musician Don Hannah agreed: "Things ran very well. There was no petty crime. The 'boys' let it be known that if you did anything like that, you'd be in the ground. But it wouldn't be our ground. . . . They would take you to California! Then, Howard Hughes came in and changed the whole face of things and the corporations then sneaked in. Many of the corporations were not operated any better nor did they have any more scruples." Boyer and Hannah were not alone in their opinions about the mob-run casinos. Many of the musicians said that, for them, things were better before the corporations came to town.

According to former Local 369 president Mark Tully Massagli, the prevailing attitude of the early casino owners was that gamblers were superstitious. If the band was good and the casino was making money, leave things alone. The owners did not expect the lounges to be profit centers, and the open lounges created excitement. They wanted you to drink, gamble, and stay over. They wanted to keep you in the hotel. Johnny Haig agreed. "The way 'the boys' worked was simply this: Get the people to come here. Lure them into the hotel, treat them like a king and let nature take its course. They will drop everything they've got . . . even if they have to lie, they will tell everybody how much money they won." Music and entertainment directors were not questioned about the number of musicians they needed. The money was there to pay for what was deemed necessary for the show. As long as the musicians arrived on time, did their job, and minded their own business, all was well. D. Gause put it this way: "Show up, do your business. . . . Just do your job."

Most musicians also remembered that the old casino owners were nicer to them in general. Mark Tully Massagli remembered that when his parents were sick in 1957 one of the casino owners came over and put $100 in his pocket, "[because] I know you are having a tough time." He said the boys always treated the musicians well. Tom McDermott added, "The 'boys' knew everybody . . . from the dishwasher, all the way up."

Other factors were also at play. Don Hannah remembered the old MGM (now Bally's) opening a show called "Hallelujah Hollywood!" with the band in the basement. The stage set was so large that there was simply no room for the band on the stage. The bandleader kept the show together by watching the performers on a closed-circuit television; the sound was artificially mixed and amplified. Hannah remembered seeing the mixing board the MGM was using and thinking, "That thing was obsolete five years ago." With the balance of the band no longer controlled by the bandleader or the band, they were at the mercy of the sound technicians. One musician observed that "many soundmen were not musicians," which had a negative effect on the overall band sound. In other words, the band sounded bad. Many of the musicians felt isolated and missed feeling they were part of the show.

Dave Hawley said that, without a doubt, his worst gig ever was in the basement of Bally's for "Hallelujah Hollywood!" and later "Jubilee!" He remembered, "The worst thing about it was the fact that we were in the basement and there was no contact with the audience at all. It was horrible and the guys were very unhappy on that band. It was hard for me because I believe in being positive and being happy. . . . I like to be in the moment and be happy. . . . It was just negative. . . . Everybody was in one way or another, going kind of nuts down there, it just made people crazy."

By the time Beth Lano got a position in the "Jubilee!" show band, the musicians had already been moved to the basement. "I looked around that room and saw that the conductor was conducting with headphones, a click track and a monitor. The headphones and the click track didn't bother me nearly as much as the monitor did, because I remember thinking 'This is the death knell.' And it was." Since the musicians were not shown, there was no longer any reason to dress up for work. She said,

> Now there was a certain beauty in being able to go to work in your jammies or whatever you happened to wake up in. But, no, I'd rather dress like a 'hoochie mama' and be seen. Orchestras should be seen. . . . When you emerged from that basement and went out you were like rats coming out of the sewer. But it was still a good time. It's about as close to an assembly line job as you can get, but yet you still have a certain camaraderie with people who are in the same boat, or basement as the case may be, as you.

Frank Leone also thought that moving the Bally's band to the basement was one of the early signs of trouble and said that the union opposed it. "People couldn't see the band. This paved the way for complete replacement, at least in production shows, with pre-recorded tapes. . . . Once musicians are out of public eye the next step is to replace them with taped music."

Once the "Jubilee!" audience stopped hearing the real band sound and could not see the actual band, they never noticed when the live band was replaced by a machine. With the altered sound, the live band had sounded every bit as canned as the taped music, so there seemed to be no practical advantage for having live musicians there for the audience. Don Hannah figured that one of the people in charge decided that since no one saw the band, why have one? Since the audience was only hearing a poor reproduction of the band sound, they thought a recording sounded better anyway.

Frank Leone stated that it was

the advent of technology, better technology, that led up to the strike of 1989. As the sound improved, it got to the point that you could replicate so faithfully. . . . The point is, prior to recorded sound, musicians were not merely musicians, they were magicians. That was a magical thing that happened when someone came in and played the flute or clarinet. You were a magical person because you had this magical ability to transform the mood. Recorded sound put an end to that because it made it commonplace. . . . Musicians get treated with indifference because they've made your magical art commonplace, and readily available because of technology. And the end result is that you are treated with indifference. Someone thinks, "Oh, I can go buy that." . . . The musicians failed to realize technology was getting better and better.

The musicians were quick to point out the problems with the use of taped music. Sharon Street-Caldwell said, "There *is* an advantage [with live musicians] . . . because the band can adapt to the dancer's problems, or vamp when the juggler loses his things. . . . You lose that with the tape." Professional musicians adjust to unusual events onstage and create nuance based on the performance as it is happening. "But one glitch [with a tape] and it all comes to a crashing halt," said conductor Tony Costa.[3] Another musician, Bill Callanan, remarked, "Putting tape music to back up a Las Vegas spectacular show is not money saving but money wasting and any show that uses that practice is going to be a second rate show. Why don't they just make a videotape of dancers and eliminate all human beings from the show? They could save a fortune."[4]

In the spring of 1989, the Musicians Union was set to begin new collective bargaining agreement negotiations with the Tropicana, the Hilton, the Flamingo, Caesars Palace, and Bally's (referred to by the media as the "Big Five"). The various other unionized casino employees had already begun their new contract negotiations in late May, including the two largest: Culinary Workers United Local 226 and Bartenders United Local 165. These negotiations were quickly settled.

The musicians' union wanted to protect what it had, maintain the status quo, and keep the same number of musicians working, but the hotel management saw an opportunity to get rid of the musicians completely. As the hotel owner's position became clear, the union decided it had no choice but to take action. Frank Leone, who was not the union president at that time, said, "The case had already been won in the Supreme Court, where employers could not be denied the use of technology. . . . The only method that we have of dealing with those entities that would take advantage of the professional musician is the withholding of services." So the union decided to strike at the Tropicana Hotel in June of 1989.

On June 3, 1989, the very day that the International Alliance of Theatrical Stage Employees (IATSE) Local 720 (known as the Stagehands Union) unanimously approved their contract offer, the musicians went on strike at the Tropicana Hotel. The Big Five were asking for unlimited use of tape-recorded music and synthesizers, something that was unacceptable to the musicians. Hotel officials were expected to meet with the union on June 3, but instead sent a letter requesting a meeting on June 5. In the letter, there was nothing that indicated a willingness to negotiate over the use of taped music, according to Musicians Union president Mark Massagli. Massagli, speaking for the musicians, said, "What we're looking for is job security so our people can make a living at this business. We don't want to be phased out."[5] Si Zentner, the bandleader at the Tropicana, thought there was no choice but to strike. "It was either do it today or do it tomorrow. They want to replace our band with tape and I'm quite concerned we can't let that happen."[6]

From the beginning, most of the musicians believed that the strike would not last long. Many, like Bill Trujillo, expected to picket for no more than a few weeks and then go back to business as usual. It soon became clear that the hotel owners were seeking dramatic change, however. According to *Las Vegas Review-Journal* reporter David Finnegan, about fifty members of the union picketed on the first night. The strike meant that the "Folies Bergere" show at the Tropicana had to be abruptly cancelled for an indefinite period. The musicians were hoping that the hotel management would eventually see things their way. "We're not after money," said Tropicana woodwind doubler Jay Volney. "They want to replace us with tapes. They want to take our jobs away."[7]

Tropicana president John Chiero responded in a prepared statement:

"The union has steadfastly demanded that the show be prohibited from using modern tape technology which will enhance the quality of sound for the show. There are no longer any legitimate reasons . . . to accede to the union's outdated prohibitory demands." The statement did acknowledge that, as a result, there would be an inevitable dislocation for thirteen members of the house band. The hotel executives proposed offering severance pay but refused to back away from their stance on using tapes and synthesizers without restrictions.[8] Within the week, the Big Five offered a similar buyout plan to musicians who would be displaced by technology.[9]

Many musicians were surprised by the strike. Trombone player Dick McGee recalled,

I showed up to the Tropicana to work and I was told by colleagues of mine in the union that we were striking . . . and I was not happy about that. They had been in negotiations for several months. We were all under the impression that the hotels were taking a hard stance on a lot of issues. . . . Everybody on the musicians' side thought that as it got closer to the zero date that we would just make a deal and go on. . . . A strike vote was not taken by the rank and file. . . . I don't mind telling you that I was not happy about it. I thought it was ill-advised.

Quite a few people agreed that the musicians had become complacent. There had never been problems before in the negotiations for contracts, so most people were not worried. There had been other strikes, including one in 1976 and one in 1984. Both of these strikes involved four unions: the Stagehands Union, the Culinary Union, the Bartenders Union, and the Musicians Union. This time, the musicians were on their own. A ninety-day clause in their new contracts prevented the other unions from striking.

The Tropicana Hotel responded by locking out the musicians. Dave Hawley was one of the musicians the hotel management told to come pick up his instruments. He was one of the few who saw the writing on the wall. "You knew it was over." Bill Trujillo said that he did not. "I figured we would go out . . . [and] get a $25.00 raise or something."

Dick McGee thought that all the strike accomplished was to accelerate the hotel's timetable. "When it comes right down to it, the union really only has one weapon . . . : withholding their services. . . . I got out of the car with

my horn and the next thing I knew, I was walking up and down the sidewalk with a picket sign, and I didn't want to be there." A week or so into the
strike, he got on the committee. "It seemed to me that [our president] was
representing us well." He thought that the union lawyer, local Dennis Sab-
bath, was "totally outclassed. I'm thinking, these people were trying to get
rid of the bands . . . so we left?"

Tom Wright, who had worked at the Tropicana for ten years, said that
when he got to work on the night of the lockout, there was a security guard
there keeping everyone out. Eventually the band members were allowed
in, but only to collect their belongings. "I've heard so many different stories about what went down, I don't know what really happened. I was looking at guys who were 50 and I was thinking, 'I'm glad I'm 30.'" Wright, who
had been frustrated already, began to fill out applications for other jobs even
as he walked the picket line. "I figured that if I found a job and I liked it,
I might not go back."

According to Kim Glennie, her husband at the time, Tom, had just gotten the Tropicana trumpet job, "the highest-paying job for trumpet in town
at the time." When the strike started only a week later, they were in disbe-
lief. Both walked the picket lines and Glennie said she did not cross the
picket line to work in any of the hotels involved in the lockout. Because of
the strike she was working very little, and her husband was not working at all.

The Stardust Hotel was one of the few hotels to sign a new contract with
the musicians. "At the Stardust, we believe that live music is a critical part
of an authentic stage production show," said Robert Boughner, the Boyd
Group senior vice president.[10] Soon afterward the Union Plaza Hotel also
reached an agreement with the musicians, followed by the Riviera. Desert
Inn conductor Lewis Elias said, "The Desert Inn is abiding by the old contract and we're just going along."[11]

El Cortez owner Jackie Gaughan believed that taped music was not
good for Las Vegas's image. As the conflict between the hotel musicians
and the corporations heated up, he noted, "We signed with the Musicians
Union already. As far as the stars are concerned, I don't think they'd work
with tapes. I think they should have live music. I'm for the musicians and
union."[12]

The musicians tried to point out how the loss of musician jobs would affect the culture of the Las Vegas community. "Almost every person in the symphony and the opera orchestras are employed at Las Vegas resorts. Culturally, Las Vegas would be a wreck," said Mark Massagli. "Putting it all together, every business person, every resident, every school kid who wants to be a musician will be affected."[13] Denis Applenan, a percussionist from the "Folies" show band agreed:

> We're all going to leave town is what's going to happen. What's going to happen when they try to have an opera? The symphony orchestra is going to go down the toilet. There won't be any jazz in the park because there won't be any jazz players to play it. The way they're going, they're going to drive all the musicians out of town. We can't play the fun things if we don't play the bread and butter gigs. Those of us who play in the house orchestras also support the arts. These hotels, by getting rid of us, are going to destroy the pool of creative musicians in this town.[14]

In spite of the striking musicians and the exchanges in the press, the Tropicana Hotel announced that it would reopen "Folies Bergere" with taped music. Mark Massagli responded that taped music cheapened the show. "Las Vegas spectaculars ought not to be gourmet meals with plastic knives and forks," he argued.[15]

Nevertheless, many musicians remained optimistic, believing that the public would not accept a lesser product. "I think the Musicians Union is going to win this battle," said keyboardist Ronnie Simone. "I think the tourists and the people of Las Vegas are entitled when they come to this town to the best entertainment in the country."[16]

The Musicians Union responded to the Tropicana by running an ad in the *Los Angeles Times* to warn potential tourists of the strike and how it might affect their travel plans to Las Vegas. The Nevada Symphony Orchestra and several other arts groups took out advertisements in Las Vegas newspapers supporting live music. In response, John Giovenco, director of Hilton Hotels Corporation and later president of Hilton Nevada Corporation, pulled his financial support from the orchestra.[17]

With negotiations at an impasse and bad feelings increasing on both sides, it soon became clear that the success of the strike depended on two things: getting tourists to avoid the hotels being struck and convincing the star headliners not to perform at those hotels. In the early days of the strike, most of the famous entertainers were firmly on the side of the striking musicians. "I don't want to see my friends the musicians go the way of the dinosaurs," said Robert Goulet. He warned that corporate thinking meant that "even the men's room has to make a profit." Sammy Davis Jr. said, "We can't have this town, which was built on live entertainment, live music, go the other way. Don't let them do this thing to us. . . . There's no way I could have made it in this business without the guys and girls in the back. I've been a saloon singer for sixty years. Without the ladies and gentlemen of the orchestra I wouldn't have been there sixty days."[18] Jerry Lewis remarked, "If we lose live music in this town, you have serious problems."[19]

An article the following month in the *Los Angeles Times* included further remarks from singer Robert Goulet: "I've been working with musicians all my life, and, holy mackerel, you just can't compare it. A singer like Sinatra needs to have his string sections, he needs to have the beautiful background music and balance. Performers such as myself, Tony Bennett, and Andy Williams may want to change tempo. We're not robots, we use our emotions and we just can't perform to taped music."[20]

The vice president of Human Resources at Bally's responded by saying, "We feel taped music is appropriate for production-type shows."[21] Tom Bruny, the publicity coordinator for Bally's, pointed out that "Jubilee!" had used an orchestra located two floors underground, out of the view of the audience, and that this orchestra was already being enhanced by the use of tapes.[22] What real difference would it make if they were replaced? And even the headliners who were supportive of the musicians did occasionally admit that they could see the value of using taped music in certain situations, though not in the celebrity rooms.

By the end of July the musicians prepared to play their last live "Jubilee!" show at Bally's. Bally's switched immediately to using taped music with only one day off, which was the normal dark night of the show. That same night, the musicians began striking at Bally's. As the Big Five hotels continued to negotiate as a unit, musicians at the Flamingo Hilton were preparing for the worst. Soon they joined the other striking musicians. By now, the ongoing strike was front-page news every day, with no resolution in sight. Dean Martin cancelled his engagement in the Bally's showroom as picketers carried signs saying "Keep Live Music in Las Vegas" twenty-four hours a day.[23] This line was in addition to the picket line at the Tropicana, which had been active since early June. News of Martin's cancellation appeared in the *Boston Globe*. "I'm saddened by the musicians' union strike which occurred today at Bally's and by the effect it has had on many people. Any time people are out of work, it is personally upsetting," Martin said.[24]

Information about the strike began to appear in other national newspapers as well, such as *USA Today*. The first article was written before the official strike began. Joe Delaney, a *Las Vegas Sun* columnist, was reported as saying, "With tapes, it's not a live performance anymore. This isn't an assembly line here." The representative for the hotels claimed otherwise, saying that the use of tape and synthesizers would trim orchestra sizes and cut costs, while not harming the spectaculars. "We just want to utilize what everybody else is utilizing," said Ira Sternberg of the Tropicana Hotel.[25] Another briefing appeared in *USA Today* once the strike began. The president of the Musicians Union of the United States and Canada, J. Martin Emerson, was moved to comment on the news from Las Vegas. "If the casino hotels get their way and continue to eliminate musicians in their main showrooms and replace live music with records and tapes, it will have a devastating effect on both the music industry and indeed, our entire American culture."[26]

Opinions vary as to whether the public was or was not supportive during the strike. McGee believed that "everybody was sympathetic with the musicians. . . . That part of our history would go by the wayside." When musicians Lisa Vazzana and Sharon Street-Caldwell stood on Tropicana street and held up signs that read, "Honk If You Love Live Music!," a Las Vegas newspaper published a photo of the two. Many people did respond with a blaring horn. "It may sound corny, but sometimes that's the only thing that encourages us," said Dave Ringenbach on the picket line, as he held the hand of his four-year old son.[27] Frank Leone also recalled that there was a lot of sympathy for the picketing musicians from the hotel clientele who would say things like, "I'm sorry that I'm here." McGee added, "It was very, very encouraging[, but] it wasn't going to change the minds of the hotels."

Many local residents were also supportive. "The guy who ran Shakey's

Pizza decided to help out the musicians," said Gary Queen. The owner offered some of the musicians work as performers in his restaurant. Queen played banjo music at Shakey's during the day and then walked the picket line from ten at night until two or even four in the morning. While banjo was not his first instrument, "I learned early on in this thing [business], you never say no. You say, 'Yes, I can do that!'"

Dave Hawley saw it differently. "In my opinion, they [the press] were biased for the hotels. . . . And to be fair . . . strikes always look to the outsider like the people on the street look like they are wrong." The casino owners put out press bulletins that made the strikers seem "unreasonable. I think it is very rare for the public to side with strikers. Because the other people have all the power of the press . . . they just look like they are right. You are doing something unseemly. . . . You are causing problems. It was very sad."

The union paid rotating groups of picketers to walk twenty-four hours a day at the hotels and was using up its money reserves quickly. With several resort hotels being struck twenty-four hours a day, the union soon was forced to pay picketers who were not musicians to fill in the gaps. Musician Denis Wilson remarked, "The music business has gone from a full-time job to a part-time job. There's a number of musicians that have full-time day jobs. They have families. They don't have time to be out here."[28] Dick McGee said, "I would go teach during the day, and I would walk a shift at night. The hotels knew that all they needed to do was to hold out."

By now, forty-five musicians had been fired and replaced with taped music and synthesizers. More headliners cancelled their appearances at Bally's, such as singer Connie Francis and comedian Rodney Dangerfield. Caesars Palace had been added to the picketing lines, forcing the cancellation of the Dionne Warwick and Burt Bacharach shows. Johnny Haig, who was working at Caesars Palace as music director, recalled the night the Caesars Palace strike was called. "Burt, to his credit, said, 'If we're on strike, we're on strike together.'" He ordered up some alcohol for everyone and took the night off. When Haig told the hotel management that the band could not work, they still kept him on the payroll. Caesars Palace violinist Carlene San-Filippo said, "We want to work, we don't want to be on strike. The rehearsal last night was very depressing. We were hoping management would start talking. But we have to fight for live music."[29] Bacharach issued a statement supporting the musicians. "I'm a musician, I always have been and I'm very supportive of them. A musician's work is his or her life and I feel terrible to see them have their work potential diminished."[30]

Eventually, some stars did cross the picket line. The first was illusionist David Copperfield, though his opening act, singer Bill Medley, cancelled his appearance. "This is a very difficult decision," said Copperfield. "My first responsibility is to the audience, especially when people come from out of town with their families to see my show, which has been previously advertised." Copperfield was sympathetic with the musicians and did donate money to the union strike fund.[31]

In August two labor organizations cancelled their conventions because of the strike: the Assembly Democratic Caucus, scheduled at Caesars Palace, and the International Brotherhood of Painters and Allied Trades, scheduled at Bally's. The union and the hotels both spun the story different ways, with the union claiming huge financial losses for the hotels, and the hotels denying any significant financial impact.

Also in August, Caesars Palace officials were surprised by the appearance of an additional 350 picketers sent from the National Treasury Employees Union (NTEU), who were attending their national convention at the Riviera Hotel. According to an article in the *Las Vegas Sun*, "(NTEU public directions director George King said the government workers union is dedicated to stopping automation when it interferes with or inhibits human contact." [32]

The first real break for the musicians came when the other union locals said that they would consider honoring the union's picket line if the talks remained stalled. The ninety-day grace period that prevented the other unions from striking was almost over. Many of the unions were considering action. In the meantime, the Tropicana officials indicated that they would seek court action to prevent a sympathy strike or walkout. Still, the discussions among members of the other unions prompted the hotels to send an attorney to meet with the Musicians Union. In return, the other unions promised to keep working as long as the negotiations continued in good faith.[33] In the meantime, George Carlin also refused to cross picket lines, though he said he was not lobbied by either side. "Obviously the easiest way to explain it is I'm sympathetic with the strike. I'm not crossing their picket line." Carlin added, "No one wants to be a rat or a scab or a fink. I've never done it and I don't want to do it now."[34]

The news continued to make national headlines. Michael Greene, the president of the National Academy of Recording Arts and Sciences, made a statement supporting the musicians. "We are here to contest the erosion of live musicians from the music-entertainment scene as a whole, not merely the Las Vegas part of it. I don't want to be a part of a generation that witnesses the genocide of an entire spectrum of performing musicians."[35] He added, "The live musicians helped make these hotels and showrooms vital, prosperous businesses. We urge all parties to do the right thing and opt for quality and keep Las Vegas a showcase for live entertainment."[36]

It got harder to get people to walk the picket line. Dave Hawley said, "It was tough." Because of the heat, he would put a bag of ice on his head under his cap to try to keep cool. Another musician walking the picket line, trumpet player Jimmy Monroe, described it this way: "This is like having a terrible score you have to play over and over again, something that stinks from the first note. It just keeps dragging on. You get sick of it, you hate it, but it's got to be done because we can't let them do this." Musicians tried to keep their spirits up by offering impromptu concerts.

One family with two musicians working on the Strip had a very negative experience with the picketing. Speaking anonymously, one of the couple said, "The union, I have harsh words. The union turned inward on itself and it punished people that were working for them. I got called in for not spending enough time on the picket line. I had been out there at one point with my two little kids in strollers and we were getting egged by people passing by." Soon, the family was sinking fast. The couple could not afford to pay for a sitter for both of them to walk the picket line, so they would take turns. "There were times when [one of us] would stay home and [the other] would go captain the line." After being reprimanded by the union, this musician was very upset. "I went, 'Are you guys nuts?'"

Percussionist Howard Agster was also on the picket line when somebody threw a water balloon out the window that hit his wife and really hurt her. He chased the car for two blocks but could not catch up to it. Another musician recalled being hit with dozens of frozen eggs. "A couple of the guys chased them down and threw them a party." Of the strike, Agster said, "It was a losing cause."

"For some reason or another, I don't know why, they decided to make me a line captain," said Gary Queen. His only job, he said, was to give strikers permission for bathroom breaks. "That was why they paid me the big bucks," he said. In other words, he made $10.00 an hour instead of $5.00.

On August 25 negotiations came to an abrupt halt fifteen minutes after they started when the hotel attorney said that the hotels would not respond to the union's proposal until September 11. Claude "Blackie" Evans, executive secretary of the Nevada AFL-CIO (American Federation of Labor and Congress of Industrial Organizations) said, "They [the hotels] said they had pressing matters to attend to. There's nothing more pressing than having people on the picket line. Eighteen days, nineteen days is too long to wait. It [negotiations] should be tomorrow. We were prepared to sit in there until midnight."[37] He contended that it was unreasonable for the hotels to take so long to respond to a compromise offer. A strike or walkout of all union employees seemed imminent. "Obviously we want to do everything we can to support the musicians and this [a sympathy strike] may be the step," said Dennis Kist, secretary treasurer of the Stagehands Union Local 720. "We have quite a few [members] biting at the bit to do what they can do."[38] The Culinary Union was supportive, but hoped that sympathy strikes were unnecessary. The Painters Union Local 159 spokesperson also indicated that a sympathy strike might be in the works.

The new proposal from the musicians at the end of August called for rehiring the forty-five fired musicians, a pay increase (after no increase for the six previous years), and a yearly retainer for musicians who worked the showrooms instead of a guaranteed number of workweeks. The idea of a retainer was a new one, and something that the hotel management determined was actually more costly than guaranteeing a certain amount of work. The hotel management responded angrily in the press, saying that the offer was not a compromise but an escalation of financial demands. The hotel executives were infuriated and the union officials were angry, too, and accused the hotels of bad faith negotiations. Blackie Evans said the delay in negotiations showed that the hotels were not negotiating in good faith.[39] A hotel executive anonymously remarked, "They knew where

we stood. They said in the press they were coming up with something creative. But what they showed us was regressive, in a big way."[40] John Giovenco, president of Hilton Nevada Corporation, was particularly scathing
about the idea of retainers. "We don't want anybody on a retainer. We really
don't want a house orchestra." Giovenco also claimed that the Las Vegas
Hilton lost $3 million annually in its celebrity room and wanted to elimi-
nate the band. He added that the strikes were having no effect on the resorts
and that the use of taped music was not a problem. "Our experience at the
Flamingo is the customer thinks that the tape we have is great and the customer is king," he said.[41]

The main issue of contention was still the use of taped music and synthesizers. With negotiations stalled again, the union called for Governor
Bob Miller to assist both sides in reaching a resolution. On August 31 the
Las Vegas Sun reported that Miller was sending his top aide to a meeting
that had already been scheduled with the Las Vegas labor leaders.

Then the hotel owners hired a high-profile attorney, Peter S. Pantaleo.
Pantaleo was, and still is, considered a top professional in the anti-union-
ism field. He would later go on work for the Las Vegas MGM Hotel to stop a
union drive in 1997.[42] His contempt for organized labor, combined with his
serious legal skills, made him a formidable opponent. With the help of Pantaleo, the Big Five dropped a bombshell: the other unions were still bound
by a no-strike clause in their contracts. "That's our legal position," said management attorney Peter S. Pantaleo, quoted for the first time in print. In a
cleverly worded remark, he added that the other unions had negotiated
"happily, without any picketing. It would be ironic if an inability to reach
an agreement with striking musicians forced the Tropicana and the other
four to close, putting thousands of union employees out of work." Pantaleo
then indicated that the hotels would "fire the employees who honored the
picket lines and sue the unions for damages."[43]

While acknowledging that the legal issue of a no-strike clause could be
interpreted many different ways, the union leaders realized that the only
way to settle the issue at that time was in a court of law, with a process that
could take years. The other unions could not take the risk that their workers would be unemployed for such a long period, and the idea of a walkout, sympathy strike, or other job action was now out of the question. "We

certainly don't want to get anyone fired," said Blackie Evans.[44] This was a serious blow to the strikers; with the arrival of the hotel attorneys came the first significant indication that the musicians might not win.

According to Thom Pastor, the Musicians Union Local 369 secretary treasurer as of this writing, this strategy was nothing new:

> The simple answer is that after 1976 there was a slow yet systematic negotiation tactic utilized by the Nevada Resort Association to "divide and conquer." Originally, many labor contracts expired simultaneously. The hotels saw how dangerous this could be when in effect the whole Strip was shut down in 1976. They began offering sweetheart deals to unions with expiration dates staggered in months and in some cases years. By the time 1989 rolled around, we, the musicians, were pretty much out on a limb. The other labor unions had 90-day clauses in their agreements preventing any sympathy work stoppages. There's more, but like I said, that's the short answer.[45]

On a meeting of the leadership from the hotels and the musicians held on August 31, the musicians agreed to return to the negotiating table and discuss a new proposal from the hotels. Though there was still no movement from either side on the issue of taped music, both sides were willing to discuss the number of musicians per hotel.[46]

By September 2 the hotel attorneys, Lawrence D. Levien and Peter S. Pantaleo, were speaking for all five hotels to the press. Levien, a high-powered attorney (trained at Harvard Law School), was also a specialist in labor relations. Using legal expertise culled from similar cases, the two lawyers sought to put holes in the musicians' case. While the other unions had decided against sympathy strikes, they did assist the musicians by walking the picket lines with them and convincing other unions not to hold their annual conventions in Las Vegas hotels. Blackie Evans had harsh words for the hotel lawyers, noting that, as outsiders, they cared nothing for the community of Las Vegas. "We think we're doing what's good for the town," said Evans. "It looks like we got a war going on."[47]

Dick McGee stated, "The hotel side had a lawyer who was very aggressive, a very expensive attorney . . . [with] a long list of credits. Nobody liked this guy, he was like Darth Vader . . . but the fact of the matter is that he was good. I wish we would have had him on our side." He also observed that the hotel lawyer used a divide-and-conquer strategy by forcing each of the hotel bands to negotiate separately.

Negotiations were eventually resumed with the governor's chief of staff in attendance. Many members of the labor groups had been urging Miller to become more involved. Evans said, "He ought to twist some arms and say this is bullshit."[48] The union backed away from the idea of retainers for showroom musicians and a guaranteed number of services, a major concession. They did, however, still demand strike pay, which the owner of the Flamingo and Las Vegas Hilton hotels referred to as "featherbedding." "They want to get paid for doing nothing," he said. "They keep saying we're against live music. That's not true." The hotel counteroffer was equally offensive to the musicians: they offered to rehire the musicians, but as computer programmers or chefs. Bill Callanan responded, "I've got a master's degree in music. I don't want to be a chef."[49] Jim Trimble also addressed this issue: "Would you send a doctor, who spent his whole life training to be a doctor, down to get a job at a gas station—which incidentally, he knows nothing about?"[50]

The musicians then gave up the demands for strike pay, but still held out for the rehiring of the musicians who had been fired. By this time, the fired musicians were really beginning to struggle financially. Reporter Joan Burkhart wrote a Labor Day weekend report on trombonist Jim Trimble and conductor Dick McGee. McGee, who had left his secure teaching position in Colorado to move his family to Las Vegas, said that if he had known that the Tropicana was going to drop the house band for taped music, "I never would have come." To keep afloat, the Trimbles cashed in his retirement account and took out a home equity loan. They also lost their insurance. "It's very stressful," said Mary Trimble, "knowing you're not going to have health insurance. . . . If someone goes to the hospital we'll have to declare bankruptcy. We have no more savings." The McGees were also concerned about their children. "They may not understand all the intricacies of the issues . . . but there's no way to hide it from my kids. It's on TV. The kids see I'm not going to work."[51]

It was clear to all at this point that there might never be a settlement. While they could not participate in a sympathy strike, the other unions still recognized what was at stake. "Today, it's the musicians, tomorrow it'll be the stagehands and the painters and the carpenters," said one labor leader.[52]

Still, many of the headliners were supporting the strike and were sympathetic to the musicians. Burt Bacharach, George Carlin, Rodney Dangerfield, Sammy Davis Jr., Connie Francis, Tom Jones, Jerry Lewis, Dean Martin, Willie Nelson, and Dionne Warwick were among the many performers who cancelled their Las Vegas appearances rather than cross the picket line.

Enter Wayne Newton. While still refusing to cross the picket lines, Newton decided to attempt to bring the two sides together. "I think that as long as there's communications, things can be resolved," he said. Mark Massagli acknowledged that this added a new dimension to the negotiations. "Wayne is a resident. He lives here. He has a boulevard named after him. He's one of us." If Newton made the decision to cross the picket lines, however, "it might make it a little easier for others to do the same." Beth Lano added, "He's in a position where he has a good relationship with the musicians and the hotels. He's in a unique position of being able to bring both sides together."[53]

The casino representatives were hoping for something else. One hotel executive said that the officials at the Big Five believed "a flood of performers" would cross the picket line if Newton did so. "At least that's what our hope is. Maybe it's wishful thinking on my part. . . . These people [the entertainers] are, above all, businessmen. This is costing them money." Some thought that the only weapon the union had at this point was the ability to keep headliners from performing. Burt Esterman, a Local 369 business agent, said, "I don't know that [Newton] is the last card we can play, but it certainly is an important one. He's a major factor in this. It hinges on him."[54]

On September 9 Governor Bob Miller and Wayne Newton met with both sides, hoping to end the labor dispute, but they did not reach an agreement. Still, many people pinned their hopes on Newton. "I don't think anyone else could have done the things he has done to bring the two sides together," Miller said. "He's been an ambassador for Las Vegas."[55] Newton, who lost $750,000 from cancelling his three-week engagement with the Las Vegas Hilton, initiated another informal meeting on September 12 between himself, Massagli, and Giovenco. Newton said, "I sincerely hope that my efforts will ultimately have a positive effect on both sides and that negotiations will continue to a successful conclusion."[56] All participants agreed not to comment to the press on the proposals until all sides had had a chance to examine them.

Around the same time, the first musician crossed the picket line: country singer Randy Travis. The union announced that they would file charges against Travis with the national union. This meant that he and his band could be expelled from the Musicians Union and fined for crossing a picket line. This event was reported in the press.[57] Ultimately, no charges were filed. Meanwhile, Diana Ross cancelled her engagement because of the strike.

For a week or so, both sides studied the proposals and the musicians seemed hopeful. By September 18, however, the *Las Vegas Sun* reported that the hotels were "unresponsive" in spite of the major concessions made by the Musicians Union. An unnamed source from the musicians said, "The hotels' position changed only in the smallest of ways. This is the most down I've been since the talks began." The new offer from the musicians required the hotels to rehire the striking musicians for at least one year. At the end of that year, though, the hotels could use taped music in their production shows and fire half of the musicians if they wanted to. They also asked to allow the existing band to make the tape and receive royalties from its use.[58]

As the musicians waited for the hotels to respond to this offer, Mark Massagli indicated that there were few, if any, concessions left for the musicians to make. Even Governor Bob Miller called Giovenco and encouraged him to make some movement and come back with a new proposal.[59]

On September 22 the *Las Vegas Review-Journal* reported that the Big Five had given the union their "best and final" offer. The use of taped music continued to be a problem and the hotels offered only twelve weeks of severance pay to the displaced musicians.[60] The musicians rejected this offer. "We couldn't even put it to a vote," Musicians Union Local 369 president Mark Tully Massagli said. "The members said, 'We don't want to even consider this.' What management proposed to use was resoundingly rejected."[61] Union spokesperson Beth Lano said, "Everybody was totally incensed at the offer. I think signing this proposal would be the end [of live music]." John Giovenco responded, "I've got $385 million in construction projects. At this point I could care less about the musicians." He also said he would not meet again with the musicians, even at the governor's request. "No," he said, "There is nothing to talk about. There's nothing to discuss. Taped music is no longer an issue. They've already conceded taped music. The only issue now is how many jobs they are going to keep. . . . Who suffers? Wayne Newton suffers. Bill Cosby and all the other entertainers suffer. We could have people come in who don't need music. Perhaps we can do a magic show . . . [or] a play."[62] Giovenco even suggested that the Musicians Union could be decertified as the bargaining agent for the musicians.

A greater blow to the musicians came from the news that Wayne Newton planned to cross the picket line. At first, neither side was sure how this would affect the strike. Some of the picketing musicians were upset. "It's a shame if he did perform tonight," said Fred Haller a Bally's musician of twelve years. "We thought Wayne was trying to help us but if he went in, it's obvious that he's a turncoat and there's nothing worse than a union musician who works behind picket lines." Musician Larue Boenig added, "It's a real downer after hearing Giovenco say all those things about how he could care less about musicians. Maybe he [Newton] felt threatened."[63] Another source said that Newton feared that Giovenco would end the star room shows where Newton worked.[64]

The Musicians Union did agree not to censure Newton after Giovenco agreed not to pursue union decertification. Newton's manager, Mark Moreno, said that Newton was primarily concerned with preserving live music on the Strip. "We're looking out for this form of entertainment as an art form. If you want to protect live entertainment, you protect live music."[65] Picketing was stopped at the Hilton because both sides were considered to be negotiating again in good faith. Twenty-two union musicians joined Newton's road band for the September 30 performance. "I'm glad we're going back to work," said Sam Cernuto, a trombonist at the Hilton. "But I don't know the terms of the agreement. We're still in the dark about it being old or new contract. We're anxious to get back to work with Wayne."[66] Unfortunately, the negotiations broke down quickly and the picket line was reestablished. Massagli blamed lawyer Larry Levien for putting a stop to the arrangement with the Hilton. He also indicated that Newton had broken his word to the Musicians Union by crossing the picket lines when the negotiations were no longer continuing in good faith.[67] Adding to the view that

Newton had betrayed the musicians, Newton agreed to fill in for Anne Murray, who had cancelled her engagement because of the strike.[68]

In one of the more bizarre moments, a group of striking musicians picketed Newton's home as he was hosting a party.[69] The Musicians Union indicated that they would file charges against Newton until it was determined that Newton's membership had lapsed and therefore he was not subject to any union disciplinary action. Instead, members of his orchestra who continued to work with him were targeted by the union.[70]

USA Today noted that Frank Sinatra would not cross the picket lines at Bally's unless the strike had been settled first. According to Frank Sinatra Jr., who worked as his father's musical director, Sinatra Sr. felt "obligated not to violate the picket line for the musicians I have worked with since the '40s."[71] *The Economist* picked up the story in November, noting, "Some of the old-style entertainers have backed the union. Mr. Sinatra has said that he will not cross the picket line. So, at first, did Mr. Wayne Newton, the embodiment of Las Vegas lounge-lizardry. He changed his mind after trying, and failing, to arbitrate the dispute." *The Economist* also correctly predicted that the musicians would ultimately fail. "The dispute, now in its sixth month, has become a war of attrition, which means the union will probably lose. For every entertainer who will not cross the picket line, another will."[72]

The union reduced its picketing to half-day picket lines at the five major hotels, both to save money and because the picketers were tired. "It appears that it's going to be a long fight," said Mark Massagli.[73] The press focused on which entertainers were honoring the picket line and which were not. Both sides speculated in the newspapers over the impact of the entertainers who honored the strike. The Pointer Sisters crossed to perform at Caesars Palace while comedian Rodney Dangerfield told Bally's that he would honor the picket lines.[74] Dean Martin joined the other prominent entertainers who refused to cross the lines, while Sheena Easton did cross the picket lines. A group of longtime Las Vegas entertainers and other unexpected celebrities (Ed Asner, Wilford Brimley, Hal Linden, and Henry Mancini) put on a benefit concert to help the Musicians Union. Mancini remarked that he could not perform in Las Vegas with taped music himself. "I wish the boys [in the Musicians Union] the best. I don't know if it [taped music] is inevitable or not. Everything is pretty much at a stalemate."[75]

Gary Queen recalled that as the strike continued into the winter the conditions were no better. "It gets cold at night in the desert." To keep warm, Queen set up a tent with blankets and a little heater. He got his power from the base of the Hilton sign. He says Hilton workers never noticed.

As the strike dragged on, even the strongest supporters of the musicians saw the writing on the wall. The *Globe and Mail* included a brief item when Frank Sinatra eventually gave in to the pressure to cross the picket lines. "The holiday season is here and it's time for everyone to get back to work," said Sinatra.[76] This was viewed as a potential death knell, in spite of the musicians' hopes. Then the singer abruptly cancelled his six-day engagement at Bally's, taking everyone by surprise. "I am informed that a settlement of the strike is possible before the holidays," Sinatra said. "If such is the case, I do not want to jeopardize these conversations and am deferring my decision to perform in Las Vegas for the moment. Leave the fighting to [Roberto] Duran and [Sugar Ray] Leonard."[77]

Seeking to fill the showrooms, the hotel owners attempted to hire foreign acts, filing suit against the government to reverse a ban on foreign entertainment during labor strikes. A federal judge ruled that the musicians could fight this move and the lawyers got to work. On December 15 a federal judge heard arguments from the musicians and the office of U.S. Immigration and Nationalization on one side, and the Big Five on the other.[78] In the end, the injunction was lifted, clearing the way to hire foreign entertainers during the strike. News of the ruling was reported in a brief in *USA Today*.[79]

The new year started with the same old story, though it seemed that with every passing day there was less hope for the musicians. According to a source quoted in the *Las Vegas Review-Journal*, "The Musicians Union has basically caved on most everything." Another hotel executive added, "In light of the preliminary injunction on the INS thing, they've basically thrown their last stone."[80] The musicians still held on. In a meeting where the hotel executives were expecting major concessions, the musicians did not act as expected. "We went into the meeting thinking there would be only five or six minor issues in the way of a settlement and that amnesty would be the major issue. What we got was a nice, little five-hour philosophical discussion and no movement on the substantive issues," said one hotel executive. "We thought there was going to be a lot of movement on the tape issue and a lot of movement on the guaranteed work issue, but there wasn't."[81]

Entertainers were increasingly crossing the picket lines and that further weakened the position of the musicians. Many of these entertainers thought that they had no choice. Rodney Dangerfield issued a statement: "I fully support the union, as I have proved, but my appearance at this time will have no influence on the outcome of the strike."[82] Led by Larry Levien, the hotels began talking about even further concessions, such as doing away with the "onerous" rates paid to musicians involved in taping, filming, or recording television programs and movies. A national union official pointed out that all Musicians Union Local 369 rates and regulations had to remain uniform with the international organization and could not be part of the Las Vegas negotiations. "He [Levien] obviously doesn't understand what the AFM [Musicians Union] clause is all about."[83]

Amnesty for the musicians who crossed the picket line remained the last major obstacle to the settlement of the strike by the end of January. At first the International Musicians Union refused to accept any side agreements, and Mark Massagli said that the local affiliate had no authority to override this refusal.[84] Massagli remarked, "They [the hotels] would have us impose no charges or fines. That's difficult from our perch because some of our members were walking the picket line for eight months. They can hardly be expected to say to those who crossed, 'We forgive and forget.'"[85] After several days of discussion, the parent organization agreed to limit fines against musicians who crossed the picket lines.[86] The union had nothing left to offer.

On January 22, 1990, after seven and a half months, a tentative settlement was reached to end the strike. The striking musicians were forced to back down on almost every issue. Nevertheless, the members were expected to approve the agreement. Union negotiator Hugh Lovelady remarked, "The rank-and-file will accept it. We will get on with our lives and most will sever their connections with the hotels."[87] The agreement called for severance payments of about $28,000 to each of the forty-five musicians who had lost their jobs, but allowed the use of taped music and synthesizers for stage productions. Only a few musicians were to be rehired, and none with a guaranteed number of services.[88] The agreement included a 5 percent pay raise.

Many of the musicians expressed disappointment, bitterness, and sadness. Bruce Armstrong, who had led the orchestra at the Flamingo Hotel show "City Lites," said, "Usually, when a strike is over, people go back to work." Bill Callanan, orchestra leader for the Stardust, added "This is the conquest of a small, tiny union, that's what it amounts to. The hotels have taken a small union and beaten it into the ground. I hope they're happy." The hotel executives responded that the musicians were the victims of changes in the industry.[89]

Mark Massagli, described by the *Las Vegas Review-Journal* as "one of the most respected and well-liked labor leaders in Nevada," met for a final time with reporters. When asked if the months of striking and negotiations had been worthwhile, he responded, "There's nothing I know of that would make an eight-month strike worthwhile."[90] Musician Archie LeCoque added, "When you're getting a payoff to leave your livelihood, what's the value of that?"[91]

On January 24, 1990, the union musicians voted to ratify a four-year contract with the Big Five, officially ending the strike. Massagli walked to the Tropicana to hug the last remaining picketer, union business agent (later secretary treasurer) Thom Pastor. Their hug was the symbolic end to a long struggle, one that ended badly for the musicians.[92] Hotels could now use taped music and synthesizers for anything they wanted. Even acts like Earth, Wind, and Fire that wanted to use an orchestra were refused, according to Tom McDermott. The hotel management said, "We don't want to get that started again." When the bands were fired, severance pay was all the union was able to negotiate.

Dick McGee recalled that the dancers at the time were not happy. Now they had to work with a recording that could not adapt to their movements, but there was nothing they could do about it. Added Sharon Street-Caldwell, "The stagehands missed us, bless their hearts."

Other hotels that had not been a part of the negotiations took advantage of the changes. Even seemingly secure groups like the Johnny Haig orchestras were affected. Ralph Pressler recalled, "It seemed to be steady work for a while, and then it started . . . well, maybe three weeks a month, two weeks a month, one week a month. And then it was a few days a month, and then a few days every other month. So that was pretty much the end of Haig's orchestra" . . . and the end of an era.

The Mirage, opened during the 1989 strike, used a recording for the "Siegfried and Roy" show. Before coming to the Mirage, the magicians took their show on the road. Because the magicians were used to working with the talented musicians of Las Vegas, they were not willing to settle for less while traveling. Once on tour, however, they could not always count on having a good band, or even a band at all. So they hired studio musicians in Los Angeles to produce a high-quality recording with which to tour, and it was this tape that they continued to use when they started working at the Mirage in 1990.

For Beth Lano, one of the most unfortunate results of the strike was the loss of so many talented musicians. "It was a watershed moment for musical history in this town. We lost a lot of good people. . . . People just kind of started trickling out of town." Bill Trujillo was one of them. "A lot of people left town. I went on the road with Frank Sinatra Sr., then Jr." Howard Agster was able to work briefly as a substitute for the Riviera show but was eventually forced to collect unemployment after that to support his family with eight children. "I thought it was sort of a waste. We [the union] lost all our money, we lost our property." Woodwind doubler Fred Haller put his house up for sale in the hopes of regrouping. "I will stay here until my daughter Cindy is out of high school. She *will* go to college."[93]

Dick McGee added that while the strike did not break the union, it almost bankrupted it. "I don't see it going back the way it was. . . . There are musicians working in this town, but I don't see it going back to what it was before." Frank Leone pointed out that, before the strike, every marquee posted names of their entertainers. Now, he said, the marquees advertised the buffet equally with the entertainers and the hotel was the celebrity. Kim Glennie concluded, "I miss the musicians I used to see all the time. . . . Every day was a story." The hotels, she continued, "don't want the musicians there. . . . They don't want them."

Some musicians blame the union leadership from that time. Said one, speaking anonymously, "It was stupid. We would still be in hotels today. The hotels just wanted to cut down. It was badly done." Others point to the hotel corporate management. When the strike finally ended, *Las Vegas Review-Journal* reporter Dave Palermo, a frequent writer on the strike, presented his own analysis of the events. "Few have been able to comprehend, for instance, why the hotels took a hard line in dealing with one of the city's smallest labor organizations. . . . If the labor dispute did not hurt the resorts financially, as executives maintained, it certainly tarnished their images, leaving the impression—truthful or erroneous—that they have little regard for quality entertainment. . . . Others contend that the union erred in taking such a firm stand against the use of taped music and synthesizers."[94] Palermo thought that the union had succeeded in generating publicity and in making the debate about the use of taped music. He said that many thought the heads of the resorts resented the musicians' success in generating favorable press coverage.

Labor observers were baffled by the hotels' move to use taped music and synthesizers in July, a move that forced the union's hand. Others thought that the lack of solidarity with the other major unions, such as Culinary, were the defining factor. "If you want solidarity, go to Poland," said musician Dave Ringenbach.[95] Many blamed the stars that crossed the picket lines. "If no star had ever crossed, it could have ended considerably differently," said Massagli.[96]

In the end, the (taped) band played on. The musicians began to reevaluate their careers in Las Vegas and the news coverage gradually ceased. Entertainment continued on the Strip and few people seemed to notice or care about what had been lost. Musician Fred Haller believed that the end of the strike marked a major turning point for Las Vegas. "They did the same thing in Atlantic City. . . . I saw the clouds on the horizon but I didn't think they'd go all out to destroy us."[97]

NOTES

1. Dave Palermo, "Settlement Called 'End of an Era,'" *Las Vegas Review-Journal*, January 23, 1990.

2. Interview with Ken Harkins by Bill Willard, April 12, 1976, Box 38, Folder 10, Bill Willard Collection, MS 2001-17 ("They excluded us"); notes written by Bill Willard, April 12, 1976, Box 38, Folder 10, Bill Willard Collection, MS 2001-17.

3. Mike Weatherford, "Musicians Fear Worst in Future of Las Vegas," *Las Vegas Review-Journal*, June 11, 1989.

4. "Musicians OK Contract at Stardust," *Las Vegas Review-Journal*, June 14, 1989.

5. Timothy Chansud, "Musicians, Stagehand Unions' Future at Stake in Negotiations," *Las Vegas Sun*, May 8, 1989.

6. Timothy Chansud, "Strike Closes Folies," *Las Vegas Sun*, June 4, 1989.

7. David Finnegan, "Tropicana Musicians Strike; Stagehands OK Contract," *Las Vegas Review-Journal*, June 4, 1989.

8. Ibid. ("The union has").

9. Weatherford, "Musicians Fear Worst in Future of Las Vegas."

10. "Musicians OK Contract at Stardust."

11. Mike Weatherford, "Caesars, Desert Inn Say Lack of Contract Won't Stop Shows," *Las Vegas Review-Journal*, July 29, 1989.

12. Moody, "Jackie Gaughan."

13. "Musicians Chief Says LV labor Dispute Threatens Community Culture," *Las Vegas Sun*, June 12, 1989.

14. Reeves, "Musicians on the Brink."

15. "Tropicana to Reopen 'Folies Bergere,'" *Las Vegas Review-Journal*, June 25, 1989.

16. Timothy Chansud, "Folies Bergere Stages Comeback without the Striking Band," *Las Vegas Sun*, June 26, 1989.

17. "LV Musicians Take Protest to Los Angeles," *Las Vegas Sun*, July 1, 1989.

18. Finnegan, "Strip Headliners Rap Taped Music" ("I don't want," "We can't have").

19. Timothy Chansud, "Entertainers Come Out in Support of Musicians," *Las Vegas Sun*, July 7, 1989.

20. Mark Chalon Smith, "Las Vegas Musicians Still Walk the Beat: 11-Week Strike to Retain Live Music 'Just Keeps Dragging On,'" *Los Angeles Times*, August 19, 1989.

21. Finnegan, "Strip Headliners Rap Taped Music."

22. Smith, "Las Vegas Musicians Still Walk the Beat."

23. Dave Palermo, "LV Musicians Union Strikes Bally's," *Las Vegas Review-Journal*, July 28, 1989.

24. Don Aucoin, "Bleaker Street; Names and Faces," *Boston Globe*, July 30, 1989.

25. Jefferson Graham, "Las Vegas battles over taped music," *USA Today*, July 11, 1989 ("With tapes," "We just want").

26. Chansud. "Bally's Showroom to Be Dark."

27. Smith, "Las Vegas Musicians Still Walk the Beat."

28. Dave Palermo, "Paid Pickets March for Idled Musicians," *Las Vegas Review-Journal*, August 5, 1989.

29. Dave Palermo and Mike Weatherford, "Musicians Strike Caesars," *Las Vegas Review-Journal*, August 3, 1989.

30. Timothy Chansud, "Caesars Hears Sounds of Silence," *Las Vegas Sun*, August 3, 1989.

31. Dave Palermo, "Illusionist Copperfield to Cross Caesars picket line," *Las Vegas Review-Journal*, August 7, 1989.

32. "Musicians Strike Garners Support," *Las Vegas Sun*, August 18, 1989.

33. Dave Palermo, "Hotels Agree to Talk with Musicians," *Las Vegas Review-Journal*, August 18, 1989.

34. Timothy Chansud, "Carlin Won't Cross Caesars Picket Line," *Las Vegas Sun*, August 22, 1989.

35. Dave Palermo, "Musicians Plan Labor Day Job Action," *Las Vegas Review-Journal*, August 26, 1989.

36. Michael L. Campbell, "Unions seek harmony on Strip," *Las Vegas Sun*, August 26, 1989.

37. Palermo, "Musicians Plan Labor Day Job Action."

38. Timothy Chansud, "Musicians' Talks Strike Sour Chord," *Las Vegas Review-Journal*, August 25, 1989.

39. Ibid.

40. Dave Palermo, "Hotels Angered by Musicians' Proposal," *Las Vegas Review-Journal*, August 29, 1989.

41. Timothy Chansud, "Giovenco: Union Lying about Hotels' Aims," *Las Vegas Sun*, August 30, 1989 ("We don't want," "Our experience at").

42. Steven Greenhouse, "Unions, Bruised in Direct Battles with Companies, Try a Roundabout Tactic," *New York Times*, March 10, 1997.

43. Dave Palermo, "Hotels Say Unions Can't Aid Strikers," *Las Vegas Review-Journal*, August 31, 1989 (all quotes).

44. Ibid.

45. E-mail interview with Thom Pastor, Local 369 secretary-treasurer, March 18, 2011.

46. Timothy Chansud, "Musician Discussing Latest Offer from Hotels," *Las Vegas Sun*, September 1, 1989.

47. Michael L. Campbell, "Other Unions Won't Honor Tropicana Picket Line," *Las Vegas Sun*, September 2, 1989.

48. Michael L. Campbell, "Miller Urged to Enter Strike Fray," *Las Vegas Sun*, September 3, 1989.

49. Dave Palermo, "Musicians Decide against Labor Day Work Stoppage," *Las Vegas Review-Journal*, September 2, 1989 ("featherbedding," "They want to get," "I've got a master's").

50. Joan Burkhart, "Striking Musicians Feeling the Blues," *Las Vegas Review-Journal*, September 3, 1989.

51. Ibid. (all quotes).

52. Dave Palermo, "Fear Keeps Labor from Joining Strike," *Las Vegas Review-Journal*, September 6, 1989.

53. Dave Palermo, "Newton a Player in Dispute," *Las Vegas Review-Journal*, September 14, 1989 (all quotes).

54. Ibid. (all quotes).

55. David Finnegan, "Governor, Newton Seek Strike's End," *Las Vegas Review-Journal*, September 20, 1989.

56. Michael L. Campbell, "Wayne Newton Joins in Musicians Talks," *Las Vegas Sun*, September 13, 1989.

57. "Musicians' Union May Expel Travis," *Globe and Mail* (Canada), September 9, 1989.

58. Michael L. Campbell, "Hotels Fail to Move on Union Offer," *Las Vegas Sun*, September 18, 1989 (all quotes).

59. Michael L. Campbell, "Musicians, Hotels Resume Talks," *Las Vegas Sun*, September 21, 1989.

60. Dave Palermo, "Musicians Handed 'Final Offer,'" *Las Vegas Review-Journal*, September 22, 1989.

61. Dave Palermo, "Musicians Board Rejects Hotels 'Final, Best' Offer," *Las Vegas Review-Journal*, September 25, 1989.

62. Campbell, "'Last Offer' A Sour Note for Musicians" ("Everybody was totally," "I've got $385 million," "There is nothing").

63. Howard Stutz and Dave Palermo, "Newton Returns to Hilton Stage," *Las Vegas Review-Journal*, September 27, 1989 ("It's a shame," ""It's a real").

64. David Finnegan, "Newton Gets Musicians' Blessing," *Las Vegas Review-Journal*, September 28, 1989.

65. Ibid.

66. David Finnegan, "Musicians Halt Hilton Picketing," *Las Vegas Review-Journal*, September 29, 1989.

67. Mike Weatherford, "Newton Crosses Picket Line for First Time," *Las Vegas Review-Journal*, September 30, 1989.

68. Dave Palermo, "Musicians Trying to Keep Stars Out of Big Hotels," *Las Vegas Review-Journal*, October 3, 1989.

69. Harold Hyman, "Musicians Picket Idol's LV Home," *Las Vegas Sun*, October 1, 1989.

70. Michael L. Campbell, "Newton's Union Membership Had Lapsed," *Las Vegas Sun*, October 3, 1989.

71. "Sinatra, True-Blue to Unions," *USA Today*, October 13, 1989.

72. "Las Vegas; Music Dies," *The Economist*, November 11, 1989 ("Some of the," "The dispute").

73. Michael L. Campbell, "Musicians Scale Back Pickets at Four Resorts," *Las Vegas Sun*, October 14, 1989.

74. "Musicians Lose One, Win One," *Las Vegas Sun*, October 24, 1989.

75. Mary Hill, "Musicians Benefit Boosts Strike Coffers," *Las Vegas Sun*, November 22, 1989.

76. "Sinatra Will Cross Vegas Picket Line," *Globe and Mail* (Canada), November 24, 1989.

77. Howard Sturtz, "Sinatra Cancels Show at Bally's," *Las Vegas Review-Journal*, November 30, 1989.

78. Phil LaValle, "Musicians' Battle Plays Federal Court," *Las Vegas Review-Journal*, December 16, 1989.

79. Brief, *USA Today*, December 18, 1989.

80. Dave Palermo, "Musicians' Talks Target End of Strike," *Las Vegas Review-Journal*, January 3, 1990 ("The Musicians Union," "In light of").

81. Dave Palermo, "Move to End Musicians' Strike Stalls," *Las Vegas Review-Journal*, January 4, 1990.

82. "Dangerfield Will Perform Next Month," *Las Vegas Sun*, January 13, 1990.

83. Dave Palermo, "Attorney: Hotels Want to Cut 'Premium' Musician Rates," *Las Vegas Review-Journal*, January 13, 1990.

84. Dave Palermo, "Musicians Strike Talks Break Down," *Las Vegas Review-Journal*, January 18, 1990.

85. "Musicians, Resorts to Return to Bargaining Table within 2 Weeks," *Las Vegas Sun*, January 5, 1990.

86. Mike Weatherford, "Parent Union OKs Musician 'Amnesty,'" *Las Vegas Review-Journal*, January 20, 1990.

87. Adrian A. Havas, "Curtain Falls on Strip Strike," *Las Vegas Sun*, January 23, 1990.

88. Dave Palermo, "Musicians Strike Ends," *Las Vegas Review-Journal*, January 23, 1990.

89. Dave Palermo, "Settlement Called 'End of an Era,'" *Las Vegas Review-Journal*, January 23, 1990.

90. Dave Palermo, "Musicians Knew Power Was Waning," *Las Vegas Review-Journal*, January 24, 1990 ("one of the most," "there's nothing").

91. Adrian A. Havas, "Musicians Formally Accept Contract," *Las Vegas Sun*, January 25, 1990.

92. Dave Palermo, "Musicians Ratify New Four-Year Contract," *Las Vegas Review-Journal*, January 25, 1990.

93. Adrian A. Havas, "Strike Finale Leaves Musicians Bitter," *Las Vegas Sun*, January 28, 1990.

94. Palermo, "Musicians Strike Ends on Foul Note."

95. Ibid.

96. Adrian A. Havas, "Union Leader Admits Star Crossings Hurt Musicians Strike," *Las Vegas Sun*, January 25, 1990.

97. Ibid.

CHAPTER EIGHT

Old Las Vegas
Is Gone Forever

I miss the musicians I used to see all the time.
Every day was a story.

KIMBERLY GLENNIE, Musician

Old Las Vegas is gone forever.

ED BOYER, Musician

WHEN THE STRIKE was finally over and the union had lost, musicians went anywhere they could get work. Anyone lucky enough to get a job offer elsewhere left the city. The remaining musicians fended for themselves as best they could. In the immediate aftermath of the strike, it was unclear what would happen next. At first, only a few musicians moved away. "It hasn't been a mass exodus," said Beth Lano in 1991. "People are just trickling out of town. People had the severance [$28,000] to live on. Others have wives who are working. A large number still are waiting around to see what is going to evolve. But it's starting to snowball."[1]

Some were able to continue playing in places like Caesars Palace, while others took full-time teaching positions. Many musicians had to find non-music jobs to stay afloat. "People worked it out for themselves," said Johnny Haig. Everybody Haig knew had to have a day job: a percussionist was doing lawn work, a trombonist became a pool man, while a trumpeter became an eye doctor.

Tom Wright began working for Farmers Insurance. He took the opportunity when it was offered because "I kind of realized you couldn't get a job . . . if you didn't have some other kind of work history than 'I used to play really loud on the Strip.' After they shut us down at the Trop, I put the horns in the case and didn't take them out again for three or four years." Bassist Bill Bailey worked for a local hospital admitting department. Interviewed in 2011, he remarked, "This was supposed to be the part-time job. But it's slowly reversed itself over the years. I'm fortunate to have it."[2]

Some players wished that they had seen the writing on the wall sooner. "After the strike of '89, there was no more gig," said Dave Hawley. "I wish I had done what I had done [initially in Las Vegas] and left town sooner, around 1982. The real goal was Los Angeles." Eventually, however, Los Angeles went through the same strikes for the same reasons. "The bottom fell out and things really changed," Hawley remarked. The music business, for better or worse, was going to be different everywhere now.

Today, the music industry continues to face many of the same challenges as it did in the late 1980s. Not only do working musicians have to fight for live music, but they also have to fight to keep studio work from being offshored to countries where production costs are cheaper. The price-saving measures seem reasonable until you consider the vast amount of profits made in Hollywood, for example. Writer Michelle Chen noted,

> Hollywood is the home of the big-name blockbuster. But in many ways, Los Angeles is a classic company town, where one industry supports legions of creative workers. For one particular class of artists, however, the business threatens to do an especially efficient job of turning their passion into penury: the recording musicians who bring you those dramatic orchestral swells of the cinematic experience are in danger of losing their jobs, as production companies go overseas for post-production work. So while film corporations ring up mega-profits, the "offshoring" of film scoring . . . is muting the city's vibrant community of working musicians. [According to the Musicians Union,] the off-shoring of soundtrack scoring for just four Lionsgate films between 2008 and 2010 resulted in a total loss of lifetime compensation estimated at $10 million for thousands of domestic musicians including wages, and no payments were made into the AFM [Musicians Union] retirement and health care plans. Meanwhile the company has gobbled up tens of millions of dollars

in tax credits from localities—a common scheme of local govern-
ments subsidizing entertainment business projects in the name of
"incentivizing" development.[3]

Just as in Las Vegas, Los Angeles as a community suffers when its musicians are put out of business. In the beginning, movie recordings were
beneficial for the entire city. "Orchestras, chamber music, club dates, and
music education in the schools all thrive because of the residual effect of
the recording industry," remarked Los Angeles violinist Rafael Rishik. Now,
if the offshoring of music continues, Los Angeles's cultural life will be negatively impacted. Chen wrote, "Public culture has driven a false dichotomy
between art and industry, viewing creative professionals more as individual
talents than as a craft workforce, which in turn undermines creative workers' leverage against a notoriously predatory business."[4]

After the Las Vegas strike, the union took a tremendous hit from which
it has yet to fully recover. To help pay for legal costs the union was forced to
sell its Tropicana property that had served as its headquarters. By 1991 several of the top positions in the union had been eliminated or consolidated to
cut costs. "It's an effort to trim the operation, which is good business," said
Musicians Union Local 369 president Mark Massagli. "It's also intended to
help us recover from the large expenditures associated with the strike. And,
as a third point, the employment is no longer here. I believe it will return
eventually, but it's not here now."[5]

The first years following the strike were grim. A *Las Vegas Review-
Journal* article written about a year after the strike ended detailed the
changes that were taking place in the music business of Las Vegas. "Most of
the people I know of, or worked with, or have worked with in the past, are
out of the business," said union negotiator Hugh Lovelady. Lovelady was
a reed player for the Flamingo Hilton production of "City Lites" until the
summer of 1989 when the band was fired and replaced by taped music and
synthesizers. "This town, entertainment wise, is rapidly becoming a joke.
Entertainment capital of the world? Ha. It's the hype capital of the world,"
he said. "What happened was inevitable," said Bruce Armstrong, former
conductor for "City Lites." "I had a good 15 years. Las Vegas was steady
employment. But it's just no longer a viable option for musicians."[6]

Bill Callanan, the former conductor for the Stardust "Lido" show, was one of the musicians who still held out hope in 1991. "In the long run, I'm sure it's going to change," Callanan said. "I'm not a doomsday type. My house is paid for. My kids are raised. I got money in the bank. I'm never leaving this town."[7] Gradually, small groups began to appear again. The Rio Hotel got a Sinatra-sized band. Shows started coming back. It seemed that perhaps live music was not dead after all. Don Hannah thought so when he was interviewed in 2005. "There will be live music," he said. "Not to the degree that we saw it at one time, but it will be here."

The musicians who continued to work on the Strip in Las Vegas during the aftermath of the strike were not treated the same way as before. The perks of the past for the headliners and bands were cut out completely as the corporate managers looked to save every nickel and dime. One sternly worded memo circulated at the Dunes Hotel stated that only certain performers were eligible for a 50 percent discount in the Savoy Room restaurant, and that everyone would be required to pay full price for the Savoy's International Buffet or Dome of the Sea Restaurants.[8] Interdepartment correspondence from Ben T. Sasaki, dated April 12, 1991, made specific note of what was allowed for the lounge performers: "Please be advised that I will permit the entertainers that are playing in the Oasis lounge to get sodas in between shows from the Oasis Bar rather than going all the way to Staff Dining as long as they do not abuse this privilege. Please instruct your bartenders to ring up on a casino comp *SOFT DRINKS AND COFFEE ONLY* (no beer or hard liquor). *THIS IS FOR THE MEMBERS OF THE BAND ONLY* (no friends and family)."[9]

The types of shows were changing, too, and now the focus was on jaw-dropping circus and magic acts with large sets and numerous special effects. Siegfried and Roy were now headliners at the Mirage Hotel, a hotel owned by Steve Wynn. Their show was spectacular, with costumes, sets, and stage effects that were bigger than ever. Reviewer Andres Martinez wrote, "The show is an exhausting, overwhelming assault on the senses, with statuesque dancers, fire-spitting steel monsters, the two aging German magicians, and some of the most majestic animals you have ever seen."[10] Donn Arden, who died in 1994, would have no doubt appreciated the concept.

Siegfried and Roy's new style production opened the door for Cirque du Soleil, a Canadian entertainment company that now presents eight Las Vegas shows. Their first show, "Mystère," found a home at Steve Wynn's Treasure Island in late 1993. It was a mixture of circus acts, dancers, live music, comedy, and an incredibly elaborate set; it was an immediate success. The production featured primarily live music with only a few taped samples.[11] Cirque du Soleil took as much care with their music as they did with all other aspects of "Mystère," and, as usual, their success led to more of the same in other hotels.

In addition to "Mystère," other productions began to hire musicians. In 1994 the *Las Vegas Review-Journal* heralded the news that live music was returning to town. In particular, there was a short-lived trend of productions based on country music. Dan Trinter, president of the Musicians Union Local 369 at that time, noted several of the country music shows were using live music: "Country Tonite" at the Aladdin Hotel, "Country Fever" at the Golden Nugget, and "Nashville USA" at the Boomtown Resort.[12]

Still, many musicians did not believe that live music was coming back in a significant way. Las Vegas conductor Jack Eglash saw no real progress, but remained hopeful. In 1994 he said, "I don't see any drastic changes, but I would hope that the opening of the new showrooms might encourage the use of more live music instead of electronics. It might get a little bit better by sheer numbers." Joe Lano was cautiously optimistic: "The groups are getting a bit bigger and we're all in favor of that. If the audience has a choice of going to a taped lounge show or a live show, I know they would gravitate to the live show because of the immediacy and presence of a live band. Tape just doesn't cut it."[13]

In spite of the optimism, there were more cuts to come. By 1996 musicians who were still working on the Strip were again struggling to keep their careers alive. Bill Callanan, who had worked for the Rio Hotel for twenty-three years, was finally a casualty of band cuts that took the seven-piece band down to only five players. "I don't want to make any real comment at this time except to say that these guys are friends and great musicians. I've enjoyed my time at the Stardust, but yes, I'll miss it." It began to seem as if things could not get much worse. "It's sad," said Dan Trinter. "A guy that once played Frank Sinatra can end up playing at your party for a very reasonable price." He continued, half-jokingly, "I think hotels wouldn't mind getting rid of entertainment completely and just playing a tape of coins clinking from the machines."[14]

In 1998 the *Las Vegas Review-Journal* ran an article called "Vanishing Musicians" that described the life of former Strip trombonist Jim Kositchek who was running a pool cleaning service. Having a full-time business made it difficult to keep practicing, though he could always take time off if a music job came up. He said, "There's so little [work] left I don't think it would make much difference if I quit or not." Kositchek even turned down an offer for full-time work in a showroom. "This is my security," he said of his business. "I'm looking to retire sooner rather than later—and the trombone isn't the answer."[15]

More than one of the musicians who stayed in town struggled with depression and anxiety. Woodwind doubler and sax player Jay Volney was one of these. After the strike, he went into a downward spiral, though he still played the occasional gig and working as the morning DJ for the classical music station. When new management took over the radio station, though, Volney lost his job there too. After the death of his mother and a series of other misfortunes, he became so depressed that he hung himself in the garage. "He never came out of it," said D. Gause. And while the loss of work after the strike was certainly not the only reason for Volney's suicide, it was a contributing factor. Musician and friend Tim Bonenfant remarked, "D. is right, but it was a long and drawn out spiral of events that took him to that dark place. . . . I would certainly say that Jay missed making a living a doing what he trained to do, and was good at. He tried to stay in 'the music business' even if that meant not being a performer. . . . But in his heart, he was a player, and that got taken away from him."

Musician Bill Bailey expressed the sadness he felt about working outside of the music field to survive. "There's something inside me that doesn't feel like a musician because I'm not playing," Bailey said. "I want to feel like a musician. . . . I'm really fortunate to have that Strip gig, but as I get older, I'm on the fringes. . . . I think most of the guys I've had my connections with are either dead or just don't play anymore."[16]

Ironically, Las Vegas was once again experiencing massive growth with new casino hotels appearing in quick succession. In 1996 the Stratosphere and the Monte Carlo were completed on the Strip, and the Orleans opened off the Strip. The Monte Carlo built a 1,200-seat theater for master magician Lance Burton. New York New York appeared in 1997, the Bellagio in 1998, and Mandalay Bay in 1999. The Bellagio, another Wynn hotel, featured the second Cirque du Soleil show on the Strip, a sensational water production called "O." Like "Mystère," this show used a group of talented musicians who were able to improvise on a moment's notice if the circus performers needed them to do so. Another new hotel, Mandalay Bay, hired the Blues Brothers (at that time made up of Dan Aykroyd, James Belushi, and John Goodman) for opening night in March 1999.[17] While individuals and small groups of musicians were still being hired, there were no regular hotel bands any more and recorded music was used for many productions.

Though most people were excited by the rapid growth of both the Strip and Las Vegas as a whole, some old-timers were skeptical. Bill Willard was one of these. Willard wrote disparagingly about the "new" Las Vegas in a letter to a friend:

> I'm not so sure that you could abide contentedly in this people/ traffic bloated 'destination,' controlled by the corporate mobsters and wacko execs (dig Sheldon Adelson of Venetian supplanting the dear old Sands, plus the ugly billion-dollar Bellagio on the Dunes corner and its blahblah owner s.a.w.). So where does one go after Vegas? . . . Lucy and I are stay-at-home, the steamy nights very much out of the loop. And so it goes and went. I still remember the town when I saw it. . . . [It was a] quaint little burg then. Let's all hope for the best.[18]

Willard also had changed careers, moving from writing reviews to heading the Arnold Shaw Center for Popular Music at the UNLV. He explained why in a letter to Mitzi Shore: "Cahners Entertainment Group, which publishes dozens of mags, bought *Variety* four years ago from the original Silverman family casting adrift many of the personnel, some of whom had been with *Variety* for several decades. I happen to have been on the payroll longer than most although as you may have noticed, the news and show reviews from Las Vegas fell off to a great extent in 1991."[19]

The biggest success story was (and still is) Cirque du Soleil. The tremendous smash hit "Mystère," followed by the equally triumphant "O," guaranteed that more Cirque shows would follow. As of 2015 there were eight Cirque du Soleil productions in Las Vegas: "Mystère," "O," "Kà," "Zumanity," "Criss Angel Believe," "The Beatles Love," "Michael Jackson One," and "Zarkana." Other hotels picked up on the formula and developed their own Cirque-type shows. It is interesting to note that Cirque du Soleil usually uses live music and that the performers and musicians improvise out of necessity. Perhaps it is this live energy that helps to make the Cirque shows so compelling. With eight Cirque shows in town, however, some might argue that it is time for a new idea.

By 2003 all the top "must-see" shows, with the exception of "Siegfried and Roy," were using live musicians rather than taped music. The groups were much smaller, and not like the full-sized big bands of the past. Still, the change was noticeable. Michael Gill, Las Vegas theater manager and consultant, said that when new producers came to him with a show, one of the first questions they asked was, "Can we do it to a track?" Though it was usually legal to do so, Gill said, "My advice is that it's not a good idea. From a marketing standpoint, it's just a nightmare."[20]

There were a number of new hotels built, beginning with the Palms in 2001, Wynn and South Point in 2005, Encore in 2006, and the Palazzo in 2008. The 2008 recession hit Las Vegas hard, especially in the housing market, but one project on the Strip was still completed between 2009 and 2010 when the City Center opened in phases with the new hotels Aria, Vdara, Mandarin Oriental, and the Cosmopolitan.

The musicians working in Las Vegas today earn their living in a variety of ways. Some are still in the lounges, some are professional players, and some are teachers. Many of the string players teach in the school system and are able to play for different acts once or twice every few months, working for whoever is brought in to the casino. The big stars usually travel with their own conductors, pianists, and drummers, and do not use a house band.

The star policy show rooms still use bands, but not on a regular basis. For example, rock-and-roll groups or country music singers usually do not need any extra musicians. It is more common for a hotel to hire a self-contained act, one that travels with its own musicians. The groups that work every night are much smaller, like those who play for the Cirque du Soleil shows. The entire genre changed: the audiences and the stars that made Las Vegas what it was have also all grown older. Dick McGee said that the hotels have every advantage now. "The star rents the room [called four-walling], then they pay for the band, the waiters, and everything else." The hotel is released from all responsibility. "The hotels don't want to take a gamble. The mentality is . . . every square foot has to make money. You and I know that forty years ago, there was no way that these shows were paying for themselves, but they were bringing people in to the casino. . . . They made their money in other ways."

Johnny Haig agreed. "The casinos don't have shows and entertainers as before. They don't want large orchestras. I'm geared down now." Haig could still put together a big band when needed. "On a recent corporate job, I made one phone call for each chair, everybody was available." Beth Lano added, "Thank God for some of the younger people coming up [that are using larger orchestras]." Tom Wright was one of the musicians who was able to start playing his instrument again, still keeping his day job at the insurance company. "You have to be the dog act," said Lisa Viscuglia. "I do my own bookings, I have my chick string group, I play in an Irish band. I have to do a little bit of everything to be employed."

Though Rebecca Ramsey was able to keep working at Caesars Palace until 2000, she also worked to create opportunities for herself. She remembered that her last show at Caesars Palace was with Steve and Eydie. "They were tearing it down as we were finishing that show." Ramsey was prepared for the inevitable because she saw that the hotels began using the band less and less. "During those years [1989–2000], it was dwindling off. They weren't using nearly as many acts that needed bands." The contract for a certain size of house band cut the band every year until there were only about four employees. (Ramsey was one of them.) "I do play for a lot of weddings. . . . Now it's really big in Vegas. I'm on the 'vendor list' for the J. W. Marriott." Ramsey also became a contractor herself, hiring string players for larger shows. "I started writing my own music. . . . I have my own CD out. I've been lucky, it is played quite often on the classical music station here." She has a Web site and makes musical arrangements. "As a musician, in order to survive, you've got to move with the times. Now it's computers and Web sites, and contracting, being on vendor lists. None of this was part of my life when I first started. . . . For me, the most difficult part is . . . self-promotion. Boy, do I hate it! It's time consuming, it's thankless, it's embarrassing. I think that even if I had stayed in college that there is no training for that." Still, this work paid off. Ramsey's CD was entered in a worldwide contest by CD Baby, a Web site for independent musicians. "As it turned out, there were 10,000 entries and it took these people a year to listen to everything." She won third place for best instrumental CD. In spite of the political maneuvering and grasping of some Las Vegas musicians, Ramsey firmly believes, "Good quality will win out. . . . Your reputation and your professionalism will win out." Even with this success, it was still hard for Ramsey not to miss what she did before the strike happened. "Last night I played with one of the greatest pianists, Ronnie Simone. . . . We had a marvelous time, just the two of us playing whatever we wanted. We had a fabulous time! It brought me back. When you get to play with a great artist like he is, that's what makes it fun."

Ronnie Simone also made the transition smoothly after the end of his job at the Tropicana. "The times had changed and they [other musicians] failed to realize it," said Simone. "Change is inevitable. I always knew that I would work. If you play piano, one way or the other, you're going to work."

Harpist Kim Glennie performs frequently, playing for weddings and corporate functions. She still gives her best, though the audiences for these events do not seem to be able to tell much difference. "In truth, you can be fabulous on these gigs and people don't know 'fabulous' from 'okay.' I think we try to be fabulous but they don't know. . . . That's just the way it is. I miss the musicians I used to see all the time. . . . Every day was a story." Thom Pastor, recently retired union secretary treasurer, thought that "in retrospect, cooler heads should have prevailed [during the strike]."

"Old Las Vegas is gone forever," said Ed Boyer. "I was there when they built it!" Now, he continued, "I would say that I am enjoying my retirement. Something that's very personal to me: I'm a Buddhist . . . for about 30 years now." He said that being a Buddhist "has really helped my life. I'll do this always. It works for me."

D. Gause now teaches clarinet and theory for the community college, continues to play in Strip shows as needed, and runs a contemporary music festival. "That's my baby. . . . Some women have children, I have a festival." The strike itself led to new opportunities for Beth Lano. While the strike was taking place, she began putting clippings and press kits together to give to the Musicians Union. Soon, she became their public relations director. The contacts she made eventually led to her first job in radio, and that turned into a career in advertising and radio work that she mixes with performing gigs.

After the strike, Bill Trujillo went on the road first with Frank Sinatra, and later with Frank Sinatra Jr. He then began teaching at a Las Vegas music store while continuing to do concerts and master classes around the world. "I started in jazz, I'm going to end up in jazz. Now I don't want to play those shows anymore. I was grateful, and I'll never knock Las Vegas with all those shows I had to play, because it was great experience. I'm playing better now than ever. When I played for those thirty years every night, I didn't practice much. I didn't want to see that horn!"

When interviewed in 2006, Gary Queen was working "an absolutely wonderful job" with Tom McDermott. "We can call tunes that we've never played before, we can do standards. . . . Nobody tells us what to do, where to stand. . . . The only comments we get are from people who love what we're doing. Actually, right now . . . things for me are better than they have ever been."

Mark Tully Massagli, who led the Musicians Union Local 369 for many years, was elected to serve as president for the national union in the summer of 1991. His departure from Las Vegas marked the end of an era for many people. "We've been through wars together. We've been in jail together," said Dennis Kist, president of the Southern Nevada Central Labor Council. "When you've gone through something like that, you form a bond." Blackie Evans, executive secretary of the Nevada AFL-CIO, said, "He's always been a steadying influence on the labor leaders in this state. Articulate. Intelligent. A real gentleman. I consider Mark to be one of the most outstanding labor leaders in the country."[21]

Johnny Haig bought land when property was cheap, excellent investments that paid off when Las Vegas became the fastest-growing city in the United States. Sharon Street-Caldwell said that the change in Las Vegas has been huge. "It seemed like there were always two different kinds of musicians: those who worked a lot, and knew this business, and they invested well, and they did well. . . . The other half . . . [thought] 'this is fun,' and they have absolutely nothing to show for it." While some musicians like contractor Haig bought property and did very well, others did not invest. "I was one of those," said Street-Caldwell. "I never expected the valley to grow."

Matt Saporita still regrets not buying property when he first came to Las Vegas in the 1940s. Back then he met a hotel desk clerk who offered to sell him some land. Saporita and a few others went to look at the site, where they could have bought five to ten acres of land for $25 down. When his band mates saw the deserted sand lot, covered with tumbleweeds and sagebrush, they roared with laughter. Saporita, however, really wanted to buy the property but was too embarrassed to do it, so he passed it up. Later, he told his father the story. Saporita remembered that his father was furious. "You had the money in your pocket and didn't buy? Stupido, stupido!" Saporita thought his father might have been right: that land is now where the Hilton Hotel and Las Vegas Convention Center are located.

In addition to the Cirque shows, several other types of productions have tested the waters in Las Vegas since the 1990s. Many people believed that Las Vegas might become the Broadway of the West based on the temporary success of several musicals in the 2000s, but that has since proven to be unsustainable on a large scale. The most successful so far was "Phantom" at the Venetian that ran for six years beginning June 12, 2006. "The Lion King" at the Luxor replaced the equally successful "Mamma Mia!" until it, too, closed in 2011. Some other musicals were also a moderate success: "The Producers" and "Spamalot" both had fairly good runs. While not all musicals seem to make it in Las Vegas, those that have made it provide great jobs for musicians. All of these shows have had orchestras of some type. These orchestras are sometimes enhanced by tapes, and synthesizers still are used to replace some instruments, but the shows provided steady work for a number of musicians living in Las Vegas.

New faces are in the pits for some of these productions. Alan Lawson is a woodwind doubler who performed with the orchestra for "Phantom." He arrived in 1978 on the advice of friends and the desire to see if he "could hang with the big boys." He is grateful to have been able to sustain a success-ful career in music, thanks, he says, to his teachers who gave him an excep-tional music background. His résumé includes over thirty Broadway shows and headliners such as Cheap Trick, Tony Bennett, and Frank Sinatra Jr., who all use live orchestras for their shows. "Although we all know the eco-nomic situation of the world today, I would certainly hope Vegas once again will become a place for lots of musicians to earn a respectable living. Maybe the general public is a bit tired of the Circus type shows and of headliners appearing with a just a trio."

Flutist Alexander Viazovtsev arrived in 2007, after winning the princi-pal flute position with the Las Vegas Philharmonic Orchestra. Things were tough in the beginning, because the Las Vegas Philharmonic is a part-time orchestra. He started teaching flute students but was finding it difficult to build a studio until he was given the chance to audition for "The Lion King." Viazovtsev was interviewed for this book while the show was still running:

> I am playing the most interesting flute book in the best show on the Strip. Talk about getting lucky! After hearing about the audi-tion for "The Lion King" I did not even think to try out—no one in the show world knew me. Right before the audition, a very good friend of mine (an old timer in Las Vegas) told me to contact Jack Gaughan [the music director] and tell him that I'd like to audi-tion. . . . I was very pessimistic about it but did it anyway. The rest is history. Jack was very nice welcoming me to the Las Vegas scene.

Viazovtsev was invited with six others to the audition. Then he had to find eight out of the twelve flutes required for the show to prepare the excerpts for his audition in order to demonstrate his abilities on each for the conductor. Viazovtsev said, "That was a quest in itself—searching the Inter-net, researching the flutes." After the audition, Viazovtsev did not believe that he would get the job. "Where else can I be so lucky to play classical music [the field I was trained in] in the great Las Vegas Philharmonic AND to play in the best show EVER? Not many places provide such an amazing variety for a classical musician. I feel very blessed indeed!" Unfortunately, "The Lion King" closed in December of 2011 to make way for yet another

Cirque du Soleil show. "Mamma Mia!" returned in 2014, this time at the Tropicana Hotel, only to close after three months of slow ticket sales.[22]

One popular type of entertainment today in Las Vegas is the large arena concert. Touring rock groups and major stars perform in the special hotel arenas, just as they do in other cities, though Las Vegas has more arenas than most. In addition to these major concerts, large showrooms have been built to house major entertainers such as Céline Dion permanently, allowing these entertainers to avoid constant touring by bringing their fans to Las Vegas. Lounge entertainment with major performers like Louis Prima is largely a thing of the past.[23]

Superstar headliner Céline Dion appears in the $95 million-theater built especially for her in Caesars Palace: the Colosseum. The humidity is reportedly kept at 55 percent under a $2 million bubble to protect her voice. Dion has a private elevator and an eight-room suite underneath the theater for her family.[24] When Dion is not performing, other big-name stars use the theater: Elton John, Bette Midler, Jerry Seinfeld, Rod Stewart, and Shania Twain, among others. In this way, Caesars is keeping the old tradition of headliner shows alive and many local musicians are part of the orchestras and back-up bands. There is one major difference between these current headliner shows and those from the 1950s and 1960s: today's ticket prices are much more expensive.

Steve Wynn himself is the creator of his new production "Steve Wynn's Showstoppers," running at the Wynn hotel since December 2014. Well-known celebrity journalist Robin Leach was very enthusiastic about the show:

> The simplicity of Steve's idea to present a jukebox medley of Broadway hit musical numbers comes to life brilliantly with the enthusiasm of the entire cast and orchestra under conductor Dave Loeb. It makes you feel exuberant even before you leave the theater, a wonderful rush of emotions, memories and lovely spine-tingling moments.
>
> I know younger kids who love the thump, thump of nightclub EDM numbers will scoff at my enthusiasm for the olden day aspects of this show, but they are missing out on yesteryear's magic. I hope

the pendulum swings full circle, and they come to realize that this is where the marriage of music, lyrics and storytelling began.

Slowly the message has been getting out there. More and more people have turned out for sell-out houses, and Steve has told me that his $10 million bet on a Broadway-themed show has begun to pay off.[25]

One show producer, David Saxe, has reclaimed the traditional Vegas-style entertainment with two productions inside the Miracle Mile Shops at Planet Hollywood: "V–The Ultimate Variety Show" and "Vegas! The Show at Saxe Theater." These shows are more reasonably priced and use smaller, less-complicated theaters. Saxe comes from a Las Vegas family of old-style performers. His father, Richard Saxe, was a woodwind doubler who worked in the relief bands. "My dad would open the front door, and he'd be in his tux," Saxe said. "He would come home after working all night, working all of the lounges. Two, three lounges a night. He worked until sunup, every day. I thought it was the coolest thing. . . . That was my routine, I thought it was normal that dads came home in tuxes at 6 in the morning, looking beat after working all night."[26]

His mother, Kathy Saxe, was a showgirl for years with "Folies Bergere" at the Tropicana, dancing her final show in 1968 while pregnant with David. Saxe is one of the few producers fighting the Cirque influence in Las Vegas. While he appreciates the impressive Cirque productions, he believes that they are "faceless and foreign." Saxe said, "I just think you have too many executives jump on the bandwagon, saying, 'I got an idea! You know what this town really needs? Another Cirque show!' . . . I know, this has happened in the past, with magicians, impressionists, everybody jumping on the bandwagon. I started [the adult dancing school] Stripper 101, and I've had one, two, three copycats. It's the same with Cirque. One worked, and they said, 'Let's do another one, and another one!'" Saxe believes there is room in Las Vegas for other types of entertainment. "Cirque is Cirque. I don't want to be Cirque. I don't want to compete with Cirque. I'm not jealous of Cirque, I actually appreciate what they've done."[27]

Another recent production that used live music was "Frank: The Man. The Music," a tribute show sung by impressionist Bob Anderson at the Venetian Hotel. This production closed in November of 2015, but provided a number of musicians work performing the great music of Sinatra's original orchestra, using many of the same charts. The advertisements prominently mentioned the phrase "featuring a live 32-piece orchestra."[28]

Las Vegas still relies on tourism as its main industry, on the top of a list that also includes Orlando and Atlantic City.[29] More than 41 million people visited in 2014, and there had already been more than 31 million by the end of September 2015.[30] One of the biggest moneymakers in Las Vegas now is nightlife. The clubs with their DJs, celebrity hosts, and rock stars attract hundreds of people every night. Wander through a major casino after dinner and you will witness a constant parade of scantily dressed women and skinny jeans-wearing men all headed to the line for the club. The flow of traffic gets heavier the later it gets. These (mostly) young people take the advertising slogan "What happens in Vegas, stays in Vegas" seriously. The stiletto heels are five or six inches high, the dresses are short and low cut. Cocktail servers dance on the tables in the casinos, most looking bored and distant, ignoring the patrons who are usually ignoring them in turn while they gamble. In the summer the clubbing centers around the pools, some of them allowing guests to go topless. And the expenses for a night out like this are high, including the costs for tables, drinks, and VIP perks like bottle service or line privileges. Some visiting celebrities and wealthy patrons "make it rain," throwing hundreds of dollars into the air, making the crowds scramble to catch a few.

The financial success of many hotel-casinos in Las Vegas is still built on the backs of all the workers, and not just the musicians. Employees of the corporate casinos in Las Vegas today are still experiencing problems. Authors Susan Chandler and Jill B. Jones interviewed a number of female casino workers in Reno and Las Vegas, from the lowest-paid cocktail servers to the few casino executives. Their subjects expressed an overwhelming sense of frustration and anxiety throughout the interviews quoted in the book, even as many fought the system, most notably through the Culinary Union. In a review of this work, writer Liz Benston stated, "The authors discovered a world where workers pop tranquilizers, antidepressants and pain medications to function. A world where financial dependence upon the job fuels paranoia and tension among co-workers competing for shifts. A world where stress, overwork, and embarrassment fuels self-loathing and alienation from family, friends, and other activities outside of work. The stories of this world are gaming industry stories, Nevada stories. But, taken together, they tell a larger tale of deep disenchantment with corporate America."[31]

A housekeeper interviewed by Benston gave just one example of the poor treatment she experienced when a corporation bought out the hotel where she works. "They're very tight and very cheap," said the woman. "In my department, they prohibit us to talk when we work. Why? I'm just working with my hands. They say, 'No, because we lose production.' They don't care about employees like a human being. . . . They think we're robots."[32] Pit boss Edna Harmon said, "It's all corporate politics. I mean, they have no feeling—there's no thought—no caring for the employees. They're just a commodity. They're something that you throw away when you're through with them."[33]

These feelings of despair can infect an entire locality. Susan Chandler elaborated, "Companies that are no longer equipped to treat people as individuals create an atmosphere of despair and low self-esteem that permeates the community. It does something really terrible to your well-being and the atmosphere of the community is to just keep your head down."[34]

It remains to be seen whether Las Vegas will continue to follow the corporate model of profits before people, or whether individual owners like Steve Wynn can bring back the more personal style of management. The Culinary Union is strong in Las Vegas, so strong that Las Vegas is sometimes referred to as "the last Detroit." It continues to fight for fair wages and fair treatment for its workers, and Las Vegas is one of the last places where a blue-collar worker can still make a good living. The casino workers in Reno, for example, have none of these protections. The Las Vegas Musicians Union, much smaller than the Las Vegas Culinary Union, still has to struggle and fight for the musicians, with mixed results.

Las Vegas will always be in flux. Nevada historian Hal Rothman put it like this: "Even in moments of great success, Las Vegas had a powerful sense of impermanence, a strong intuition that whatever ruled today might well not tomorrow."[35] There is simply no predicting what the next trends will be or whether other visionaries like Wynn will arrive with new ideas.

One constant is that a successful idea will always be copied. For this reason, musicians remain hopeful that live music will remain viable here as long as there is successful entertainment that uses it. In 1994, conductor Dick Palombi explained it like this: "Like so many other businesses, there are a few leaders but a lot of followers. If someone comes in and builds a hit using live music, you can bet that others will follow."[36] Old Las Vegas is not coming back, but perhaps future Las Vegas will offer something even better for its musicians, and perhaps this will be a return to live music.

Once a person has acquired the taste for live music, there is no going back to the stale and dead sounds of synthesizers, CDs, and tapes. Hearing live music is a bit like eating a tomato fresh from the garden: there is simply no comparison between the rich flavor of a freshly grown tomato versus the bland, tasteless version sold in most grocery stores. The bland tomatoes are cheaper, but they do not really satisfy. Audiences who pay top dollar for spectacular experiences should not be cheated. Hearing great artists perform with live music is truly the experience of a lifetime. For these reasons, many people hope that live music on the Strip is here to stay.

NOTES

1. Dave Palermo and Mike Weatherford, "LV Musicians Face the Music," *Las Vegas Review-Journal*, January 21, 1991.

2. Sonia Padgett, "Longtime Musicians Remember Days When Gigs Were Plentiful in Las Vegas," *Las Vegas Review-Journal*, September 25, 2011.

3. Michelle Chen, "Entertainment Companies Get $1.5 Billion in Tax Breaks Each Year—Yet They're Offshoring Musicians' Jobs," *The Nation*, May 14, 2014.

4. Ibid. (all quotes).

5. Dave Palermo, "Musicians Union Weighs Cuts," *Las Vegas Review-Journal*, June 8, 1991.

6. Palermo and Weatherford, "LV Musicians Face the Music" (all quotes).

7. Ibid.

8. Memo from Lisa Baker, Convention Services Manager, 1991, Box 5, Folder 9, Dunes Hotel Collection, MS 93-08.

9. Interdepartment correspondence from Ben T. Sasaki to Tim Lager, April 12, 1991, Box 5, Folder 9, Dunes Hotel Collection, MS 93-08.

10. Andres Martinez, *24/7: Living It Up and Doubling Down in the New Las Vegas* (New York: Dell, 1999), 101; Gragg, *Bright Light City*, 125. Pg. 101 in the Martinez, first read in the Gragg

11. Michael Paskevich, "Live Music Returning—On A Smaller Scale," *Las Vegas Review-Journal*, July 24, 1994.

12. Ibid.

13. Ibid. (both quotes).

14. Michael Paskevich, "Musicians Continue to Struggle to Keep Careers Alive," *Las Vegas Review-Journal*, July 14, 1996 (all quotes).

15. Carol Cling, "Vanishing Musicians: Jim Kositchek," *Las Vegas Review-Journal*, September 6, 1998 (all quotes from Kositchek).

16. Padgett, "Longtime Musicians Remember Days When Gigs Were Plentiful."

17. Niemann, *Las Vegas Legends*, 226.

18. Letter to "Joe" written by Bill Willard, September 7, 1998, Box 11, Folder 4, Bill Willard Collection, MS 2001-17.

19. Letter to Mitzi Shore written by Bill Willard, November 14, 1991, Box 11, Folder 2, Bill Willard Collection, MS 2001-17.

20. Mike Weatherford, "Live Music Debate Revisited," *Las Vegas Review-Journal*, February 9, 2003.

21. Dave Palermo, "Massagli Preparing for New National Gig," *Las Vegas Review-Journal*, July 21, 1991 ("We've been through," "He's always been").

22. John Katsilometes, "'Mamma Mia!' Closes in Less Than Three Months at Tropicana," *Las Vegas Sun*, July 22, 2014.

23. Moehring and Green, *Las Vegas*, 220.

24. Parker, Munier, and Reynolds, *The Sordid Secrets of Las Vegas*, 190.

25. Leach, Robin. "Review: Revamped 'Steve Wynn's Showstoppers' is showbiz wow, razzmatazz at its finest," *Las Vegas Sun*, June 9, 2015.

26. John Katsilometes, "Show Producer David Saxe Is on a Mission to Bring Vintage Vegas Back," *Las Vegas Weekly*, January 12, 2012.

27. Ibid. (all Saxe quotes this paragraph).

28. Venetian Hotel, http://www.venetian.com/entertainment/shows/frank.html

29. Parker, Munier, and Reynolds, *The Sordid Secrets of Las Vegas*, 86.

30. Las Vegas Convention and Visitors Authority, http://www.lvcva.com/stats-and-facts/visitor-statistics/.

31. Susan Chandler to Liz Benston, "The Toll and the Silence," *Seven*, December 22, 2011–January 4, 2012 (quote); Susan Chandler and Jill B. Jones *Casino Women: Courage in Unexpected Places* (Ithaca, NY: Cornell University Press, 2011).

32. Chandler to Benston, "The Toll and the Silence" (quote); Chandler and Jones *Casino Women*.

33. Chandler and Jones, *Casino Women*, 172.

34. Susan Chandler to Liz Benston, "The Toll and the Silence"; Chandler and Jones, *Casino Women*.

35. Katsilometes, "Show Producer David Saxe Is on a Mission."

36. Paskevich, "Live Music Returning—On a Smaller Scale."

Bibliography

BOOKS

Ainlay, Thomas, and Judy Gabaldon. *Las Vegas: The Fabulous First Century.* Charleston, SC: Arcadia, 2003.

Bailey, Dr. William H. "Bob." *Looking Up! Finding My Voice in Las Vegas.* Las Vegas: Stephens Press. 2009.

Berman, Susan. *Lady Las Vegas: The Inside Story behind America's Neon Oasis.* New York: A&E Network and TV Books, 1996)

Binkley, Christina. *Winner Takes All: Steve Wynn, Kirk Kerkorian, Gary Loveman, and the Race to Own Las Vegas.* New York: Hyperion, 2008.

Bracey, Earnest N. *The Moulin Rouge and Black Rights in Las Vegas A History of the First Racially Integrated Hotel-Casino.* Jefferson, NC: McFarland, 2009.

Chandler, Susan, and Jill B. Jones. *Casino Women: Courage in Unexpected Places.* Ithaca, NY: Cornell University Press, 2011.

Coakley, Deirdre, with Hank Greenspun, Gary C. Gerard, and the staff of the *Las Vegas Sun. The Day the* MGM *Grand Hotel Burned.* Seacaucus, NJ: Lyle Stuart, 1982.

Ferrari, Michelle, with Stephen Ives. *Las Vegas: An Unconventional History.* New York and Boston: Bulfinch Press, 2005.

Geran, Trish. *Beyond the Glimmering Lights: The Pride and Perseverance of African Americans in Las Vegas.* Las Vegas: Stephens Press, 2006.

Gragg, Larry. *Bright Light City: Las Vegas in Popular Culture.* Lawrence: University Press of Kansas, 2013.

Hopkins, A. D., and K. K. Evans, eds. *The First 100: Portraits of the Men and Women Who Shaped Las Vegas.* Las Vegas: Huntington Press, 1999.

Knepp, Donn. *Las Vegas: The Entertainment Capital.* Menlo Park, CA: Lane, 1987.

Land, Barbara, and Myrick Land. *A Short History of Las Vegas.* Reno: University of Nevada Press, 1999.

Martinez, Andres. *24/7: Living It Up and Doubling Down in the New Las Vegas.* New York: Dell, 1999.

Moehring, Eugene P. *Resort City in the Sunbelt,* 2nd ed. Reno: University of Nevada Press, 2000.

Moehring, Eugene P., and Michael S. Green. *Las Vegas: A Centennial History.* Reno: University of Nevada Press, 2005.

Neimann, Greg. *Las Vegas Legends: What Happened in Vegas*. San Diego, CA: Sunbelt, 2011.

Papa, Paul W. *It Happened in Las Vegas: Remarkable Events That Shaped History*. Guilford, CT: Morris Books, 2009.

Parker, Quentin, Paula Munier, and Susan Reynolds. *The Sordid Secrets of Las Vegas*. Avon, MA: Adams Media, 2011.

Roman, James. *Chronicles of Old Las Vegas: Exposing Sin City's High Stakes History*. New York: Museyon, paperback, 2011.

Rothman, Hal. *The Making of Modern Nevada*. Reno: University of Nevada Press, 2010.

———. *Neon Metropolis: How Las Vegas Started the Twenty-First Century*. New York and London: Routledge, 2002.

Rothman, Hal K., and Mike Davis, eds. *The Grit Beneath the Glitter: Tales from the Real Las Vegas*. Berkeley and Los Angeles: University of California Press, 2002.

Schumacher, Geoff. *Sun, Sin & Suburbia: An Essential History of Modern Las Vegas*. Las Vegas: Stephen Press LLC, 2004.

Sheehan, Jack. *Quiet Kingmaker of Las Vegas: E. Parry Thomas*. Las Vegas: Stephens Press, 2009.

Weatherford, Mike. *Cult Vegas: The Weirdest! The Wildest! The Swingin'est Town on Earth!* Las Vegas: Huntington Press, 2001.

Wright, Frank. *Nevada Yesterdays: Short Looks at Las Vegas History*. Las Vegas: Stephens Press, 2005.

ARTICLES

Aucoin, Don. "Bleaker Street; Names and Faces." *Boston Globe*. July 30, 1989.

Bacon, James. "Unexpected Hotel Appearance: Frank Surprises Vegas." *Las Vegas Review-Journal*. December 16, 1963.

Benston, Liz. "The Toll and the Silence." *Seven*. December 22, 2011–January 4, 2012.

"Bill Reddie's Original Work to Highlight Sunday Program." *Las Vegas Review-Journal*. January 17, 1960.

Burkhart, Joan. "Striking Musicians Feeling the Blues." *Las Vegas Review-Journal*. September 3, 1989.

Campbell, Michael L. "Hotels Fail to Move on Union Offer." *Las Vegas Sun*. September 18, 1989.

———. "'Last Offer' a Sour Note for Musicians." *Las Vegas Sun*. September 25, 1989.

———. "Miller Urged to Enter Strike Fray." *Las Vegas Sun*. September 3, 1989.

———. "Musicians, Hotels Resume Talks." *Las Vegas Sun*. September 21, 1989.

———. "Musicians Scale Back Pickets at Four Resorts." *Las Vegas Sun*. October 14, 1989.

———. "Newton's Union Membership Had Lapsed." *Las Vegas Sun*. October 3, 1989.

———. "Other Unions Won't Honor Tropicana Picket Line." *Las Vegas Sun.* September 2, 1989.

———. "Unions Seek Harmony on Strip." *Las Vegas Sun.* August 26, 1989.

———. "Wayne Newton Joins in Musicians Talks." *Las Vegas Sun.* September 13, 1989.

Chansud, Timothy. "Bally's Showroom to be Dark in Wake of Musicians' Strike." *Las Vegas Sun.* August 2, 1989.

———. "Caesars Hears Sounds of Silence." *Las Vegas Sun.* August 3, 1989.

———. "Carlin Won't Cross Caesars Picket Line." *Las Vegas Sun.* August 22, 1989.

———. "Entertainers Come Out in Support of Musicians." *Las Vegas Sun.* July 7, 1989.

———. "Folies Bergere Stages Comeback without the Striking Band." *Las Vegas Sun.* June 26, 1989.

———. "Giovenco: Union Lying about Hotels' Aims." *Las Vegas Sun.* August 30, 1989.

———. "Musician Discussing Latest Offer from Hotels." *Las Vegas Sun.* September 1, 1989.

———. "Musicians, Stagehand Unions' Future at Stake in Negotiations." *Las Vegas Sun.* May 8, 1989.

———. "Musicians' Talks Strike Sour Chord." *Las Vegas Review-Journal.* August 25, 1989.

———. "Strike Closes Folies." *Las Vegas Sun.* June 4, 1989.

Cling, Carol. "Vanishing Musicians: Jim Kositchek." *Las Vegas Review-Journal.* September 6, 1998.

"Cook's Crew: Vegas Band Captures U.S. Crown." *Las Vegas Review-Journal.* November 23, 1960.

"Dangerfield Will Perform Next Month." *Las Vegas Sun.* January 13, 1990.

Devor, Les. "Vegas Vagaries." *Las Vegas Review-Journal.* January 19, 1960.

———. "Vegas Vagaries." *Las Vegas Review-Journal.* January 21, 1960.

Digilio, Don. "The Aladdin Comes to the Front." *Las Vegas Review-Journal.* August 17, 1967.

———. "Angry Sinatra Quits at Sands." *Las Vegas Review-Journal.* September 11, 1967.

———. "Sinatra Loses Teeth in Strip Hotel Brawl." *Las Vegas Review-Journal.* September 12, 1967.

Duke, Forrest. "Dunes Benefit Show for Injured Performer." *Las Vegas Review-Journal.* July 10, 1968.

———. "Martin, Sinatra, Bishop in Ring-a-Ding Gasser." *Las Vegas Review-Journal.* April 15, 1966.

———. "Salute to Sinatra." *Las Vegas Review-Journal.* January 19, 1960.

Finnegan, David. "Governor, Newton Seek Strike's End." *Las Vegas Review-Journal.* September 20, 1989.

———. "Musicians Halt Hilton Picketing." *Las Vegas Review-Journal*. September 29, 1989.

———. "Newton Gets Musicians' Blessing." *Las Vegas Review-Journal*. September 28, 1989.

———. "Strip Headliners Rap Taped Music." *Las Vegas Review Journal*. July 7, 1989.

———. "Tropicana Musicians Strike; Stagehands OK Contract." *Las Vegas Review-Journal*. June 4, 1989.

"First Jazz Concert on Set on Saturday." *Las Vegas Review-Journal*. May 10, 1961.

Friess, Steve. "The Quiet Storm: Bill Harrah's Impact on Gaming." *Desert Companion*. August 2011.

Fuller, Thomas R. "Life Begins for Harold." *Sir Knight*. Vol. 1, no. 5, 12, Box 1, Folder 19, Minsky's Burlesque Collection, MS 87–97, Special Collections, UNLV Libraries, University of Nevada, Las Vegas.

"'Gotta Get to Vegas!' Opens at Dunes Tonight." *Las Vegas Review-Journal*. October 19, 1962.

Graham, Jefferson. "Las Vegas Battles over Taped Music." *USA Today*. July 11, 1989.

Greenhouse, Steven. "Unions, Bruised in Direct Battles With Companies, Try a Roundabout Tactic." *New York Times*. March 10, 1997.

Hansen, Ken. "Ocean's 11 Cast's Sands Perfect Success." *Las Vegas Review-Journal*. February 6, 1960.

Havas, Adrian A. "Curtain Falls on Strip Strike." *Las Vegas Sun*. January 23, 1990.

———. "Musicians Formally Accept Contract." *Las Vegas Sun*. January 25, 1990.

———. "Strike Finale Leaves Musicians Bitter." *Las Vegas Sun*. January 28, 1990.

———. "Union Leader Admits Star Crossings Hurt Musicians Strike." *Las Vegas Sun*. January 25, 1990.

Hertz, Murray. "Lounges Boast Biggest Names in Business." *Las Vegas Review-Journal*. July 5, 1963.

———. "Minimums in Lounges Next for Las Vegas???" *Las Vegas Review-Journal*. November 5, 1963.

Hill, Mary. "Musicians Benefit Boosts Strike Coffers." *Las Vegas Sun*. November 22, 1989.

"Hughes Takes DI Reins." *Las Vegas Review-Journal*. April 1, 1967.

Hyman, Harold. "Musicians Picket Idol's LV Home." *Las Vegas Sun*. October 1, 1989.

"Jazz and Jim Crow." Editorial. *Las Vegas Review-Journal*. May 21, 1962.

Joncich, Paul. "The Life and Times of a Casino Boss' Wife." Channel 8 News Now: KLAS TV Las Vegas. February 9, 2014.

Jones, Florena Lee. "Bravos Still Echo." *Las Vegas Review-Journal*. March 16, 1969.

Katsilometes, John. "'Mamma Mia!' Closes in Less Than Three Months at Tropicana." *Las Vegas Sunday*. July 22, 2014.

———. "Show Producer David Saxe Is on a Mission to Bring Vintage Vegas Back."
Las Vegas Weekly. January 12, 2012.

Koch, Ed. "Another Stardust Tale." *Las Vegas Sun.* November 12, 2006.

Koch, Ed, and Manning, Mary. "Mob Ties." Las Vegas Sun History of Las Vegas.
May 15, 2008. http://www.lasvegassun.com/news/2008/may/15/mob-ties/.

Krane, Elliot S. "Orchestra Leaders of the Strip: 6. Al Ramsey of Caesars Palace." *Las
Vegas Sun Magazine.* March 18, 1981.

"Las Vegas; Music Dies." *The Economist.* November 11, 1989.

LaValle, Phil. "Musicians' Battle Plays Federal Court." *Las Vegas Review-Journal.*
December 16, 1989.

Lawry, Barbara. "Las Vegas May No Longer Play the Starring Role in Modern 'Tale
of Two Gaming Cities.'" *Las Vegas Sun.* July 22, 1984.

Levitan, Corey. "Top Ten Scandals." *Las Vegas Review-Journal.* March 2, 2008.

"LV Musicians Take Protest to Los Angeles." *Las Vegas Sun.* July 1, 1989.

MacKinlay, Colin. "Divorce Decreed Here: Louie, Keeley Split." *Las Vegas Review-
Journal.* October 4, 1961.

Moody, Bill. "Jackie Gaughan: Others Move, But He Keeps the Faith on Fremont
Street." *Nevadan.* September 17, 1989.

Morrison, Jane Ann. "From the El Rancho to Atlantic City." *Nevadan.* June 19, 1977.

"Musicians Chief Says LV Labor Dispute Threatens Community Culture." *Las Vegas
Sun.* June, 12, 1989.

"Musicians Lose One, Win One." *Las Vegas Sun.* October 24, 1989.

"Musicians OK Contract at Stardust." *Las Vegas Review-Journal.* June 14, 1989.

"Musicians, Resorts to Return to Bargaining Table within 2 Weeks." *Las Vegas Sun.*
January 5, 1990.

"Musicians Strike Garners Support." *Las Vegas Sun.* August 18, 1989.

"Musicians' Union May Expel Travis." *Globe and Mail* (Canada). September 9, 1989.

Nelson, Valerie J. "Mary Kaye, 83: Singer Brought All-Night Lounge Acts to Las
Vegas." *Los Angeles Times.* February 20, 2007.

"Nevada." *USA Today*, December 18, 1989.

"Nevada Show for Guys, Dolls." *The Times-News* (Hendersonville, NC). June 24,
1955. http://news.google.com/newspapers?nid=1665&dat=19550624&id=gvQZAAAA
IBAJ&sjid=XSMEAAAAIBAJ&pg=4252,8303574.

Padgett, Sonia. "Longtime Musicians Remember Days When Gigs Were Plentiful in
Las Vegas." *Las Vegas Review-Journal.* September 25, 2011.

Palermo, Dave. "Attorney: Hotels Want to Cut 'Premium' Musician Rates." *Las Vegas
Review-Journal.* January 13, 1990.

———. "Fear Keeps Labor from Joining Strike." *Las Vegas Review-Journal.*
September 6, 1989.

———. "Hotels Agree to Talk with Musicians." *Las Vegas Review-Journal.* August 18, 1989.

———. "Hotels Angered by Musicians' Proposal." *Las Vegas Review-Journal.* August 29, 1989.

———. "Hotels Say Unions Can't Aid Strikers." *Las Vegas Review-Journal.* August 31, 1989.

———. "Illusionist Copperfield to Cross Caesars Picket Line." *Las Vegas Review-Journal.* August 7, 1989.

———. "LV Musicians Union Strikes Bally's." *Las Vegas Review-Journal.* July 28, 1989.

———. "Massagli Preparing for New National Gig." *Las Vegas Review-Journal.* July 21, 1991.

———. "Move to End Musicians' Strike Stalls." *Las Vegas Review-Journal.* January 4, 1990.

———. "Musicians Board Rejects Hotels 'Final, Best' Offer." *Las Vegas Review-Journal.* September 25, 1989.

———. "Musicians Decide against Labor Day Work Stoppage." *Las Vegas Review-Journal.* September 2, 1989.

———. "Musicians Handed 'Final Offer.'" *Las Vegas Review-Journal.* September 22, 1989.

———. "Musicians Knew Power Was Waning." *Las Vegas Review-Journal.* January 24, 1990.

———. "Musicians Plan Labor Day Job Action." *Las Vegas Review-Journal.* August 26, 1989.

———. "Musicians Ratify New Four-Year Contract." *Las Vegas Review-Journal.* January 25, 1990.

———. "Musicians Strike Ends." *Las Vegas Review-Journal.* January 23, 1990.

———. "Musicians Strike Ends on Foul Note." *Las Vegas Review-Journal.* January 28, 1990.

———. "Musicians Strike Talks Break Down." *Las Vegas Review-Journal.* January 18, 1990.

———. "Musicians' Talks Target End of Strike." *Las Vegas Review-Journal.* January 3, 1990.

———. "Musicians Trying to Keep Stars Out of Big Hotels." *Las Vegas Review-Journal.* October 3, 1989.

———. "Musicians Union Weighs Cuts." *Las Vegas Review-Journal.* June 8, 1991.

———. "Newton a Player in Dispute." *Las Vegas Review-Journal.* September 14, 1989.

———. "Paid Pickets March for Idled Musicians." *Las Vegas Review-Journal.* August 5, 1989.

———. "Settlement Called 'End of an Era.'" *Las Vegas Review-Journal.* January 23, 1990.

Palermo, Dave, and Mike Weatherford. "LV Musicians Face the Music." *Las Vegas Review-Journal.* January 21, 1991.

———. "Musicians Strike Caesars." *Las Vegas Review-Journal.* August 3, 1989.

Paskevich, Michael. "Live Music Returning—On a Smaller Scale." *Las Vegas Review-Journal.* July 24, 1994.

———. "Musicians Continue to Struggle to Keep Careers Alive." *Las Vegas Review-Journal.* July 14, 1996.

———. "Publicist Fondly Recalls Casino's Heyday." *Las Vegas Review-Journal.* May 19, 1993.

Las Vegas Review-Journal. Photograph. August 18, 1967.

"Progress!" *The Voice.* April 15, 1954. Alice Key Papers, MS 95–47, Special Collections, UNLV Libraries, University of Nevada, Las Vegas.

Puit, Glenn. "MGM Grand Fire: The Deadliest Day." *Las Vegas Review Journal.* November 19, 2000.

Reeves, David. "Musicians on the Brink." *Las Vegas Sun,* June 16, 1989.

Shawhan, Casey, and James Bassett. "Costly Floor Shows Frost Las Vegas Gambling Cake." *Oakland Tribune.* July 21, 1953.

"Sinatra, True-Blue to Unions." *USA Today.,* October 13, 1989.

"Sinatra Will Cross Vegas Picket Line." *Globe and Mail* (Canada). November 24, 1989.

Smith, Mark Chalon. "Las Vegas Musicians Still Walk the Beat: 11-Week Strike to Retain Live Music 'Just Keeps Dragging On,'" *Los Angeles Times.* August 19, 1989.

Solomon, Phil. "Lights of Las Vegas." *Jack Cortez' Fabulous Las Vegas Magazine.* June 15, 1971. Dunes Hotel Collection, MS 93-08, Box 5, Folder 6, Special Collections, UNLV Libraries, University of Nevada, Las Vegas.

Spaniel, William. "Bosoms Bug Musicians." *Las Vegas Review-Journal.* August 20, 1967.

Sturtz, Howard. "Sinatra Cancels Show at Bally's." *Las Vegas Review-Journal.* November 30, 1989.

Stutrz, Howard, and Dave Palermo. "Newton Returns to Hilton Stage." *Las Vegas Review-Journal.* September 27, 1989.

"Symphony Concert Will Benefit NSU." *Las Vegas Review-Journal.* January 17, 1960.

"Tropicana to Reopen 'Folies Bergere.'" *Las Vegas Review-Journal.* June 25, 1989.

Weatherford, Mike. "Bandleader Johnny Haig Dies of Cancer." *Las Vegas Review Journal.* August 8, 2007.

———. "Caesars, Desert Inn Say Lack of Contract Won't Stop Shows." *Las Vegas Review-Journal.* July 29, 1989.

———. "Live Music Debate Revisited." *Las Vegas Review-Journal.* February 9, 2003.

———. "Musicians Fear Worst in Future of Las Vegas." *Las Vegas Review-Journal.* June 11, 1989.

———. "Newton Crosses Picket Line for First Time." *Las Vegas Review-Journal.* September 30, 1989.

———. "Parent Union OKs Musician 'Amnesty.'" *Las Vegas Review-Journal.* January 20, 1990.

Willard, Bill. "Computer Colorless Sub for Old-Time Vegas Boss." *Variety*, October 26, 1976.

———. "5,500,000 Gamble and Gambol Spa Is Writ on The Sands of Las Vegas, Where a Preem Means Four Days." *Variety*, December 24, 1952, 45.

———. "Las Vegas Luck Riding Out Bad Time: 3 New Casino-Hotels Set to Bow." *Variety*, January 11, 1956.

———. "Vegas' $164,000,000 Question." *Variety*, July 13, 1955.

———. "Vegas' New Year's Eve in July." *Variety*, July 22, 1953.

———. "Vaudeville: Nat'l Spotlight Feeds More Fuel to Vegas 3 G's—Gambling, Glam & Garble." *Variety*, January 14, 1953.

INTERNET RESOURCES

"A Byte Out of History: The Kidnapping of Frank Sinatra, Jr." http://www.fbi.gov/news/stories/2013/december/the-kidnapping-of-frank-sinatra-jr/the-kidnapping-of-frank-sinatra-jr.

"About the El Rancho Vegas Exhibit." http://gaming.unlv.edu/ElRanchoVegas/entertainment.html.

"American Experience, Las Vegas: An Unconventional History, People & Events, PBS." http://www.pbs.org/wgbh/amex/lasvegas/peopleevents/p_entertainers.html.

Chen, Michelle. "Entertainment Companies Get $1.5 billion in Tax Breaks Each Year—Yet They're Offshoring Musicians' Jobs." http://www.thenation.com/blog/179865/entertainment-companies-get-15-billion-tax-breaks-each-year-yet-theyre-offshoring-musici#.

"Desert Inn Las Vegas NV A CHORUS LINE 1982." http://www.worthpoint.com/worthopedia/desert-inn-las-vegas-nv-a-chorus-line-12-pg-prog.

"Dreaming the Skyline: Thunderbird." http://digital.library.unlv.edu/skyline/hotel/thunderbird.

"History of the Dunes / Bellagio." http://www.a2zlasvegas.com/hotels/history/h-bellagio.html.

"The Fabulous Flamingo Hotel History from the 1960s–1980s." http://classiclasvegas.squarespace.com/a-brief-history-of-the-strip/?currentPage=8.

"Frontier Hotel History: The Hotel Last Frontier/The New Frontier/The Frontier/The New Frontier." http://classiclasvegas.squarespace.com/display/ShowJournal?moduleId=1093544&currentPage=5.

"The El Rancho Vegas Story." http://gaming.unlv.edu/ElRanchoVegas/story.html.

"Las Vegas Caesars Palace Opening Week." http://classiclasvegas.squarespace.com/a-brief-history-of-the-strip/2008/7/20/las-vegas-caesars-palace-opening-week.html.

"Lido at the Stardust." http://digital.library.unlv.edu/collections/showgirls/lido-stardust.

"Local Notes." *Las Vegas Age*, December 21, 1907, http://digital.lvccld.org/cgi-bin/queryresults.exe?CISOROOT1=%2Flvccg&CISOFIELD1=itemye&CISOBOX1=1907&CISOFIELD2=itemmo&CISOBOX2=december&CISOFIELD3=itemda&CISOBOX3=21&CISOMODE=grid&CISOSTART=121.

"Local Notes." *Las Vegas Age* August 7, 1909, http://digital.lvccld.org/cgi-bin/queryresults.exe?CISOBOX1=1909&CISOFIELD1=itemye&CISOBOX2=august&CISOFIELD2=itemmo&CISOBOX3=07&CISOFIELD3=itemda&CISOROOT1=%2Flvccg&x=33&y=16.

"Local Notes." *Las Vegas Age* August 21, 1909, http://digital.lvccld.org/cgi-bin/queryresults.exe?CISOBOX1=1909&CISOFIELD1=itemye&CISOBOX2=august&CISOFIELD2=itemmo&CISOBOX3=21&CISOFIELD3=itemda&CISOROOT1=%2Flvccg&x=29&y=12.

Timeline. *Las Vegas Sun.* http://www.lasvegassun.com/history/timeline/.

"The Tropicana Hotel History: Miami Comes to the Las Vegas Strip." classiclasvegas.squarespace.com/a-brief-history-of-the-strip/2008/3/23/the-tropicana-hotel-history-miami-comes-to-the-las-vegas-str.html.

"The Tropicana Hotel History: The Tiffany of the Strip." http://classiclasvegas.squarespace.com/a-brief-history-of-the-strip/?currentPage=29.

"Vegas FAQs." http://www.lvcva.com/includes/content/images/media/docs/2013-Vegas-FAQs.pdf.

FIRST-PERSON INTERVIEWS

Interviewed on audio tape by Janis McKay, Archie McKay, and Cuba McKay

Frank Leone, Musicians Union president (2000–2015), interviewed on February 1, 2005

Don Hannah, composer, arranger, tuba, bass, interviewed on February 3, 2005

Dave Hawley, woodwind doubler, interviewed on February 3, 2005

Dick McGee, trombone, conductor, interviewed on February 4, 2005

Johnny Haig, contractor, conductor, trombone, interviewed on February 9, 2005

Tom McDermott, guitar, electric guitar, bass, interviewed on February 10, 2005

Rebecca Ramsey, violin, contractor, composer, interviewed on February 15, 2005

Ken Hanlon, trombone, interviewed on February 16, 2005

Tom Snelson, trumpet, interviewed on February 22, 2005

Tom Wright, trumpet, interviewed on February 25, 2005

Patricia (Saarinen) Harrell, violin, interviewed on February 26, 2005

D. Gause, piano, arranger, conductor, interviewed on March 2, 2005
Kimberly (Kim) Glennie, harp, interviewed on March 2, 2005
Ronnie Simone, piano, interviewed on March 14, 2005

Interviewed on audio tape by Janis McKay

Beth Lano, horn, interviewed on June 6, 2006
Ed Boyer, bass, electric bass, interviewed on June 8, 2006
Ralph Pressler, trombonist, interviewed on June 8, 2006
Lisa Viscuglia, violin, contractor, interviewed on June 9, 2006
Sharon Street-Caldwell, viola, interviewed on June 9, 2006
Howard Agster, drums, percussion, interviewed on June 11, 2006
Gary Queen, guitar, electric guitar, electric bass, interviewed on June 14, 2006
Bill Trujillo, woodwind doubler, copyist, interviewed on June 14, 2006

Interviewed with notes only by Archie McKay and Cuba McKay

Matt Saporita, woodwind doubler, interviewed on February 17, 2005
Barbara Gurley, cello, interviewed on March 3, 2005
Thom Pastor, woodwind doubler, union secretary treasurer, interviewed on March 4, 2005
Frank Leone, piano, active during strike, interviewed on March 4, 2005
Joe Lano, guitar, arranger, composer, conductor, interviewed on March 7, 2005 and March 14, 2005
Tommy Check, drums, percussion, arranging, interviewed on March 8, 2005
Mark Tully Massagli, former national union president, electric bass, interviewed on March 9, 2005

Interviewed with notes only by Janis McKay, Archie McKay, and Cuba McKay

Jim Stivers, trombone, interviewed on February 16, 2005
Carol Stivers, piano, interviewed on February 16, 2005
Sam Pisciotta, woodwind doubler, interviewed on February 18, 2005

Interviewed by e-mail by Janis McKay

Alan Lawson, woodwind doubler, interviewed July 16, 2010
Alexander Viazovtsev, woodwind doubler, flute, interviewed July 16, 2010
Tim Bonenfant, woodwind doubler, interviewed July 30, 2014

ORAL HISTORIES AND INTERVIEWS

Heberling, Tracy. KNPR *Vegas I Remember* Transcripts. Box 1, MS 063. Special Collections, Nevada State Museum, Las Vegas.

Lewis, Maxine. Oral History. February 20, 1987. Special Collections, UNLV Libraries, University of Nevada, Las Vegas.

Maheu, Bob. KNPR *Vegas I Remember* Transcripts. Box 1, Folder 18, MS 063. Special Collections, Nevada State Museum, Las Vegas.

Merenda, Harry. KNPR *Vegas I Remember* Transcripts. Box 1, Folder 19, MS 063. Special Collections, Nevada State Museum, Las Vegas.

Saxe, Kathy. KNPR *Vegas I Remember* transcripts. Box 1, MS 063. Special Collections, Nevada State Museum, Las Vegas.

OTHER

Dunes Hotel Collection. MS 93-08/2010–14. Special Collections, UNLV Libraries, University of Nevada, Las Vegas.

Fluke, David. 1947–1981 Notebooks, Collection #89–29, folder 25. Special Collections, UNLV Libraries, University of Nevada, Las Vegas.

———. Collection. Box1, Folder 23; "Frontier Hotel Spends 100G for Talent in a Year, Plans Expansion." *Billboard*. October 16, 1943.

Index to *Las Vegas Review-Journal*. Special Collections, Nevada State Museum, Las Vegas.

Las Vegas Show Programs. Collection 93–28. Special Collections, UNLV Libraries, University of Nevada, Las Vegas.

Manone, Wingy. Collection. MS 2001–28. Special Collections, UNLV Libraries, University of Nevada, Las Vegas.

Morelli, Antonio. Papers, 2009–17. Special Collections, UNLV Libraries, University of Nevada, Las Vegas.

Musicians' Wives Collection, MS 2004–13. Special Collections, UNLV Libraries, University of Nevada, Las Vegas.

Tan, Mark. Collection. 1976. Special Collections, Nevada State Museum, Las Vegas.

Willard, Bill. Lecture notes. Bill Willard to the Nevada Historical Society. "The Entertainment Industry's Role in Shaping Nevada's Image." 13, Bill Willard Collection, MS 2001–17. Special Collections, UNLV Libraries, University of Nevada, Las Vegas.

———. Letter from Maxine Lewis to Brigham Townsend. Box 11, Folder 5. Bill Willard Collection, MS 2001–17. Special Collections, UNLV Libraries, University of Nevada, Las Vegas.

———. Collection, MS 2001–17, Special Collections, UNLV Libraries, University of Nevada, Las Vegas.

Index

Page numbers in *italics* indicate illustrations.

Carroll, Diahann, 51
Carson, Johnny, 51, 151
Carter, Benny, 35
Casbar Lounge or Theatre, 33, 60, 102
Cash, Johnny, 102
casino and hotel owners (mob). *See* mob
   owners
"Casino de Paris" (show), 38, 51–52, 58, 101,
   122, 128, 136
casino entertainment, decline of, 141
casino hotels: bands, golden age of, 9; construction of, 198–199; financial success
   of, 208
casino industry, corporate takeover impact
   on, 76, 144
casinos: de-emphasis on, 94; history of,
   7–8; ownership, corporate (*see* corporate owners (casino and hotel)); security at, 92
casino workers: casino ownership change
   impact on, 1, 2; income and financial
   aid to, 61–62; job satisfaction, decline
   of, 142; mob owners, relations with, 26;
   working conditions, 208–209
Cathcart, Jack, 51, 102
CDs, 201, 202, 210
celebrity DJs, 4
Cenicola, Phil, 57
Cernuto, Sam, 181
Chandler, Susan, 208, 209
Channing, Carol, 52
Charisse, Cyd, 103
Charles, Ray, 51
Charlie Teagarden and His Dixieland
   Band, 58
Cheap Trick, 205
Check, Tommy, 39, 79, 128, 130, 131, 151
Checker, Chubby, 51
cheetah, 127
Chen, Michelle, 194–195
Cher, 149
Cherry, Don, 101
Chevalier, Maurice, 41
Chicago Outfit, 96
Chick Floyd Orchestra, 10
Chiero, John, 166–167

Child Haven, 56
"Chorus Line, A" (show), 140, 147
Chuck's House of Spirits, 41–42, 67
circus acts, 196–197
Circus Maximus Orchestra, 70
Circus Maximus Showroom, 69, 101
Cirque du Soleil: shows, 158, 196–197, 199–
   200, 204, 205–206; star performers, past
   contrasted with, 4
"City Lites" (show), 185, 195
civil rights, 56–57
Clark, Petula, 70, 101
Clark, Roy, 71, 102
Clark, Wilbur, 24–25, 62
classical musicians, 205
Cleopatra's Barge, 101, 103
"click track," 97
Clooney, Rosemary, 31, 51
club music (term defined), 4, 5n8
Cohen, Burton, 139, 140, 141
Cohen, Carl, 73, 74
Cole, Natalie, 131, 151
Cole, Nat King, 24, 34, 51
Colored Citizens' Labor and Protective
   Association, 17–18
Colosseum, 206
comic musicians, 33
community, lost sense of, 89–90
Continental Theatre, 103
contract: formal, adopting of, 75; legal dif-
   ficulties over, 161; negotiations for, 167;
   pay or play, 135; work without, 2, 7, 14,
   26, 98
Cook, Jimmy, 54
Copacabana, 24, 27, 70
CopaGirl Dancers, 48, 51
Copa Room, 47, 49, 103
Copperfield, David, 173
Cornero Brothers, 9
corporate America, disenchantment with,
   208–209
corporate business model: criticism of,
   94–95; personal business model
   replaced by, 2, 90–91; profits empha-
   sized in, 86–87; shift to, 88
Corporate Gaming Acts, 1, 92

Knight, Gladys, 102
Knotts, Don, 70
Koch, Ed, 62
Kositchek, Jim, 198, 211
Kozloff, Jake, 17, 19
Krupa, Gene, 33, 41, 52
Kurland, Jerry, 40–41

Ladybirds, 77
Lady Luck Lounge, 60
Laine, Frankie, 56
Lane, Dick, 99, 102, 143
Lano, Beth: dressing up, 149–150; on large
orchestras, 201; Mathis, Johnny recalled
by, 151; music changes, impression of,
164; Newton, Wayne recalled by, 148;
production shows recalled by, 153; Sinatra, Frank recalled by, 40, 145; in strike
of 1989, 179, 180; in strike of 1989 aftermath, 186, 193, 203
Lano, Joe, 68, 122, 128, 132, 133, 197
Last Frontier Hotel and Casino: African
American performers at, 34; celebrities
at, 27; entertainment at, 10–11, 28;
Lewis, Maxine departure from, 12; photos, 124–125; racial discrimination at, 19;
as resort hotel example, 14
Las Vegas: change and growth in, 3–4, 23,
85, 89–90, 94, 98, 157, 198–199, 203–
204, 209; as corporate town, 76; decline
of, 87; as family destination, 144; first
impressions, 63; image, changing of,
73, 75; press coverage of, 27–28; pres-
tige connected with, 107; race relations
in, 17–19, 34–37
Las Vegas Courthouse, 123–124
Las Vegas Musicians Union. *See* Musicians
Union Local 369
Las Vegas Philharmonic Orchestra, 57, 59,
205
Las Vegas Pops Orchestra, 57, 58
Las Vegas Spectaculars, 29
Las Vegas: The Fabulous First Century
(Ainlay and Gabaldon), 3–4
Laughlin, Jack, 9
Lawford, Peter, 4, 47, 48, 49

Lawrence, Steve, 151
Lawson, Alan, 204–205
Lawson, Bob, 54
Leach, Robin, 206–207
LeCoque, Archie, 185
LeCoque, Ffolliott "Fluff," 36
Lee, Alan, 103
Lee, Peggy, 10, 19, 52, 69
Lee, Pinky, 29, 60
Leone, Frank: band move to basement,
views on, 164; corporate casino owner
budget cuts recalled by, 162; Flamingo
Hotel opening recalled by, 12; recorded
sound impact analyzed by, 3; in strike
of 1989 aftermath, 186; strike of 1989
recalled by, 165, 166, 171
Levien, Lawrence D., 177, 181, 184
Lew Elias Relief Band, 53, 110, 111, 127
Lewis, Jerry: appearance on Strip, 19;
Lewis, Maxine recollections of, 15; live
music, views on, 170; musician recollections of, 70–71; at Sands Hotel, 51;
in strike of 1989, 179; Viscuglia, Lisa
recollections of, 130–131
Lewis, Joe E., 15, 19, 25
Lewis, Maxine: as booker, 15, 26; as Flamingo entertainment director, 12; as
Last Frontier entertainment director,
10, 11; mob owner dealings recalled by,
16
Lewis, Moe, 103
Lewis, Tommy, 58
Liberace: appearance on Strip, 19; death,
158; hiring of, 11; jobs, getting through,
147; in Las Vegas, 15; lounge disappearance impact noted by, 87; musician
recollections of, 41; orchestra conduc-
tor, 146; at Riviera, 27; show, 120–121
"Lido de Paris" (show), 29–30, 32, 95, 97,
103, 139, 196
Lilting Strings, 60
Linden, Hal, 182
Linger, John, 112
Lionel Hampton and His Orchestra, 58
"Lion King, The" (show), 204, 205–206
"Lisa and Laszlo" act, 150

Page, Patti, 56, 101
Painted Desert Showroom, 25
Painters Union Local 159, 175
Pair-O-Dice Nightclub, 10–11
Palace Pops, 146
Palazzo Hotel, 200
Palermo, Dave, 187
Palms Hotel, 200
Palombi, Dick, 102, 108, 210
Pantaleo, Peter S., 176, 177
Parker, "Colonel" Tom, 78, 79
Parton, Dolly, 150
Pastor, Thom, 114, 150–151, 177, 202
Paul Revere and the Raiders, 102
Paul Whiteman Orchestra, 19
Pearl, Ralph, 47–48
personal business model, 2, 157
"Phantom" (show), 204
Pierre, 70
Pioneer Club, 11
Pisciotta, Sam, 42, 67, 72, 129
"Playgirls on Ice," 108
Pointer Sisters, 182
popular culture, 86
Porcino, Al, 54
Powell, Eleanor, 52
practical jokes, 121–122
Prado, Perez, 60
pregnancy, 134
Presley, Elvis, 4, 41, 78–79, 85, 99, 100–101
Pressler, Ralph: arrival in Las Vegas, 55;
   Bennett, Tony recalled by, 70; Cole,
   Natalie recalled by, 131; divide and con-
   quer tactics, commentary concerning,
   162; incidents recalled by, 122, 127–128;
   pre-corporate era recalled by, 3; social
   life recalled by, 42; strike of 1989 aftermath recalled by, 185–186; working
   conditions recalled by, 47, 155
price-saving measures, 194
Prima, Louis, 33, 51, 56, 59–60, 102, 206
"Producers, The" (show), 204
production shows: boredom, coping with,
   121–122; challenges of, 153; current
   scene, 204; decline of, 78, 89; fights
   during, 129; long-running, 29–30, 31,

66–67, 114–115, 121–122; taped music
   for, 170
profit sources, change in, 201
Prowse, Juliet, 74, 143
Pryor, Richard, 51
Puit, Glenn, 142
"Pzazz '68" (show), 51

Queen, Gary, 139, 147, 150, 171–172, 175,
   183, 203

race discrimination, 17–19, 24, 34, 117
railroad industry, 8
Ramona Room, 124
Ramsey, Al, 109, 141, 146
Ramsey, Rebecca: on female musicians,
   116–117; incidents recalled by, 149; as
   independent contractor, 201–202; on
   musician qualifications, 107, 115–116;
   practicing, 130; Sinatra, Frank recalled
   by, 40; starting out, 108–110; Viscuglia,
   Lisa recollections of, 132
Rat Pack: enduring presence of, 85; location of, 74, 96, 103; performances by,
   48, 49, 50, 59; popularity of, 72; recollections of, 4, 47; show films, 27
Rawls, Lou, 102
Ray, Johnny, 87
Ray Sinatra Orchestra, 51
Reagan, Ronald, 27
recession, 2008, 200
recording industry, 195
records and tapes, live music replaced by, 1
Reddie, Bill, 52, 57–58
Reese, Della, 60, 87
Regency Lounge, 103
relief bands, 53–54, 108, 110, 114, 127, 129,
   207
relief orchestras, xi, 108, 155
resort hotels, 14
resort industry, 8, 90
retainer, 175–176, 178
Revere, Paul, 102
Reyes, Diego Alfredo, 58
Reynolds, Debbie: at Desert Inn, 100, 101;
   elephant cleanup by, 128; Liberace